CAMBRIDGE UNIVERSITY PRESS

CAMBRIDGE ENGLISH
Language Assessment
Part of the University of Cambridge

Cambridge English

Joanna Kosta
Melanie Williams
Series Editor: Annette Capel

Prepare!

STUDENT'S BOOK

Level 3

Cambridge University Press
www.cambridge.org/elt

Cambridge English Language Assessment
www.cambridgeenglish.org

Information on this title: www.cambridge.org/9780521180542

First published 2015

Printed in Italy by Rotolito Lombarda S.p.A.

A catalogue record for this publication is available from the British Library

ISBN 978-0-521-18054-2 Student's Book
ISBN 978-1-107-49740-5 Student's Book and Online Workbook
ISBN 978-1-107-49735-1 Student's Book and Online Workbook with Testbank
ISBN 978-0-521-18055-9 Workbook with Audio
ISBN 978-0-521-18056-6 Teacher's Book with DVD and Teacher's Resources Online
ISBN 978-0-521-18057-3 Class Audio CDs
ISBN 978-1-107-49732-0 Presentation Plus DVD-ROM

Contents

1	It's a challenge!	10
2	The natural world	14
Culture	The USA	18
3	Travel: then and now	20
4	My place	24
Geography	Rivers	28
Review 1		30
5	School	32
6	It's very special	36
Culture	Secondary school in the UK	40
7	Travel and holidays	42
8	Life in the future	46
Science	The birth and death of stars	50
Review 2		52
9	Sports and games	54
10	Useful websites	58
Culture	Football (The beautiful game)	62
11	City living	64
12	Festivals and films	68
History	The history of writing	72
Review 3		74
13	Life experiences	76
14	Spending money	80
Culture	Instrument families	84
15	Free time	86
16	So many languages!	90
Design and Technology	Materials from nature	94
Review 4		96
17	Staying healthy	98
18	Expedition!	102
Culture	Mumbai, India	106
19	Different ingredients	108
20	Changes	112
Literature	Michael Morpurgo	116
Review 5		118

Exam profiles	120
Get talking!	130
Activities	135
Vocabulary list	138
Grammar reference	147
List of irregular verbs	167

UNIT	VOCABULARY	GRAMMAR	PRONUNCIATION	READING
1 It's a challenge Page 10	Adjectives of personality	Present simple and present continuous	The alphabet	Two letters to the teacher *The Merrydown Award*
2 The natural world page 14	Geographical features Animals	Verbs we don't usually use in the continuous	th: θ and ð	*The Earth: A changing planet* *The Giant Panda*
Culture The USA page 18				
3 Travel: then and now page 20	Travel Holiday vocabulary	Past simple	Silent letters	Amelia Earhart – the first female pilot to fly across the Atlantic Moscow tourist attractions
4 My place page 24	Describing a holiday Words to describe homes	Past continuous and past simple	/iː/and /ɪ/	*Our worst holiday ever* An unusual home
Geography Rivers page 28		**Review 1** Units 1–4 page 30		
5 School page 32	School words and school subjects Take *take exams*, *take a photo*	Comparative and superlative adverbs	Word patterns	*How to give a good talk* *Home school is cool*
6 It's very special page 36	Possessions and materials	Possession	Weak forms: *a* and *of*	*The Staffordshire Hoard*
Culture Secondary school in the UK page 40				
7 Travel and holidays page 42	Holiday activities Get *get back*, *get lost* Transport	Present continuous for future	Words that sound similar	Unusual holidays
8 Life in the future page 46	Household furniture and appliances Words with two meanings	Future with *will*	*will* and *won't*	*Three amazing time capsules*
Science The birth and death of stars page 50		**Review 2** Units 5–8 page 52		
9 Sports and games page 54	Sports and activities Games	*must*, *mustn't*, *have to*, *don't have to*	*must* and *mustn't*	*Mind sports*
10 Useful websites page 58	People *guest*, *old friend* Internet: nouns and verbs	Verb patterns – gerunds and infinitives	*gh*	*Teen troubles* *Six great websites for teenagers*
Culture Football (The beautiful game) page 62				

LISTENING	SPEAKING	WRITING	EXAM TASKS	VIDEO
An introduction to the Merrydown Award Dylan and Gabby talk about public speaking	Talk about yourself	Write about yourself	Speaking Part 1	
The United Kingdom Animal photos	A talk about your country EP **Get talking!** *You're so lucky! Really?*	A text about an animal	Listening Part 2	
At a hotel reception desk	A conversation asking for tourist information Talk about an adventure you would like to have	A paragraph about Amelia Earhart and Fred Noonan	Speaking Part 2	Adventures!
Five short conversations	EP **Get talking!** *By the way, It's the best way to … I don't agree, That's right*	A description of a home	Reading and Writing Part 7 Listening Part 1	Homes
Dylan practises his talk	A talk about your school Describe your perfect school	A reply to an email	Reading and Writing Part 3b Reading and Writing Part 9	School subjects
Carmen looks for something for her art class	Talk about possessions EP **Get talking!** *Actually, it's…, I think it's…*	Write about possessions Adjective order	Listening Part 2 Reading and Writing Part 4	
An adventure holiday	A perfect adventure week Plan an activity weekend		Listening Part 5 Reading and Writing Part 8	
Homes of the future	Make predictions about the future EP **Get talking!** *Why not? First of all ….*	A message for a time capsule *too, also, as well*	Reading and Writing Part 6	Time capsule
A phone conversation about dance classes A discussion about mind sports	Agreeing and disagreeing		Listening Part 3 Reading and Writing Part 4	Games
A doctor gives advice to teenagers	Give advice on a problem EP **Get talking!** *After all, Make sure …*	A description of a website	Reading and Writing Part 3a Reading and Writing Part 2	

UNIT	VOCABULARY	GRAMMAR	PRONUNCIATION	READING
11 City living Page 64	Places Signs and notices	Determiners Uncountable nouns	*the*	*Australian cities*
12 Festivals and films page 68	Instruments and types of music	Relative pronouns *who, which, that* Conjunctions	Sounds and spellings	Music festivals *Showing today at Star Cinema*
History The history of writing page 72		**Review 3** Units 9–12 page 74		
13 Life experiences page 76	Jobs Past participles	Present perfect with *ever* and *never*	Past participles	A life quiz
14 Spending money page 80	Shops Units of measurement	Present perfect with *just*, *yet* and *already*	Questions with question words	*Businesses and shops in Cardiff*
Culture Instrument families page 84				
15 Free time page 86	Free-time activities Collocations *order a pizza, pay a bill*	Present perfect with *since* / *for*	Weak forms	*A special birthday*
16 So many languages! page 90	Words to describe language learning	Present perfect and past simple	Word stress	*An amazing language learner* *Languages of the world*
Design and Technology Materials from nature page 94	**Review 4** Units 13–16 page 96			
17 Staying healthy page 98	Body parts Teen health	Pronouns *myself, yourself, herself, himself, ourselves, yourselves, themselves* First conditional	/uː/ and /ʊ/	*Teen health*
18 Expedition! page 102	Things to take on an expedition Phrasal verbs *pick up, wake up*	*may* / *might*	Sentence stress	*The Merrydown Expedition – kit list* A description of an expedition
Culture Mumbai, India page 106				
19 Different ingredients page 108	Words to describe cooking Ingredients	Present simple passive	Ways to pronounce *ea*	*Breakfast cereals* A cooking blog
20 Changes page 112	Types of building *Change* as a verb and noun	Past simple passive	Sounds and spelling quiz	*Changing buildings* Two biography fact files

Literature Michael Morpurgo page 116 **Review 5** Units 17–20 page 118 **Exam profiles** 1-5 page 120 **Get talking!** page 130

LISTENING	SPEAKING	WRITING	EXAM TASKS	VIDEO
A city quiz	Making requests and responding	A city quiz	Reading and Writing Part 5 Reading and Writing Part 1	Favourite cities
A cinema trip	A presentation on a festival EP **Get talking!** *That sounds exciting, Make sure …*	An invitation to the cinema	Reading and Writing Part 4 Listening Part 4	
The Merrydown Award – choosing who to interview	Ask and answer questions about experiences Role play three different situations		Reading and Writing Part 2 Reading and Writing Part 3a	Life experiences
A birthday picnic	Plan and make suggestions EP **Get talking!** *I suppose, If you like …*	A note	Speaking Part 2 Reading and Writing Part 9	
Birthday challenges Three young people talk about their free time	Talk about your partner's hobbies and free time activities An interview	Your partner's hobbies and activities	Reading and Writing Part 4	
Different languages	Languages you and your family speak EP **Get talking!** *unfortunately*, *at least*	Information about your English class	Reading and Writing Part 6	Different languages
A story about an accident		Conditional sentences	Reading and Writing Part 3b Listening Part 1	Health
Plans for the expedition Describing photos of the expedition	Plan an expedition EP **Get talking!** *What about you?*, *The same*	A description of an expedition		
A cooking competition	Invent and describe a new snack Decide on a recipe		Reading and Writing Part 7 Listening Part 4	Favourite foods
An interview about changing jobs	Talk about reusing a building EP **Get talking!** *You're welcome*. *All the time*	A biography		

Activities page 135 **Vocabulary list** page 138 **Grammar reference** page 147 **Irregular verbs** page 167

Welcome to Prepare!

Learn about the features in your new Student's Book

Corpus challenge Take the grammar challenge and learn from common mistakes

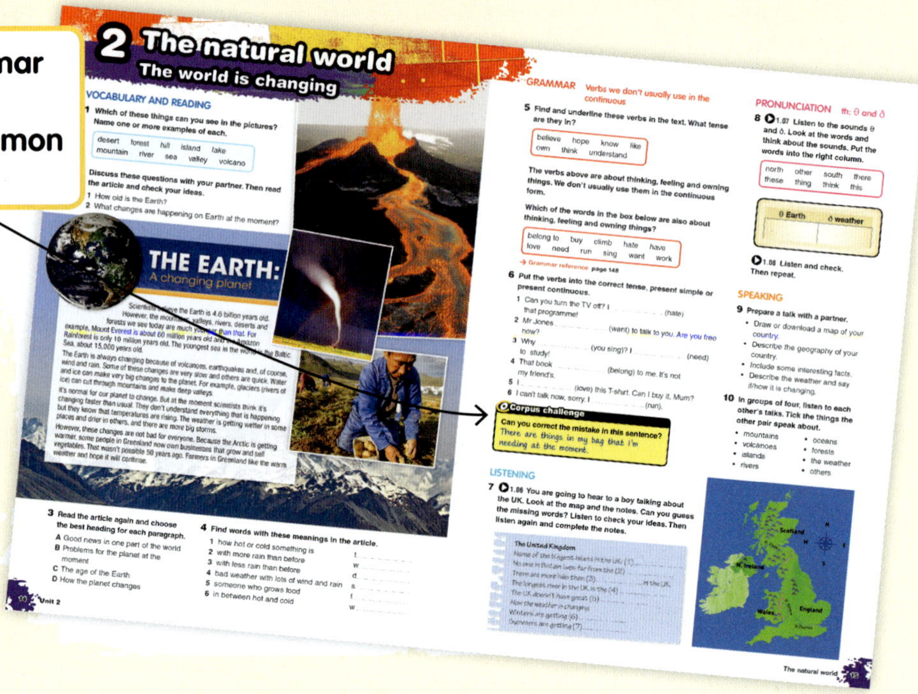

About you Talk about you and your life

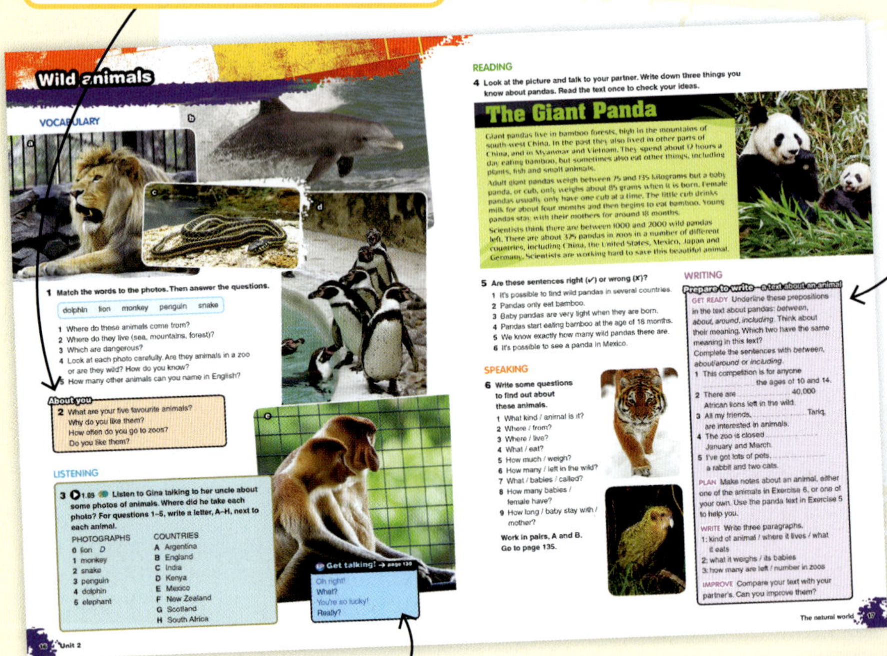

Prepare to write Prepare, plan, write and check your writing

Get talking Useful phrases to get you talking!

Video Watch interviews with teenagers like you

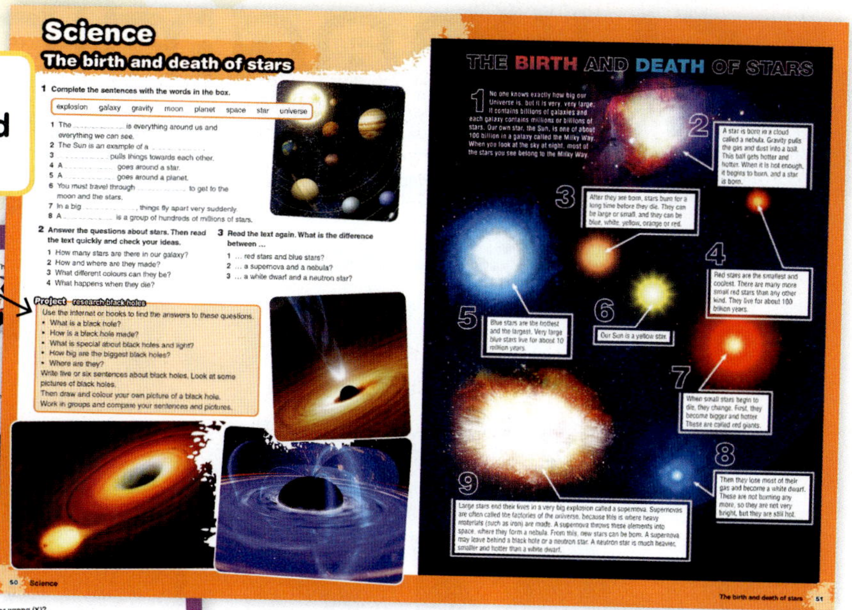

Project Work together to create something fun and expand your learning

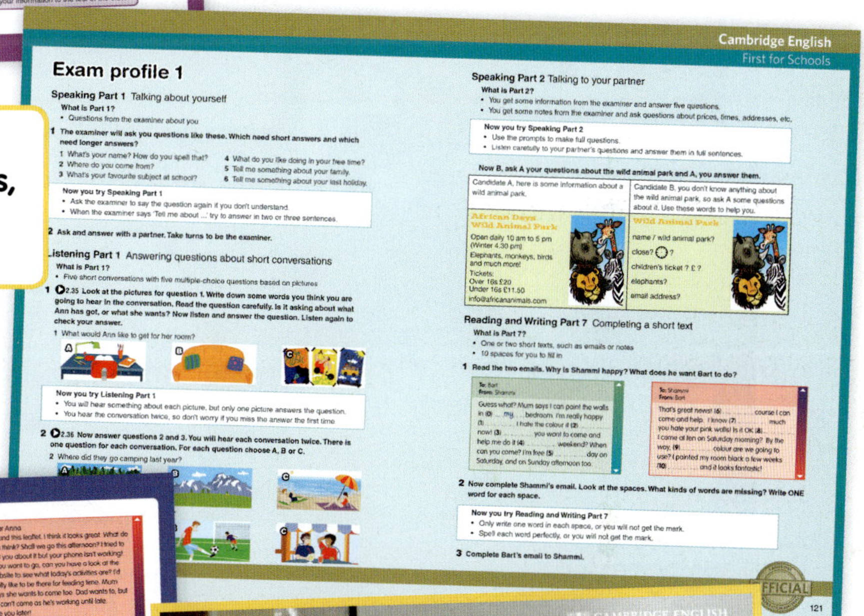

Exam profile Read useful tips, practise techniques, then try a taster exam task.

Review Check your progress

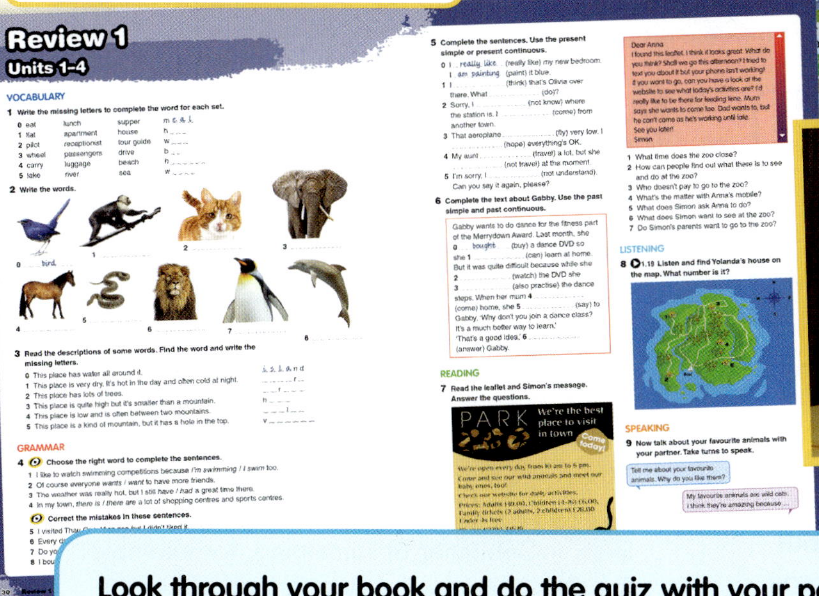

Video Watch teenagers doing speaking tasks in an exam situation.

Look through your book and do the quiz with your partner.

1. Which country can you see in the photos on page 22?
2. What is the subject you learn about on page 28?
3. Is Unit 8 about the past, present or the future?
4. In which unit do you read about free time?
5. On what page do you learn about India?

1 It's a challenge!
The adventure starts here

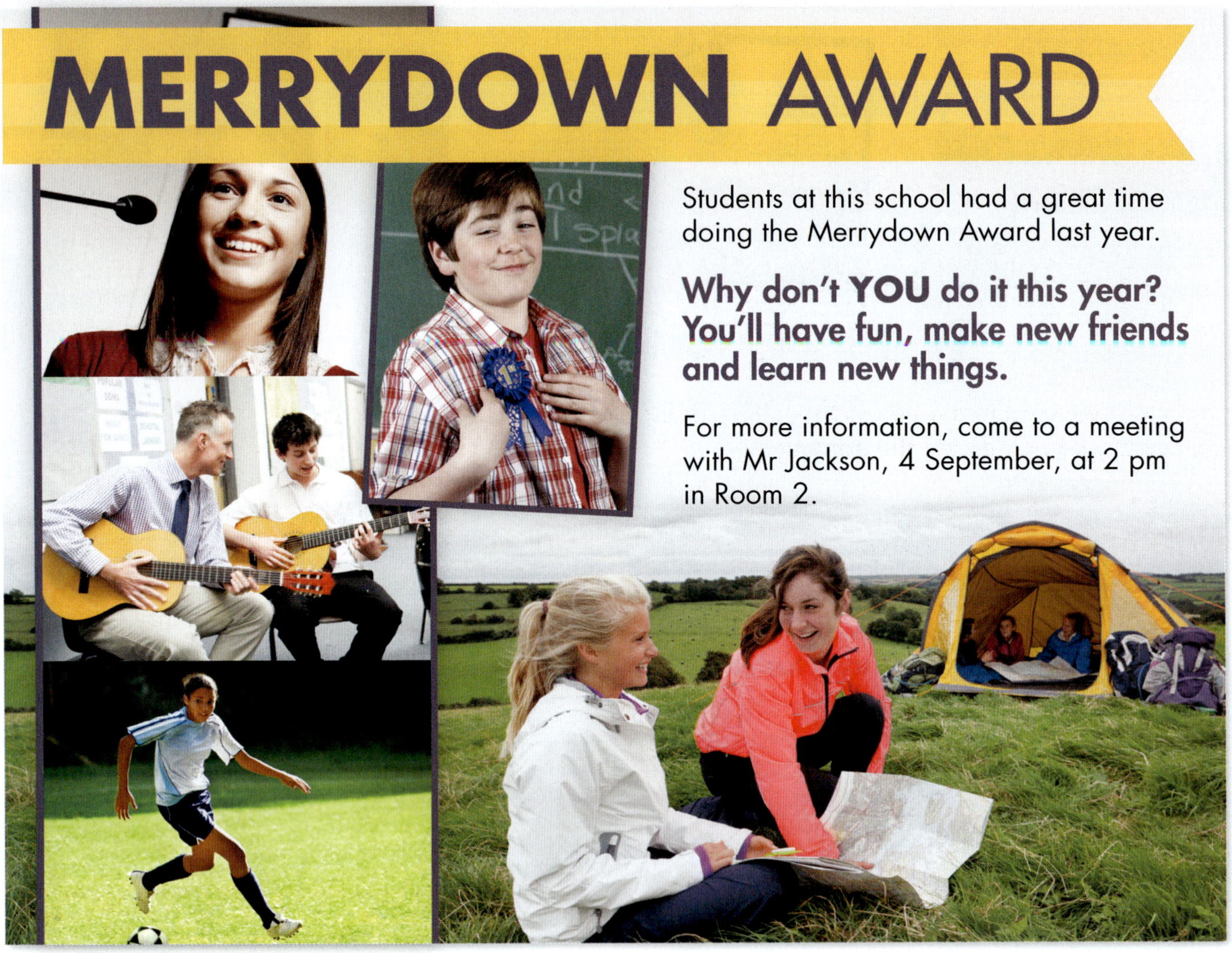

About you

1 Look at the poster.
What are the people in the pictures doing?
Which activities would you like to try?
Which wouldn't you like to try?
What do you think students have to do on the Merrydown Award?

LISTENING

2 ▶1.02 **You are going to listen to a teacher, Mr Jackson, talking to some students about the Merrydown Award. Which of these words do you think you are going to hear? Listen and check.**

business	camp	exercise	hiking
hobby	homework	money	
science	students	subject	talk

3 ▶1.02 **Read the information about the award. Then listen again. Write one word in each space.**

MERRYDOWN AWARD

The adventure begins here!

There are (**0**) ....*four*.... parts to the award:

Public Speaking – Choose a subject and talk about it for (**1**) .... minutes.

Fitness – Choose a kind of exercise to get fit, for example (**2**) .... or dance.

Skills – Get better at something, for example the (**3**) .... or piano, or find out about a job you'd like to do.

Expedition – Go camping and (**4**) .... in the countryside.

If you want to do the award, write a (**5**) .... to Mr Jackson. Describe yourself and say why you want to do it.

READING AND VOCABULARY

4 **Read the letters two students wrote to Mr Jackson.**

1 *I'm a friendly person and I'm popular at school. I'm funny – I can make people laugh easily. I usually work hard and I'm polite to the teachers. Music is important to me. I had guitar lessons last year and I'm learning to play the keyboard now. I do a lot of sport. I play hockey twice a week and I go swimming every Tuesday. I'm teaching my little brother to swim at the moment. He's really enjoying it.*

2 *I love school. Art's my favourite subject. At the moment I'm painting a picture of the sea. I'm really pleased with it. I like to be busy — I'm not a lazy person. I also like helping other people. My neighbour's quite old and I often go shopping with her. She always tells me I'm very kind. She is going to be 85 soon. My mum and I are planning a party for her.*

5 **Find the words in the box in the letters. Then use them to complete the sentences.**

busy friendly funny kind lazy pleased polite popular

1 My brother's very .... He lies in bed until midday and never does any work.
2 I was really .... when I got a good mark for my maths homework.
3 Sonia is very .... She always thinks of other people and tries to help them.
4 Everyone likes Toby. He's the most .... boy in the school.
5 Our teacher is very .... – she always makes us laugh.
6 When I speak to adults I try to be ....
7 Sara is very .... She smiles a lot and she's easy to talk to.
8 I'm really .... at the moment – I've got lots of things to do.

GRAMMAR Present simple and present continuous

6 **Complete the table with examples of present simple and continuous from the two letters.**

Present simple	Present continuous
I usually work hard.	*I'm learning to play the keyboard.*

7 **Complete the rules.**

1 We use the present .... to talk about things happening now, at the moment.
2 We use the present .... to talk about things that are always true or happen regularly.

→ Grammar reference **page 147**

8 **Choose the correct form of the verb.**

1 I *watch / am watching* Spartak Moscow play football every week.
2 What *do you usually eat / are you usually eating* for dinner?
3 Sorry, I can't talk now, I'm busy. *I'm practising / I practise* the piano.
4 We learned about rivers last term and now we *learn / are learning* about forests.
5 I'm quite lazy – *I don't always do / I'm not always doing* my homework.
6 My dad *is teaching / teaches me* how to play tennis at the moment.

Corpus challenge

Can you correct the mistake in this sentence?
It rains a lot at the moment.

WRITING

9 **Write a paragraph about yourself. Make notes first. Think of some:**

- adjectives to describe yourself
- things you like and don't like
- sports and hobbies you usually do
- things you are learning/planning/doing now.

Fill in the form with your details

MERRYDOWN AWARD

Home | News | Activities | Photos | Messages | Search

Your leader: Mr Jackson

Today you are going to start using the Merrydown Award website. This has all your details on it and it shows the activities you are doing. You can also get news and messages from Mr Jackson here.

What you need to do:

- Fill in the online form with all your details.
- Choose your activities. You have to discuss and agree these with Mr Jackson first.
- When you do your activities, take lots of photos and put them on the website.

When you finish, you can use the information to print a book about your time doing the award. This costs about £20.

PERSONAL DETAILS

FIRST NAME: Gabby
SURNAME: Hopkins
GENDER: female / male
AGE: 14
FIRST LANGUAGE: English

CONTACT DETAILS

EMAIL ADDRESS: g.hopkins@topnet.com
ADDRESS: 44 Meadow Avenue, London N24 6BG
HOME TELEPHONE NUMBER: 020 7659 2001
MOBILE NUMBER: 07561 364 883
SUBJECT FOR PUBLIC SPEAKING: not sure yet!

READING

1 Read the information from Mr Jackson. Are the sentences right (✓) or wrong (✗)?

1 Mr Jackson can put news and messages on the website.
2 Mr Jackson is going to fill in the students' forms.
3 Students need to talk to Mr Jackson before they choose their activities.
4 Students can put information about their activities on the website.
5 Every student gets a free book about their time doing the award.

2 Read Gabby's details. Match questions 1–5 to the words from the form a–e.

1 What's your family name?
2 How old are you?
3 Are you a girl or a boy?
4 Where do you live?
5 What do you speak at home?

a Address
b Gender: male / female
c First Language
d Age
e Surname

VOCABULARY

3 ▶1.03 Listen to Gabby's contact details. Then repeat them.

1 g.hopkins@topnet.com
2 44 Meadow Avenue, London N24 6BG
3 0207 659 2001
4 07561 364 883

4 Ask and answer with these contact details.

What's your (email address)?
sam.brown@yahoo.com

STUDENT A

sam.brown@yahoo.com
89 Sandy Lane, Oxford O22 3PG
Tel 01865 995478
Mob 07968 133 254

STUDENT B

jo.marsh@mac.co.uk
72 Hale Street, Manchester M4 8QT
Mob 07473 964 443

PRONUNCIATION The alphabet

5 **Practise saying the letters of the alphabet. Which letters sound similar? Complete the table.**

A B C D E F G H I
J K L M N O P Q R
S T U V W X Y Z

A	B	F	I	O	Q	R
H	C				u	

1.04 Listen and check.

LISTENING

6 **1.05 Listen to Gabby and Dylan talking to a new student called Finn. Answer the questions.**

1 What is Gabby's idea for the public speaking?
2 What is Dylan's idea?
3 How can Finn help Gabby and Dylan?

7 **1.05 Listen again to check your answers to Exercise 6. Then complete Finn's contact details.**

1 Phone number: ....
2 Email address: ....

SPEAKING

8 **Work in pairs. Ask and answer to fill in this form for each other. Spell your surnames.**

FIRST NAME:
SURNAME:
AGE:
ADDRESS:

PHONE NUMBER:

9 **Choose three questions to ask your partner.**

What are your favourite free time activities?
What are you learning about at school at the moment?
Tell me about your family.
What do you like doing on holiday?
What's your favourite food?
Tell me about your home town.

10 **Which questions were easy to answer? Which ones were difficult? Why?**

2 The natural world
The world is changing

VOCABULARY AND READING

1 **Which of these things can you see in the pictures? Name one or more examples of each.**

desert forest hill island lake
mountain river sea valley volcano

2 **Discuss these questions with your partner. Then read the article and check your ideas.**

1 How old is the Earth?
2 What changes are happening on Earth at the moment?

THE EARTH:
A changing planet

Scientists believe the Earth is 4.6 billion years old. However, the mountains, valleys, rivers, deserts and forests we see today are much younger than that. For example, Mount Everest is about 60 million years old and the Amazon Rainforest is only 10 million years old. The youngest sea in the world is the Baltic Sea, about 15,000 years old.

The Earth is always changing because of volcanoes, earthquakes and, of course, wind and rain. Some of these changes are very slow and others are quick. Water and ice can make very big changes to the planet. For example, glaciers (rivers of ice) can cut through mountains and make deep valleys.

It's normal for our planet to change. But at the moment scientists think it's changing faster than usual. They don't understand everything that is happening but they know that temperatures are rising. The weather is getting wetter in some places and drier in others, and there are more big storms.

However, these changes are not bad for everyone. Because the Arctic is getting warmer, some people in Greenland now own businesses that grow and sell vegetables. That wasn't possible 50 years ago. Farmers in Greenland like the warm weather and hope it will continue.

3 **Read the article again and choose the best heading for each paragraph.**

A Good news in one part of the world
B Problems for the planet at the moment
C The age of the Earth
D How the planet changes

4 **Find words with these meanings in the article.**

1 how hot or cold something is t..............................
2 with more rain than before w..............................
3 with less rain than before d..............................
4 bad weather with lots of wind and rain s..............................
5 someone who grows food f..............................
6 in between hot and cold w..............................

GRAMMAR Verbs we don't usually use in the continuous

5 **Find and underline these verbs in the text. What tense are they in?**

believe hope know like
own think understand

The verbs above are about thinking, feeling and owning things. We don't usually use them in the continuous form.

Which of the words in the box below are also about thinking, feeling and owning things?

belong to buy climb hate have
love need run sing want work

→ Grammar reference **page 148**

6 **Put the verbs into the correct tense, present simple or present continuous.**

1 Can you turn the TV off? I .... (hate) that programme!
2 Mr Jones .... (want) to talk to you. Are you free now?
3 Why .... (you sing)? I .... (need) to study!
4 That book .... (belong) to me. It's not my friend's.
5 I .... (love) this T-shirt. Can I buy it, Mum?
6 I can't talk now, sorry. I .... (run).

Corpus challenge

Can you correct the mistake in this sentence?
There are things in my bag that I'm needing at the moment.

LISTENING

7 **1.06 You are going to hear to a boy talking about the UK. Look at the map and the notes. Can you guess the missing words? Listen to check your ideas. Then listen again and complete the notes.**

The United Kingdom
Name of the biggest island in the UK: (1) ....
No one in Britain lives far from the (2) ....
There are more hills than (3) .... in the UK.
The longest river in the UK is the (4) ....
The UK doesn't have great (5) ....
How the weather is changing:
Winters are getting (6) ....
Summers are getting (7) ....

PRONUNCIATION th: θ and ð

8 **1.07 Listen to the sounds θ and ð. Look at the words and think about the sounds. Put the words into the right column.**

north other south there
these thing think this

θ Earth	ð weather

1.08 Listen and check. Then repeat.

SPEAKING

9 **Prepare a talk with a partner.**

- Draw or download a map of your country.
- Describe the geography of your country.
- Include some interesting facts.
- Describe the weather and say if/how it is changing.

10 **In groups of four, listen to each other's talks. Tick the things the other pair speak about.**

- mountains
- volcanoes
- islands
- rivers
- oceans
- forests
- the weather
- others

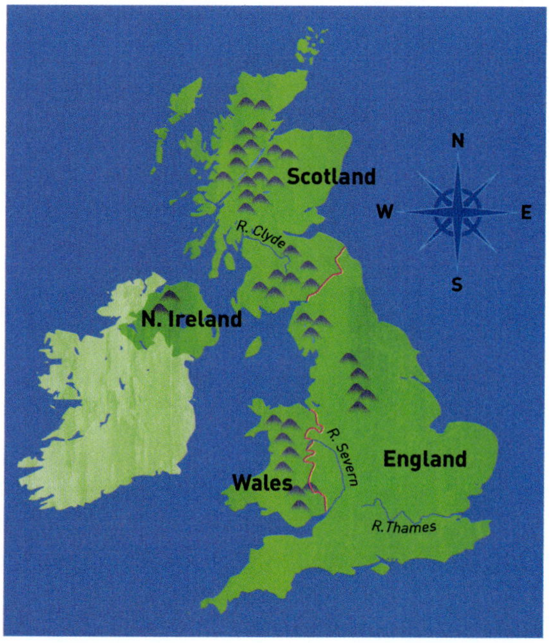

Wild animals

VOCABULARY

1 Match the words to the photos. Then answer the questions.

dolphin	lion	monkey	penguin	snake

1 Where do these animals come from?
2 Where do they live (sea, mountains, forest)?
3 Which are dangerous?
4 Look at each photo carefully. Are they animals in a zoo or are they wild? How do you know?
5 How many other animals can you name in English?

About you

2 What are your five favourite animals?
Why do you like them?
How often do you go to zoos?
Do you like them?

LISTENING

3 1.09 **Listen to Gina talking to her uncle about some photos of animals. Where did he take each photo? For questions 1–5, write a letter, A–H, next to each animal.**

PHOTOGRAPHS		COUNTRIES	
0 lion	*D*	**A**	Argentina
1 monkey		**B**	England
2 snake		**C**	India
3 penguin		**D**	Kenya
4 dolphin		**E**	Mexico
5 elephant		**F**	New Zealand
		G	Scotland
		H	South Africa

EP Get talking! → page 130

Oh right!
What?
You're so lucky!
Really?

READING

4 **Look at the picture and talk to your partner. Write down three things you know about pandas. Read the text once to check your ideas.**

The Giant Panda

Giant pandas live in bamboo forests, high in the mountains of south-west China. In the past they also lived in other parts of China, and in Myanmar and Vietnam. They spend about 12 hours a day eating bamboo, but sometimes also eat other things, including plants, fish and small animals.

Adult giant pandas weigh between 75 and 135 kilograms but a baby panda, or cub, only weighs about 85 grams when it is born. Female pandas usually only have one cub at a time. The little cub drinks milk for about four months and then begins to eat bamboo. Young pandas stay with their mothers for around 18 months.

Scientists think there are between 1000 and 2000 wild pandas left. There are about 325 pandas in zoos in a number of different countries, including China, the United States, Mexico, Japan and Germany. Scientists are working hard to save this beautiful animal.

5 **Are these sentences right (✔) or wrong (✘)?**

1 It's possible to find wild pandas in several countries.
2 Pandas only eat bamboo.
3 Baby pandas are very light when they are born.
4 Pandas start eating bamboo at the age of 18 months.
5 We know exactly how many wild pandas there are.
6 It's possible to see a panda in Mexico.

SPEAKING

6 **Write some questions to find out about these animals.**

1 What kind / animal is it?
2 Where / from?
3 Where / live?
4 What / eat?
5 How much / weigh?
6 How many / left in the wild?
7 What / babies / called?
8 How many babies / female have?
9 How long / baby stay with / mother?

Work in pairs, A and B. **Go to page 135.**

WRITING

Prepare to write – a text about an animal

GET READY Underline these prepositions in the text about pandas: *between, about, around, including*. Think about their meaning. Which two have the same meaning in this text?

Complete the sentences with *between, about/around* or *including*.

1 This competition is for anyone .... the ages of 10 and 14.
2 There are .... 40,000 African lions left in the wild.
3 All my friends, ... Tariq, are interested in animals.
4 The zoo is closed .... January and March.
5 I've got lots of pets, ... a rabbit and two cats.

PLAN Make notes about an animal, either one of the animals in Exercise 6, or one of your own. Use the panda text in Exercise 5 to help you.

WRITE Write three paragraphs.

1: kind of animal / where it lives / what it eats
2: what it weighs / its babies
3: how many are left / number in zoos

IMPROVE Compare your text with your partner's. Can you improve them?

Culture
The USA

1 **How much do you know about the USA? Do the quiz. Then check your answers with a partner.**

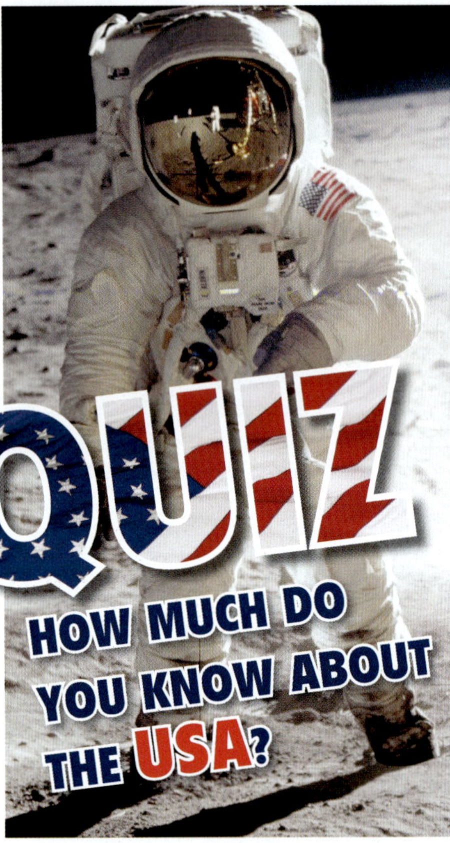

1 What's the name of the capital city of the USA?
A Los Angeles **B** New York
C Washington DC

2 Which country gave the Statue of Liberty to the USA?
A Brazil **B** France **C** The UK

3 Who started Microsoft?
A Bill Gates **B** Steve Jobs **C** Mark Zuckerberg

4 What was the name of the first man on the moon?
A Buzz Aldrin **B** Neil Armstrong **C** Michael Collins

5 What colour are the backs of the dollar notes?
A Black **B** Blue **C** Green

6 What is the national sport of the USA?
A Baseball **B** Basketball **C** American Football

There are fifty states in the United States of America. The largest is Alaska and the smallest is Rhode Island.

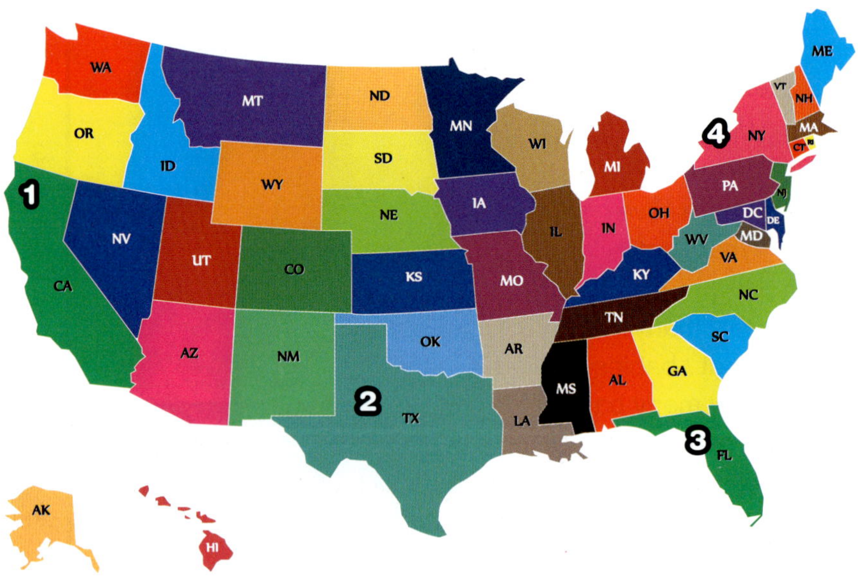

2 **Work in pairs. Can you find Alaska on the map? Use the letters to help you.**

3 **What are the names of states 1–4? Check your ideas with another pair. How many other states can you name?**

4 Read the text below quickly and check your answers to Exercise 3.

STATES OF THE USA

California

California is sometimes called *The Golden State*. It is on the west coast of the USA and more people live there than in any other state. It has several animal symbols but the most famous is the bear. You can find this animal on its flag too. The Californian poppy is the state flower. It is golden yellow and it grows all over the state. California Poppy Day is on April 6th each year.

Florida

Florida is in the south east of the USA and is famous for its beaches, for Disney World and for its oranges. The state plant is, of course, the orange tree with its beautiful flowers. The state animal is the panther, a wild cat. Florida's nickname is *The Sunshine State*.

New York

New York is on the eastern side of the USA. The city of the same name is probably more famous than the state and it is the city that gives the state its nickname, *The Empire State*. New York's animal symbol is the beaver. It lives in rivers up and down the state. The state plant is the red rose with its beautiful flowers.

Texas

Texas is the second biggest state in the USA and has the second largest population after California. Texas is in the south and has deserts and mountains as well as being next to the sea. It is often called *The Lone Star State*. The state plant, the prickly pear cactus, grows in the desert. The fruit are good to eat but very difficult to open. The state animal is the armadillo with its hard skin.

5 Read the text again and match the pictures (a–h) to the states.

6 Complete the table. Use information from Exercise 4.

State	Animal	Plant	Other name

Project a presentation on a state in the USA or part of your country

The United States has 50 *states*, but different countries use other words for parts of their country.

province (China) *département* (France) *county* (UK)

What word do you use for parts of your country?

Research a state in the USA or part of your country. Use the internet or books to find out

- where is it in the country
- if it has a nickname (if it doesn't, you can think of one)
- if it has a flag and what it looks like (if it doesn't, you can design one)
- if it has animal and plant symbols (if it doesn't, you can think of some)

Present your information to the class. Use pictures to make the presentation more interesting.

3 Travel: then and now

She loved adventure

VOCABULARY

1 How many ways of travelling can you think of? Which do you like best?

2 Check the words in blue in your dictionary. Then answer the questions.

1. Is an adventure something exciting or something boring?
2. Can you think of the names of three different aeroplanes?
3. Where do you find engines on planes? What do they do?
4. Does a flight take you into the air or under the ground?
5. Does a passenger fly the plane or fly in a plane?
6. What happens when a plane or a car doesn't have any fuel?
7. What does a pilot do?
8. Why is a radio important on a plane?

READING

3 Read the text quickly and find:

- the name of the pilot
- the name of the navigator
- the last place she took off from.

What do you think happened to Amelia Earhart?

1 In 1928 Amelia Earhart became the first female pilot to fly across the Atlantic. She loved flying and adventure. She always wanted to do new and different things. She was an amazing woman for her time.

2 Amelia decided to fly around the world. Her first flight was not successful but this did not stop her. What did she do? In 1937 she decided to try a second time. She chose Fred Noonan as her navigator. They didn't take any passengers. The aeroplane was too small!

3 Amelia and Fred took off from Oakland, California in her two-engine aeroplane, Electra on 21 May 1937. They flew over the Golden Gate Bridge in San Francisco and then travelled east across the United States and south to South America.

4 Amelia and Fred flew on across the Atlantic, Africa, the Middle East, India, Asia and Australasia. On the way they had to stop quite often. They didn't carry very much fuel on the plane. They were able to contact people by radio.

5 On Friday 2 July Amelia and Fred took off from Lae in Papua New Guinea. This was the last, most dangerous part of their flight because they were flying across the Pacific Ocean. But they never arrived at their first stop, Howland Island, and no-one ever saw them again.

6 In 2012 people thought they saw part of Amelia's plane in the sea. Where was it? It was near the tiny island of Nikumaroro, 640 km from Howland Island. They also found an old campsite on the island with fish and bird bones, two buttons and part of a pocket knife.

4 **Read the text again and answer the questions.**

1 Why was Amelia Earhart's 1928 flight special?
2 When did Amelia try and fly around the world for a second time?
3 What was Fred Noonan's job?
4 Which direction around the world did they fly, east to west or west to east?
5 Why did the plane have to stop so often?
6 Where were Amelia and Fred flying to on 2 July? Did they arrive?
7 How far is Nikumaroro Island from Howland Island?
8 What did people find on Nikumaroro Island?

5 **Discuss these questions. What do *you* think? Make notes.**

1 What did Amelia and Fred find to eat and drink on Nikumaroro?
2 Why did they build a fire?
3 What did they use the knife for?
4 How do you think they died?

PRONUNCIATION Silent letters

6 **Read these words aloud with a partner. Which are the silent letters?**

build climb flight knew knife
listen school write

1.11 **Listen and check.**

GRAMMAR Past simple

7 **Underline the past simple in these sentences from the text.**

She always wanted to do new and different things.
Her first flight was not successful.
What did she do?
She decided to try a second time.
Amelia and Fred took off from Oakland.
They flew over the Golden Gate Bridge.
They didn't carry very much fuel on the plane.
Where was it?

1 Which past simple verbs are regular?
2 Which past simple verbs are irregular?
3 Which verb never has 'did' in questions and negatives?

→ Grammar reference **page 149**

8 **Underline all the examples of the past simple in the text about Amelia Earhart.**

9 **Read questions *a* and *b* and complete the answers. Then answer questions 1–4.**

a Who did Amelia choose as her navigator?
She chose .... as her navigator.
b Who found an old campsite?
.... found an old campsite.

1 Which past simple question uses 'did', **a** or **b**?
2 What is the verb form in the other question?
3 Is the question asking about the subject or object?
4 How are the verbs different in **a** and **b**?

Choose *a* or *b* for each question.

5 Who did the boy see?
a His mother saw him.
b He saw his mother.
6 Who saw the boy?
a His mother saw him.
b He saw his mother.

10 **Complete the sentences in the past simple.**

1 In the past, people often .... (travel) by train.
2 My parents .... (not return) to the same hotel for their holidays.
3 What time .... (your aeroplane / take off) yesterday?
4 Who .... (fly) the first aeroplane across the Atlantic?
5 Mariana .... (not see) the film because the cinema .... (be) full.
6 My dad .... (find) a bottle at the beach with a message in it.

Corpus challenge

Can you correct the mistake in this sentence?
Tim, Sue, Christoph and Sabrina was here.

WRITING

11 **Look at your notes for Exercise 5. Write your ideas as a paragraph.**

I think Amelia and Fred ate … .

About you

12 Amelia Earhart's adventure was to fly across the Atlantic and then around the world.
What adventure would you like to have?
Would you like to fly in a hot air balloon, a helicopter, an aeroplane or a spaceship?
Where would you like to go?
Would you like to travel alone?

How can I help you?

LISTENING AND VOCABULARY

1 **Look at the photo. What can you see? Who are the people? What are they doing? Use some of these words.**

guest	luggage	map	on holiday	receptionist
suitcase	tourist	visitor		

I can see …   I think that …   I don't think that …

2 **1.12 Listen to the conversation between John, a student on holiday with his parents, and the hotel receptionist and check your ideas. Which city is he visiting?**

3 **1.12 Listen again. Are the sentences right (✓) or wrong (✗)?**

1 John is an only child.
2 John wants to look around the city in the afternoon.
3 The tourist information centre is a long way from the hotel.
4 The receptionist hasn't got an underground map.
5 John thinks taxis are faster than the underground.
6 John forgot his bag.
7 The guest before John had several suitcases.
8 There is a lift in the hotel.

EP Get talking! → page 130

By the way
It's the best way to …
Have a good day.
Excuse me

READING

4 **John goes to the tourist information centre and finds some information about visitor attractions. Read the information and match the places to the descriptions.**

a The Kremlin

b Red Square

c Yuri Kuklachev Cat Theatre

d Old Arbat

1 This street is more than 500 hundred years old! It's one of the oldest streets in Moscow. Come here to see the buildings and to do some souvenir shopping for friends back home.

2 This group of buildings is one of the most famous in Russia. Many years ago, the whole of the city centre was inside its walls. It's full of history and is a great place to visit.

3 This is the only show like this in the world. All the actors are, yes, cats! Come and be amazed by what the animals can do. Don't miss it.

4 This is a big open space right in the centre of the city with beautiful buildings all around it. There are always people walking around it, enjoying the sights.

5 **Which places would you like to visit? Why? Tell your partner.**

SPEAKING

6 1.13 **John phones the tourist information centre for some more information. Read and listen to his conversation. What are John and his family going to do that day?**

Clerk: Tourist information. How can I help you?
John: Hello. I'm here in Moscow with my mum and dad and my little sister. Can you give me some information about the zoo, please?
Clerk: Yes, certainly. It's open every day except Mondays.
John: Oh no. It's Monday today, so we can't go there. What about the Cat Theatre? Is there a show this evening?
Clerk: Ah, one minute. Ah, yes, there is. The theatre's near the centre and you can book online. You'll really enjoy it.
John: That's perfect. Thanks. We all want to go to see the cats. I'll tell mum and dad.
Clerk: And why don't you visit Red Square and The Kremlin before that? It's the best way to learn about the history of our country.
John: That's a really good idea. Oh, by the way, have you got any information about the Kremlin?
Clerk: Yes, of course. It's all on our website. It's in several different languages.
John: OK. Perfect. Thanks.
Clerk: Have a good day and enjoy your stay here.
John: Thanks. Bye.

7 1.14 **Listen and repeat the phrases.**

Can you give me some information about the zoo, please?
Yes, certainly.
The theatre's near the centre and you can book online.
You'll really enjoy it.
That's perfect. Thanks.
It's the best way to learn about the history of our country.
That's a really good idea.
Oh, by the way, have you got any information about the Kremlin?
Yes, of course. It's all on our website.
Have a good day.

8 **In pairs, choose a city you both know. What four places would tourists like to visit in this city?**
Role play a conversation at a tourist information centre. Use Exercises 6 and 7 to help you.

9 **Make questions. Then ask and answer them with a partner using the information below.**

1 address?
2 open every day?
3 what time / close?
4 how much / drinks?
5 web address?

TOURIST INFORMATION CENTRE

24 Green Street

Monday – Saturday
Hours: 9 am – 5 pm

Coffee, Tea and Juice: 50p

Come in for maps and a chat.

Visit: www.tinfo.com

10 **Student A turn to page 135.**
Student B turn to page 136.

4 My place
We were staying in an apartment

VOCABULARY

1 What does the word 'home' mean to you? What is a holiday home? What do people do there? Write some ideas on the word map.

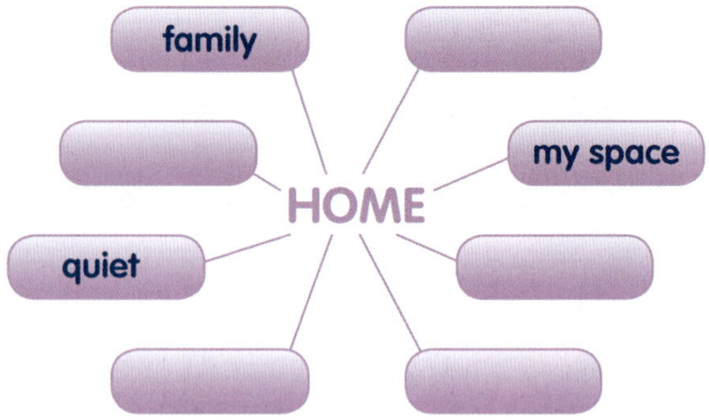

Compare your word map with another student's.

2 Look at the pictures of Elena's holiday below. What do you think happened?

Talk about each picture with your partner. Use the words in the box to help you.

I can see …   *Perhaps …*

apartment	beach	electricity	market	sand	sink	storm	suitcase	supper	surfboard

READING

a

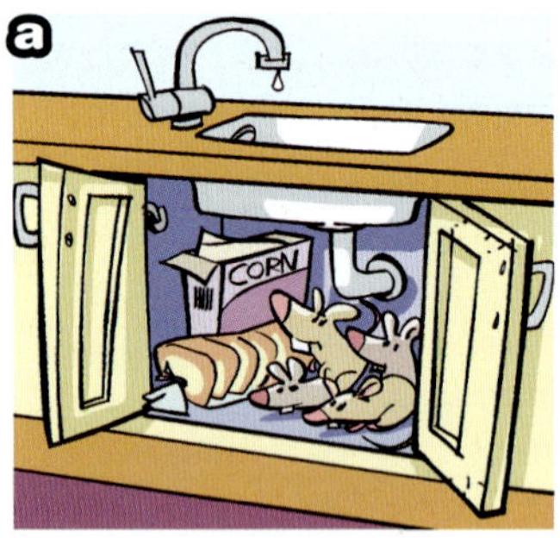

b

c

d

e

3 Read the text about Elena's holiday. Match the pictures to parts of the text. Which part of the holiday does not have a picture?

4 Write a short caption for each picture.

5 Lots of things went wrong on Elena's holiday. What other things can go wrong on holiday? Did you once have a terrible holiday or family day out? Tell the class.

OUR WORST HOLIDAY EVER!

1 It was the summer holidays and our family were renting an apartment for a week near the beach. We all went to the beach on the first day and it was fantastic! I did lots of surfing. The sea was really warm! While Mum and Dad were reading their books, my brother Pavel was building a really big sandcastle. He was happy for hours!

2 On the first evening, Mum and Dad were cooking supper while Pavel was playing with his toys. I was chatting to my friends on the internet, when suddenly my computer stopped working. There was no electricity in the apartment! We had to eat our supper in the dark! The electricity didn't come on again until the next morning.

3 On the next day, we went to the market. While we were shopping, the sun was shining and it was hot. But then suddenly dark clouds came over and it started to rain really hard. Dad drove us back to the apartment.

4 When we got back, the rain was coming into Pavel's bedroom and his bed was very wet. So for the rest of the holiday he had to share my bedroom!

5 At the end of the holiday, Mum and Dad were cleaning the apartment when suddenly Dad shouted, 'Oh, no!' Pavel and I ran into the kitchen. Dad was looking into a cupboard under the sink. We looked, and at the back of the cupboard we saw a family of mice!

6 We packed our suitcases and left the apartment very quickly! We were all really glad to get home.

GRAMMAR Past continuous and past simple

6 Look at the example sentences from the text.

a On the first evening Mum and Dad were cooking supper while Pavel was playing with his toys.
b I was chatting to my friends on the internet, when suddenly my computer stopped working.
c Then suddenly dark clouds came over and it started to rain really hard.

1 Find and underline all the verbs in the sentences. Which verbs are past simple and which verbs are past continuous?
2 Match i–iii to sentences a–c.
   i one action follows the other
   ii the actions are happening at the same time
   iii one action interrupts the other
3 Find one more example of i, ii and iii in the text.
4 Choose the right words to complete the sentence:

To form the past continuous we use the *present* / *past* simple of the verb 'be' and the *present* / *past* participle.

→ Grammar reference **page 150**

7 Work with a partner. Use the pictures from Exercise 2 to tell the story in your own words.

8 Look at the pictures and write sentences using the past continuous.

What was happening at the Jones family house when the taxi arrived?

When the taxi arrived, Ben was making sandwiches in the kitchen.

Corpus challenge

Can you correct this sentence? Choose the right answer.

I went to Kenting for my holiday. I ~~was playing~~ on Kenting's beach.

A play **B** played **C** am playing

PRONUNCIATION /iː/ and /ɪ/

9 How do you say the words in each pair?

eat	it	his	he's
fit	feet	leave	live
he'll	hill	sit	seat

▶ 1.15 **Listen and check. Then repeat.**

READING AND WRITING

10 Work with a partner. Look at this text. What kind of words are missing? How do you know? What are the missing words?

My name (1) .... Zara. I come (2) .... Bogotá in Colombia. I am fourteen years old and I (3) .... got two sisters. My favourite subjects at school (4) .... science and English, and I like history, too. Please write and tell (5) .... about you!

11 Complete these emails.

Write ONE word for each space.

Hello Tim,
How (0) ...are... you? I'm writing to tell you (1) .... my weekend. We visited my grandparents in (2) .... country. We travelled there (3) .... train. I went swimming in the river (4) .... day. I want to visit them again soon! I (5) .... a really great time.
From
Jackie

Hi Jackie,
Thanks for your email. My weekend was boring. I did (6) .... go anywhere. Mum was ill (7) .... we all stayed at home. I played my new computer game and helped my dad to (8) .... the cleaning and the washing! Mum is feeling (9) .... lot better now.
Write to (10) .... again soon.
Tim

No two homes are the same

VOCABULARY

1 Talk about the homes in the pictures. Use the words in the box.

- Which home would you like to live in? Why?
- Which home wouldn't you like to live in? Why not?

attractive	boat	cave	cold	dark	light	lorry
made of (*wood*)	pretty	unusual	useful	warm		

a

b

c

d

READING

2 Read the text. Which of the homes is it about?

Before Paula and Gary moved into their new home, they lived in a normal house. They liked their old house but they both wanted to live somewhere more interesting. So they started to look for a new home.

They were looking for a new place, when Tim, Gary's dad, had an idea. Tim had his own lorry business and he was selling one of his lorries. Paula and Gary could buy it and make it into their new home! Gary and Paula thought this was a great idea too and bought it.

Gary was building everything for their new home while Paula was working. He built cupboards, a table and he even built the bed. They didn't see each other much!

But a year ago, Gary finished the work on the lorry and they moved into it. Gary and Paula love their new place! There's no place like home!

3 Read the text again. Answer the questions.

1. Why did Gary and Paula want to leave their old home?
2. What happened when they were looking for a new place?
3. What did Gary and Paula buy from Tim?
4. Who built the things for the new home?
5. When did Gary and Paula move into their new home?
6. What do they think of their new home?

About you

4 What other unusual places to live in can you think of?
Make a list. Compare it with a partner.
How can you make them into a real home?
Write some sentences about your ideas and draw a picture.
Present your unusual home to the class.

LISTENING

5 ▶1.16 **What do the three pictures show? Now listen. What's the weather like now?**

A ☐ 
B ☐ 
C ☐ 

6 ▶1.17 **Listen to these five conversations and tick (✔) the right picture each time.**

1 What are they going to put in their sandwiches?

A ☐ 
B ☐ 
C ☐ 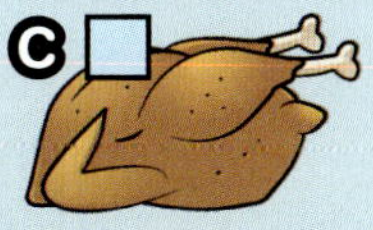

2 How much does the boy want to spend on new sunglasses?

A ☐ £ 10
B ☐ £ 12
C ☐ £ 16

3 What colour does Ben want to paint his bedroom?

A ☐ 
B ☐ 
C ☐ 

4 What's the number of the girl's house?

A ☐ 15
B ☐ 5
C ☐ 50

5 Where did James have his picnic?

A ☐ 
B ☐ 
C ☐ 

EP Get talking! → page 130

I don't agree.
I'm sorry.
That's right.
Excuse me.

WRITING

Prepare to write – a description of a home

GET READY Read Fernanda's description of her home. Which city does she live in? How many rooms does her family's apartment have?

> Hi, I'm Fernanda. I live with my family in an apartment in São Paolo, Brazil. It's on the ninth floor of a big block near the city centre. There's a kitchen, a living room, a bathroom and two bedrooms. I share one of the bedrooms with my sister, Luiza. She's fifteen. I'd like my own bedroom but it's OK sharing with Luiza. We like the same things and we enjoy talking at night.

We use pronouns instead of nouns so we don't have to repeat nouns.
Which nouns do the underlined pronouns in Fernanda's description replace?
Now replace the underlined nouns in this paragraph with pronouns.

> David lives with his family in a small house in York. The house is quite new and the house has two bedrooms. David shares his bedroom with his baby sister, Mia. Mia is two and a half. David's mum, Helen, is a doctor and his dad, Francisco, is a nurse. Helen and Francisco both work at the local hospital.

PLAN Think about your home. Where is it? What kind of home is it? Who lives there? How many rooms has it got? Do you have your own room or do you share a bedroom? Make notes.

WRITE Write a paragraph about your home. Use pronouns for some of the nouns.

IMPROVE Read your paragraph and look for mistakes. Check that you included all the information from your plan, and that you have used some pronouns.

Geography

Rivers

1 Look at the names of the four famous rivers. Do you know where they are?

Amazon Nile Volga Yangtse

a

b

c

d

Match the pictures to the rivers.

2 Think of two rivers in your country. What do you know about them?

3 Look at the diagram and complete the sentences.

1 The bottom of a river is called the ....

2 The side of a river is called the ....

RIVERS

Rivers are very important for people all around the world. Without them our lives would be very different. But what do you know about rivers? Rivers are always changing. Changes happen over a long time because of the flow of a river. Flow is the energy and speed of the moving water. Rivers always go downhill, towards the sea or a lake.

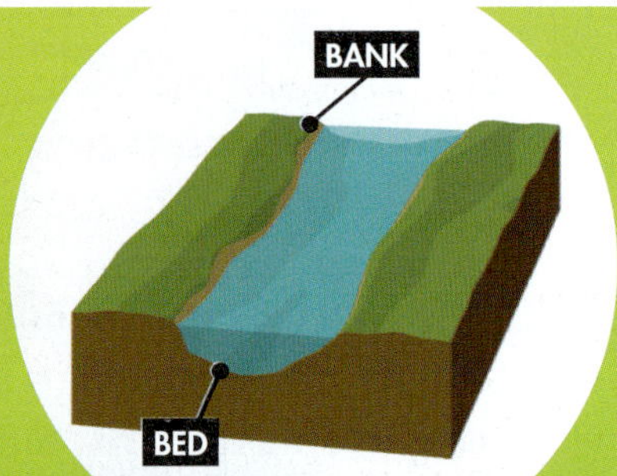

TWO THINGS CAN MAKE THE FLOW OF A RIVER CHANGE.

- Rainfall. A lot of rain means there is more water in the river, so it moves faster.
- The land. If the river is on steep land, then it moves faster. If the river is on flat land, then it moves more slowly.

When the flow of a river changes, then the form or shape of the river also changes and it looks different.

4 Read the text about rivers. Match words 1–6 to meanings a–f.

1 flow	a goes down quickly
2 rainfall	b shape
3 form	c from higher to lower ground
4 steep	d water from the sky
5 downhill	e without hills
6 flat	f energy of moving water

5 Work in pairs. Read the text again. Complete the sentences in your own words.

1 When there is a lot of rain, a river moves ....

2 A river moves .... on flat land than on steep land.

6 **Read some more about rivers.**
Match paragraphs 1–3 to diagrams a–c.

a

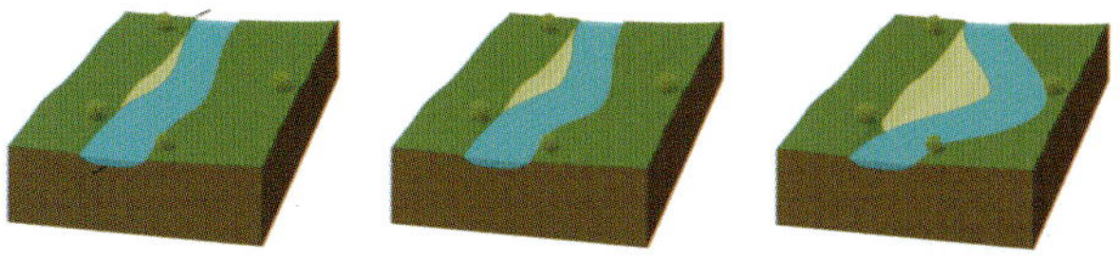

b

c

1. **Faster-flowing rivers are often on steep land. The river moves fast, so there is more energy in the water. This energy erodes the bed of the river and it becomes deeper and deeper. After many years, these fast-flowing rivers form deep V-shaped valleys.**
2. **Rivers on flatter land move quite slowly and there is less energy in the water. But there is still enough energy to make small curves, or *meanders*. These meanders become bigger and bigger as the water erodes the riverbank on one side and leaves sediment on the other.**
3. **When there is a lot of rain, a fast-flowing river moves even faster. A slow-flowing river moves faster too. But, because it is on flat land, the water comes up over the banks and covers the land around it. This is called a flood. The land around these rivers is called a flood plain.**

7 **Read about the River Thames and answer the questions.**

THE RIVER THAMES

The River Thames is 346 kilometres long and is the second longest river in the United Kingdom. It flows east into the North Sea. The Thames is not a very fast-flowing river and so does not have V-shaped valleys. The river goes through the centre of London. Can you see the meander in the photo? The last big flood of the Thames was in 1928, when the centre of London was under water. In 1984 they built the Thames Barrier and this stops the river flooding. The barrier is made of ten gates. They are as high as a five-storey building and they weigh 3,300 tonnes each!

The River Thames

The River Thames' meanders

The Thames Barrier

1. Which direction does the river go in?
2. Which sea does the river flow into?
3. Does the river flow quickly or slowly?
4. Which capital city does the river flow through?
5. Is the river on flat or steep land?
6. Why doesn't the river flood any more?

Project make a poster about a river

Choose a river in your country. Find out:

- which direction it goes in
- which sea or lake it flows into
- if it flows quickly or slowly
- if it is on flat or steep land
- if it floods and, if so, how often
- if it has a flood plain, and, if so, how big it is
- if it has meanders.

Draw the river on a map of your country. Show the main towns and cities near the river and where the river flows into the sea or a lake. Write about your river. Use the text about the River Thames to help you.

Review 1
Units 1–4

VOCABULARY

1 Write the missing letters to complete the word for each set.

0 eat	lunch	supper	m e a l
1 flat	apartment	house	h _ _ _
2 pilot	receptionist	tour guide	w _ _ _
3 wheel	passengers	drive	b _ _
4 carry	luggage	beach	h _ _ _ _ _ _
5 lake	river	sea	w _ _ _ _

2 Write the words.

0 ....bird........

1 ....

2 ....

3 ....

4 ....

5 ....

6 ....

7 ....

8 ....

3 Read the descriptions of some words. Find the word and write the missing letters.

0 This place has water all around it. i s l a n d
1 This place is very dry. It's hot in the day and often cold at night. _ _ _ _ r _
2 This place has lots of trees. _ _ r _ _ _
3 This place is quite high but it's smaller than a mountain. h _ _ _
4 This place is low and is often between two mountains. _ _ _ l _ _
5 This place is a kind of mountain, but it has a hole in the top. v _ _ _ _ _ _

GRAMMAR

4 Choose the right word to complete the sentences.

1 I like to watch swimming competitions because *I'm swimming* / *I swim* too.
2 Of course everyone *wants* / *want* to have more friends.
3 The weather was really hot, but I still *have* / *had* a great time there.
4 In my town, *there is* / *there are* a lot of shopping centres and sports centres.

Correct the mistakes in these sentences.

5 I visited Thau Cam Vien zoo but I didn't liked it.
6 Every day we doing different tests or exams at school.
7 Do you liked the competition?
8 I bought these clothes because I going to a party.

5 Complete the sentences. Use the present simple or present continuous.

0 I ...*really like*... (really like) my new bedroom. I ...*am painting*... (paint) it blue.
1 I .... (think) that's Olivia over there. What .... (do)?
2 Sorry, I .... (not know) where the station is. I .... (come) from another town.
3 That aeroplane .... (fly) very low. I .... (hope) everything's OK.
4 My aunt .... (travel) a lot, but she .... (not travel) at the moment.
5 I'm sorry, I .... (not understand). Can you say it again, please?

6 Complete the text about Gabby. Use the past simple and past continuous.

Gabby wants to do dance for the fitness part of the Merrydown Award. Last month, she **0** ...*bought*... (buy) a dance DVD so she **1** .... (can) learn at home. But it was quite difficult because while she **2** .... (watch) the DVD she **3** .... (also practise) the dance steps. When her mum **4** .... (come) home, she **5** .... (say) to Gabby, 'Why don't you join a dance class? It's a much better way to learn.'
'That's a good idea,' **6** .... (answer) Gabby.

READING

7 Read the leaflet and Simon's message. Answer the questions.

PARK ZOO
We're the best place to visit in town
Come today!

We're open every day from 10 am to 6 pm.
Come and see our wild animals and meet our baby ones, too!
Check our website for daily activities.
Prices: Adults £10.00, Children (4–16) £6.00, Family tickets (2 adults, 2 children) £28.00
Under 4s free
Phone: 02794 33529
Website: parkzoo@visit.com

Dear Anna
I found this leaflet. I think it looks great. What do you think? Shall we go this afternoon? I tried to text you about it but your phone isn't working! If you want to go, can you have a look at the website to see what today's activities are? I'd really like to be there for feeding time. Mum says she wants to come too. Dad wants to, but he can't come as he's working until late.
See you later!
Simon

1 What time does the zoo close?
2 How can people find out what there is to see and do at the zoo?
3 Who doesn't pay to go to the zoo?
4 What's the matter with Anna's mobile?
5 What does Simon ask Anna to do?
6 What does Simon want to see at the zoo?
7 Do Simon's parents want to go to the zoo?

LISTENING

8 1.19 Listen and find Yolanda's house on the map. What number is it?

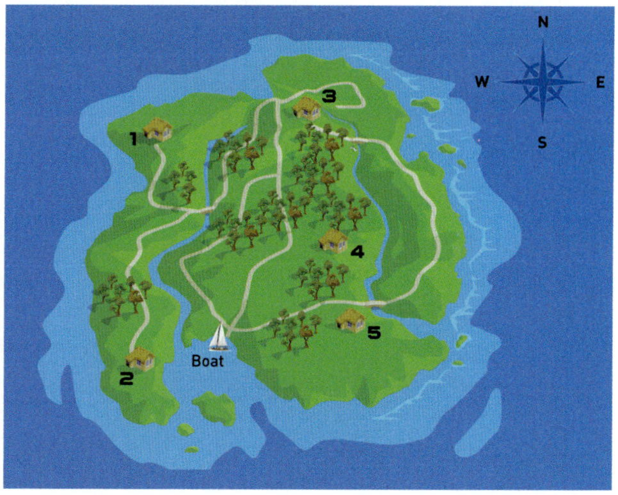

SPEAKING

9 Now talk about your favourite animals with your partner. Take turns to speak.

Tell me about your favourite animals. Why do you like them?

My favourite animals are wild cats. I think they're amazing because …

5 School

Choose your topic carefully

READING

1 **What do you like doing best in your lessons? Do you ever have to give talks?**

2 **Read the tips about how to give a good talk. Which one do you think is the most useful?**

HOW TO GIVE A GOOD TALK

BEFORE THE TALK ...

1 ....
Choose carefully. You can talk more easily about something you like and know about.

2 ....
It's often better to say less! Choose a few ideas and think about how to communicate them clearly to your audience.

3 ....
BEGINNING: It's important to start well, so think of an interesting way to begin.

MIDDLE: You should say three important things about your topic. Think the most carefully about this part of your talk as it is the longest section.

END: You don't want your talk to end badly. People often remember the ending the best, so why not plan this part of your talk first?

4 ....
Write your main ideas on a card. This helps you remember your talk better when you practise.

5 ....
Practise at home. When you can do it easily without notes, then you're ready.

WHEN YOU DO THE TALK ...

6 ....
Talk less quickly than you usually do but speak more clearly and more loudly than usual. Make sure that everyone can hear you easily.

7 ....
Talk to your audience, not to your hands or to the floor. Look quickly around the room at people's faces and check they are listening.

GOOD LUCK!

3 **Read the tips again. Match the headings to the paragraphs.**

a Don't try to say too much
b Don't speak too fast
c Get an idea
d Make notes
e Look up not down
f Plan your talk
g Prepare

GRAMMAR Comparative and superlative adverbs

4 **Look at these adverbs from the reading.**

a It's important to start well.
b Look quickly around the room at people's faces.
c Speak more loudly than usual.
d Talk less quickly than you usually do.
e Think the most carefully about this part of your talk.
f People often remember the ending the best.

Examples **a** and **b** have simple adverbs.
Examples **c** and **d** have comparative adverbs.
Examples **e** and **f** have superlative adverbs.

5 **Read the text again and find other adverbs. Are they simple, comparative or superlative? Choose the right words to complete the sentences.**

1 We usually use *than* after *comparative* / *superlative* adverbs.
2 We use *the* before *comparative* / *superlative* adverbs.

→ Grammar reference page 151

6 **Complete the table.**

Adjective	Simple adverb	Comparative adverb	Superlative adverb
bad		worse	the worst
			the best
			the most carefully
	quickly		
easy			

7 **Choose the right words to complete the sentences.**

1 Laura always does her homework *too quickly* / *more quickly* and makes mistakes.
2 Hans spoke *more quietly* / *the most quietly* of all the people in the class.
3 My dad drives *much carefully* / *more carefully* than my mum does.
4 You speak English really *good* / *well*.
5 I swim *often* / *less often* than I did when I was younger.

Corpus challenge

Can you find and correct the mistake here?
The weather was very well.

LISTENING AND READING

8 1.20 **Gabby, Dylan and Finn are planning their talks for the school challenge. Listen to Dylan practising his talk. Does he follow the advice in the text?**

9 **Gabby and Finn discuss Dylan's talk. Complete the conversation between the two friends. What does Gabby say to Finn? Write the correct letter A–H.**

Finn: Let's discuss Dylan's talk. Shall I start?
Gabby: **0** ...E...
Finn: OK. Well, the beginning was good, wasn't it?
Gabby: **1** ....
Finn: But after that, he stopped. Why was that?
Gabby: **2** ....
Finn: Perhaps he did. Anyway, then he spoke too fast.
Gabby: **3** ....
Finn: Do you remember what the third part was?
Gabby: **4** ....
Finn: That's right! And what did you think of the end?
Gabby: **5** ....
Finn: Our advice is lots more practice, then!

A I agree. It was hard to understand all his ideas.
B You're right. He started very clearly.
C He didn't remember to look at his watch.
D Wasn't it something about people being boring?
E Yes, you go first!
F It wasn't too bad, but he needs to improve it.
G Did you like the beginning as well?
H I think he forgot what to say next!

VOCABULARY

10 **Are these 'school words' or 'school subjects'?**

art biology chemistry classroom dictionary diploma music paper physics sport uniform fail/pass/take an exam

SPEAKING

11 **Give a 30-second talk about school. Choose from the ideas below, or use your own.**

Everyone should wear school uniform.
School holidays are too short.

Home schooling

About you

1 How many different school subjects do you study?
How many hours a week do you spend at school?
How many lessons do you have a day?
How much homework do you usually get each night?

READING

2 Read the blog about Oliver. Can you answer the questions in Exercise 1 about him? Why? / Why not?

Home school is cool!

A few years ago, I wasn't very happy at school and I wasn't doing well in tests. So, when I was eight, Mum and Dad decided to teach me at home.

Home schooling – great, I thought! I could stay in bed all day! Well it wasn't quite like that! My parents found out what I needed to learn. Sometimes I had lessons but most of the time I studied things I liked and found interesting. That's how home schooling works best.

My favourite hobby was playing computer games. So, with Dad's help, I began to write my own computer programs. But I didn't sit at the computer all day. I liked making models too and for that I needed … maths! At school maths was boring but now it was useful for making my models. I made a model aeroplane and a model boat and I needed to understand science and maths to do that – oh and design and technology too!

So were there any bad things about home schooling? Not really. I missed my friends. But I saw them at weekends and we talked about school! They told me about their week at school and I told them about mine. Mine always sounded more fun. Some weeks I studied more than they did. Other weeks I didn't study much at all. And I never had homework!

I'm 15 now and I'm back at school because I need to take exams. I don't mind. It's nice to be studying with my friends again. I still want to work on the space programme when I'm older.

3 Read the text again. Are these sentences right (✓) or wrong (✗)?

1 Oliver was a good student when he was young.
2 Oliver liked the idea of home schooling.
3 Oliver's parents decided what to teach him.
4 Oliver wrote computer programs alone.
5 Oliver liked maths when he was at school.
6 Oliver met his friends on Saturdays and Sundays.
7 Oliver's friends had more homework than he did.
8 Oliver isn't happy to be back at school.

4 Discuss the questions with your partner.

What are the good things about home schooling?
What are the bad things about it?
Do you know anyone who is home schooled?
Would you like to be home schooled?
Why? / Why not?

VOCABULARY

5 **What does *take* mean in this sentence?**

I'm 15 now and I'm back at school because I need to *take exams.*

Now look at the mind map. How is the meaning of *take* different each time? Can you think of an example sentence for each one?

TAKE

- A exams
- B a train
- C medicine
- D the second turning
- E a photo/picture
- F an umbrella

6 **Match the meanings of *take* in Exercise 5 to these words.**

1 carry
2 make
3 do
4 catch
5 go along
6 use

READING AND WRITING

7 **Oliver is going on a trip with his school. Read the email. How many questions does he ask? What does he want to know? Discuss your ideas.**

> **From:** Oliver
>
> Please email me about the school trip to the mountains next week. What day is it? What time do we meet? What do I need to take?

8 **Read Sam's answer to Oliver. These were the instructions for the task:**

Write an email to Oliver and answer the questions. Write 25–35 words.

> **From:** Sam
>
> The school trip to the mountains is on thursday. The bus goes from school at 8.30 o'clock in the morning. Don't forget to bring a lunch and a towel. I think it's going to be a great day.

Discuss these questions in pairs.

1 Did Sam answer all three questions?
2 Did Sam include any extra information? Was he asked to do this?
3 How many words did Sam write?
4 Are there any mistakes in the email?

9 **Read the email from your English friend Lucy.**

> **From:** Lucy
>
> Please tell me about our hockey match next Monday. Where is it? What time does it start? What do I need to bring?

Now write an email to Lucy and answer the questions. Write 25–35 words.

10 **Read your partner's email. Did they answer all the questions clearly?**

PRONUNCIATION Word patterns

11 **1.21 Listen and look at the word patterns in the table. Then put the words in the box into the right column.**

Oo	Ooo	oOoo
topic	*audience*	*communicate*

aeroplane biology chemistry
classroom comparative dictionary
favourite model technology

1.22 Listen and check. Then repeat the words.

SPEAKING

12 **Work in groups. Describe your perfect school. Make notes.**

Where is the school?
What lessons do you have?
How many students are there?
Who are the teachers?
Do you have homework?
How many lessons do you have in a day/week?
How long are the holidays?
Do you wear a uniform?
What's the food like?
Do you sleep there?

13 **Now tell the rest of the class about your perfect school.**

Take turns in your group to speak.

Video extra

6 It's very special
It belongs to a friend of mine

VOCABULARY

1 **Match the things in A to the materials in B. Some have more than one answer!**

A
bottle bowl
cup envelope
jumper necklace
ring shoes

B
glass gold
leather paper
plastic silver
wood wool

2 **Work with a partner. Have you got any of the things in Exercise 1?**

Where did you get them? What is your favourite thing? Describe it. Use the words in the box to help you.

little lovely old pretty small soft

LISTENING

3 **1.23 Listen to Carmen at her grandparents' house. She is looking for something to take to her art class. Her friend Murat is helping her. They find lots of different things.**

Who does each thing belong to? Write a letter A–H next to each thing.

Things	People
0 clock *E*	**A** aunt
1 scarf	**B** brother
2 hat	**C** cousin
3 toy bear	**D** father
4 painting	**E** grandfather
5 jacket	**F** grandmother
	G mother
	H uncle

4 **1.23 Which things in Carmen's grandparents' house are …**

1 … lovely? **2** … old? **3** … pretty?
4 … small? **5** … soft?

EP Get talking! → page 131

Actually, it's …
I don't know why …
I think it's …
That's not …

GRAMMAR Possession

5 **Who does the dog belong to? Match the pictures to the sentences.**

1 It's my brother's dog.
2 It's my brothers' dog.

Look at sentences 1 and 2. Which sentence has *'s* and which sentence has *s'*? Why?

6 **Complete the table.**

Determiners	Pronouns
my	mine
your	
his	
her	
our	
their	

→ Grammar reference **page 152**

7 **Who does the football belong to? Match the pictures to the sentences.**

1 It belongs to a friend of theirs.
2 It belongs to a friend of hers.

8 **Complete the sentences with the correct word.**

1 That's not Robert's book, it's Paula's. I can give it to ....
2 This jacket belongs to .... friend. I'm borrowing it today.
3 A cat plays in our garden sometimes, but it's not ....
4 That football is my brother's! Why did you take it without telling .... ?
5 Julie and Dave are lucky. .... house has a swimming pool.
6 Can I use .... pencil? I forgot ....

Corpus challenge

Choose the correct sentence.

1 I went to the stadium with my father and two friends of us.
2 I went to the stadium with my father and two friends of ours.
3 I went to the stadium with my father and two friends of my.

PRONUNCIATION Weak forms: *a* and *of*

9 **1.25 Listen and repeat.**

She's a friend of mine.
He's a friend of hers.
They're friends of ours.
Is he a friend of yours?

SPEAKING

About you

10 In pairs, think of three things that belong to different people in your family and how to describe them.

toy horse, surf board, earrings

The toy horse is my baby brother's. It's small and soft and he loves playing with it …

11 **Work in groups. Take turns to talk about the things from Exercise 10.**
Who do they belong to? What are they like?

WRITING

12 **Write a paragraph about the things you talked about in Exercise 11.**

I found some amazing silver jewellery!

READING

1 **Work in groups. Look at the pictures of treasure and answer the questions.**

Who usually finds treasure?
Where do they usually find it?
Who usually hides it?
What stories do you know about treasure?

About you

2 What kinds of treasure are there in museums near you?
How old are they? Where are they from?

a

b

c

d

3 **Read the text. What treasure from Exercise 1 did Terry Herbert find?**

The Staffordshire Hoard

Terry Herbert's hobby was looking for treasure, especially gold. He looked for eighteen years and found nothing important. Then one day he did! Over five days, Terry found hundreds of pieces of gold and silver treasure in a square green field not far from his house.

The field belonged to a farmer called Fred Johnson. Fred and Terry couldn't keep this national treasure, but they received a lot of money for finding it. They shared more than three million pounds! The farmer built a new house with his half of the money.

The treasure is called the Staffordshire Hoard. There are more than 3,500 pieces of gold and silver, all from the 7th or 8th centuries. Nobody knows why the treasure was in the field. Some pieces are quite small, including some beautiful gold fish and snakes. Every piece is amazing!

Most of this wonderful old treasure is at the Birmingham Museum and Art Gallery. Sometimes travelling exhibitions take pieces of the treasure to different parts of the UK and the world. Terry Herbert gives talks about how he found the treasure. At these talks it is possible to look at photos and copies of some of the treasure but Terry doesn't bring any of it with him.

4 **Read the text again and then answer the questions. Choose A, B or C.**

Example: 0 *Answer: A*

0 Terry Herbert started his hobby
- **A** 18 years ago.
- **B** five days ago.
- **C** one day ago.

1 Where was the treasure?
- **A** in his house
- **B** near his house
- **C** a long way from his house

2 Why didn't Terry keep any of the treasure?
- **A** It belonged to the whole country.
- **B** Fred wanted to keep it all.
- **C** Terry needed a new house.

3 How much of the money did Terry get?
- **A** none of it
- **B** all of it
- **C** half of it

4 People know
- **A** how old the treasure is.
- **B** why it was in the field.
- **C** who it belonged to.

5 The treasure is all
- **A** the same size.
- **B** made of gold.
- **C** very beautiful.

6 What happens to the treasure now?
- **A** Some of it moves from place to place.
- **B** None of it leaves the United Kingdom.
- **C** All of it stays in a museum in Birmingham.

7 At Terry Herbert's talks, people can
- **A** learn how Terry found the treasure.
- **B** see some of the real treasure.
- **C** take photos of Terry with the treasure.

WRITING

Prepare to write – adjective order

GET READY

To: citymuseumfinds@museum.uk

I found a big wooden box in my granddad's house. It's full of little gold coins. There are hundreds of them. I'm sending a photo. I hope it's treasure!
From
Ben

Read Ben's email to the museum. What did he find?
Put the underlined pairs of adjectives in the email under the right heading below.
- opinion • size • shape • age • colour • material

Find two other examples of pairs of adjectives in Exercise 3 and add them.
Add the pair of adjectives from the title of this lesson.

PLAN Imagine you found some treasure: • What is it? • Where did you find it? • What does it look like?
Plan your email to the museum.
What pairs of adjectives can you use to describe your object? What order do they go in?

WRITE Write an email to the museum. Describe the object and say where you found it.
Use Ben's email to help you. Write 25–35 words.
Draw a picture of your object.

IMPROVE Read your partner's email. Check for mistakes with adjectives.

Culture
Secondary school in the UK

1 Work with a partner. What do you know about secondary schools in Britain? Discuss your ideas. Read the webpage. Were any of your ideas mentioned?

HOME | PRIMARY | SECONDARY | COLLEGE | UNIVERSITY | VOCATIONAL

The secondary school system in England and Wales

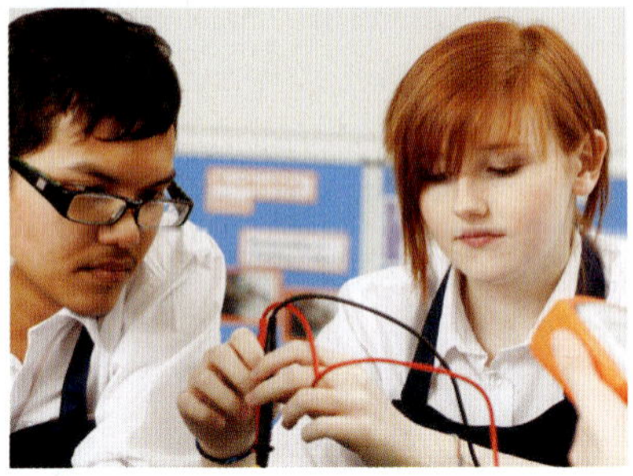

In the UK, children go to secondary school from the age of 11–16. Most secondary schools are 'comprehensives' – this means they take children of all abilities. At the end of Year 9, when they are 14, students choose the subjects they want to study at GCSE. These are national exams you take when you are 16. Everyone has to do English, maths and science and they choose another four or five subjects. There are lots to choose from, including photography, drama and food technology.

The school year

The secondary school year goes from September to July. There are three terms, and each one is about twelve weeks. There's a one-week half-term holiday in the middle of each term in October, February and May. The Christmas and Easter holidays are two weeks and the summer holiday is six weeks.

The school day

The school day at comprehensive schools goes from about 8.45 am to 3.30 pm. There's a break in the morning and another for lunch. Most British school students have to wear a uniform. This usually includes a blazer and a tie. Each school has its own colours.

Sixth form

After GSCEs, students can leave school and go to college or do other types of training course. If they stay at school for Years 12 and 13, students go into the Sixth Form. In most schools they don't have to wear a uniform any more and sometimes have their own café. In Year 12, they choose four subjects and study for exams called AS levels. In Year 13, they continue with three of those subjects for their A levels. These are high-level exams you need to pass to go to university.

Private schools

Most children go to state schools, but Britain also has private schools. Some of these are hundreds of years old and have interesting traditions. Eton, a school for boys, is an example. The Queen's grandsons, William and Harry, studied there.

2 Read the webpage again and complete the chart.

	Age	School years	National exams
Secondary school	11–14 14–16	Year 7 – Year 9 Year 10 – Year 11	2 ....
1	16–17 17–18	Year 12 Year 13	AS levels 3 ....

The School Year

First term: 4 .... to December Christmas holiday (two weeks)
Second term: January to April Easter holiday (5 .... weeks)
Third term: May to 6 .... Summer holiday (7 .... weeks)

3 Work in groups. Compare the UK secondary school system with your own.

We go to secondary school at the age of …

We don't have three terms, we have …

We have national exams when we are …

4 Read the information on the school website. Answer the questions.

W Woodedge
SECONDARY SCHOOL

Parents | Teachers | Students

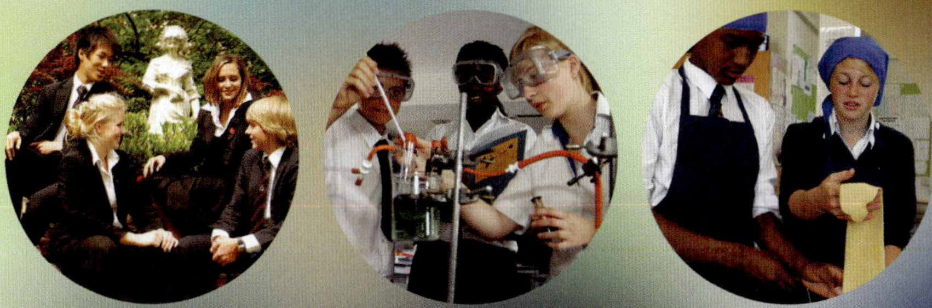

Welcome to the Woodedge School website. We are a comprehensive school for girls and boys aged 11–18. Our children come from many different cultures and backgrounds. We are a popular school and children who come here do very well in their exams. As well as excellent teaching, we offer many interesting after-school clubs, including sports, drama and dance.

School Diary

Important Dates for November

Friday 13th: Charity Day
This is a non-uniform day, so can everyone please bring £1.00. Wear your own clothes, but no hats please, and don't colour your hair. There will be things for sale, so bring in some extra money. All the money we make will go to the charity Save the Children.

Friday 20th: Autumn concert
Tickets £3.00 on sale now - maximum four per student.

Tuesday 24th: Years 7–10 Girls' indoor football competition
Sports Hall –trainers only, please.

Monday 30th: Year 11 school trip to National Theatre

1 At what age do students leave Woodedge School?
2 Where are Year 11 students going on 30 November?
3 How many tickets can each student buy for the concert?
4 What must students wear for the football competition?
5 Do students have to wear their school uniform on 13 November?
6 Why do students need to bring money to school on 13 November?

5 ▶1.26 Listen to Aleesha talking about Woodedge School. Answer the questions.

1 How many pupils are there at Woodedge?
2 What is Aleesha's cultural background?
3 What time does school finish?
4 What do students learn about in PDT?
5 What kind of food can you get at lunchtime?
6 How does Aleesha pay for her lunch?
7 What after-school clubs is she doing this term?
8 What is she making for Charity Day?

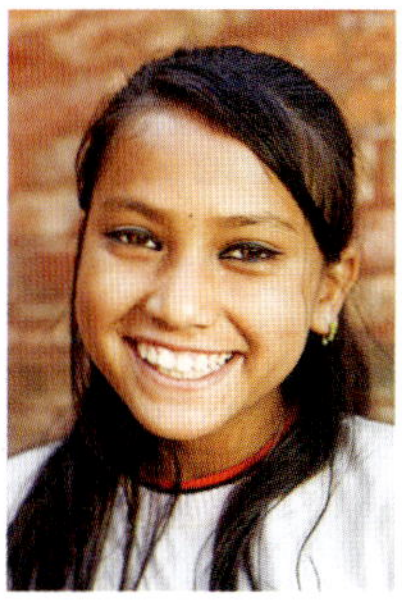

6 Compare Woodedge School with your own. Talk to your partner about these things.

- mix of cultures
- number of students
- how long the day is
- school lunches
- after-school clubs
- special days (like Charity Day)
- concerts
- school trips

Project – make a school webpage

Design a webpage for your school. Include this information:

- a description of the school
- photos of your friends and the building
- a newsletter with school events for one month

7 Travel and holidays

We're climbing next week

VOCABULARY AND LISTENING

1 **Where can you go on adventure holidays? What can you do on them? Match the pictures of the holiday activities to the words in the box.**

climbing   hiking   mountain biking   zip wiring

a

b

c

d

2 **1.27 Tara is talking to her friend Dan about her holiday plans. Listen and number the activities from Exercise 1 in the order you hear them.**

3 **1.27 Listen again. Write Tara's and Dan's holiday activities in the plan.**

Monday	Tuesday	Wednesday	Thursday	Friday

4 **Complete the sentences with the words in the box.**

get back   get lost   getting on   getting to   getting up

1 Tara's .... the airport by car.
2 Tara and Dan have to .... to the activity centre alone.
3 Tara and Dan are .... a bus early in the morning.
4 Tara and Dan are .... at 5 am on Monday morning.
5 Dan hopes he doesn't .... in the mountains.

5 **Which adventure activity would you like to do? Why? Tell your partner.**

4 Read the information on the school website. Answer the questions.

W **Woodedge** SECONDARY SCHOOL

Parents | Teachers | Students | School Diary

Welcome to the Woodedge School website. We are a comprehensive school for girls and boys aged 11–18. Our children come from many different cultures and backgrounds. We are a popular school and children who come here do very well in their exams. As well as excellent teaching, we offer many interesting after-school clubs, including sports, drama and dance.

Important Dates for November

Friday 13th: Charity Day
This is a non-uniform day, so can everyone please bring £1.00. Wear your own clothes, but no hats please, and don't colour your hair. There will be things for sale, so bring in some extra money. All the money we make will go to the charity Save the Children.

Friday 20th: Autumn concert
Tickets £3.00 on sale now - maximum four per student.

Tuesday 24th: Years 7–10 Girls' indoor football competition
Sports Hall –trainers only, please.

Monday 30th: Year 11 school trip to National Theatre

1 At what age do students leave Woodedge School?
2 Where are Year 11 students going on 30 November?
3 How many tickets can each student buy for the concert?
4 What must students wear for the football competition?
5 Do students have to wear their school uniform on 13 November?
6 Why do students need to bring money to school on 13 November?

5 ▶ 1.26 Listen to Aleesha talking about Woodedge School. Answer the questions.

1 How many pupils are there at Woodedge?
2 What is Aleesha's cultural background?
3 What time does school finish?
4 What do students learn about in PDT?
5 What kind of food can you get at lunchtime?
6 How does Aleesha pay for her lunch?
7 What after-school clubs is she doing this term?
8 What is she making for Charity Day?

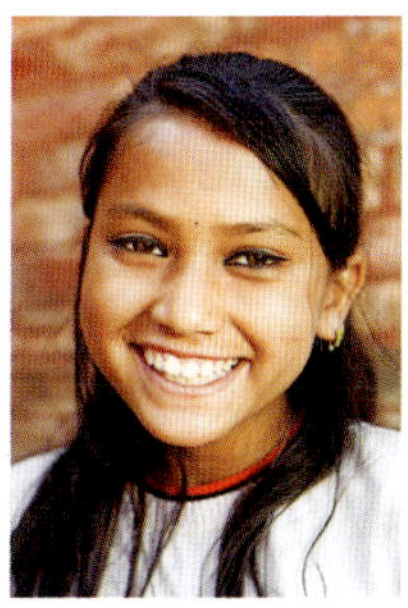

6 Compare Woodedge School with your own. Talk to your partner about these things.

- mix of cultures
- number of students
- how long the day is
- school lunches
- after-school clubs
- special days (like Charity Day)
- concerts
- school trips

Project make a school webpage

Design a webpage for your school. Include this information:

- a description of the school
- photos of your friends and the building
- a newsletter with school events for one month

7 Travel and holidays

We're climbing next week

VOCABULARY AND LISTENING

1 **Where can you go on adventure holidays? What can you do on them? Match the pictures of the holiday activities to the words in the box.**

climbing hiking mountain biking zip wiring

2 ▶1.27 **Tara is talking to her friend Dan about her holiday plans. Listen and number the activities from Exercise 1 in the order you hear them.**

3 ▶1.27 **Listen again. Write Tara's and Dan's holiday activities in the plan.**

Monday	Tuesday	Wednesday	Thursday	Friday

4 **Complete the sentences with the words in the box.**

get back get lost getting on getting to getting up

1 Tara's .... the airport by car.
2 Tara and Dan have to .... to the activity centre alone.
3 Tara and Dan are .... a bus early in the morning.
4 Tara and Dan are .... at 5 am on Monday morning.
5 Dan hopes he doesn't .... in the mountains.

5 **Which adventure activity would you like to do? Why? Tell your partner.**

VOCABULARY

5 Match the pictures to the words.

by boat on foot by helicopter by motorbike by scooter by ship by tram by underground

6 Put the words from Exercise 5 into these groups: Air, Land, Sea. What other ways of travelling can you add?

7 Complete the sentences with ways of travelling.

1 I usually go to school .... but if I'm late I go ....

2 In the past, people used to go across the sea .... but now they can do the journey ....

3 People in big cities don't always use their cars. They often travel .... or ....

SPEAKING

8 Laura is on holiday with her parents. Read the conversation. What is Laura's dad doing on Sunday morning?

Dad: Let's go sightseeing on Saturday morning, Laura.
Laura: I'm not that interested in sightseeing, Dad. How about shopping?
Dad: I'd prefer to go on a boat trip or something like that.
Laura: A boat trip. That's a great idea!
Dad: What shall we do in the afternoon? Would you like to go horse riding?
Laura: I'd love to. Where is it?
Dad: It's near the beach. It's a shame about the sightseeing. I wanted to do that. Never mind.
Laura: Why don't you go on Sunday morning with Mum, and I can sleep late, if you like?
Dad: Good idea. So, tomorrow we're taking a boat trip in the morning and …
Laura: … we're going horse riding in the afternoon!

9 ▶1.30 Listen to the conversation. Then practise it in pairs.

10 Work with a partner. Read the weekend programme for an adventure holiday and plan your activities for the weekend.

Come and join us this weekend!

SATURDAY MORNING	bike ride and picnic beach volleyball	SATURDAY AFTERNOON	boat trip barbecue	SATURDAY EVENING	night walk through the forest
SUNDAY MORNING	helicopter trip around the island races and games on the beach	SUNDAY EVENING	goodbye party with disco		

Write your name on the list or speak to John.

Have a conversation like the one in Exercise 8. Use the words in blue to make suggestions and say if you agree or don't agree. Then act it out to another pair of students.

8 Life in the future
Will homes change in 20 years?

VOCABULARY

1 Match the pictures to the words.

- Where in a home do you usually find these things?
- Which things need electricity to work?
- Which things are furniture?

5

3

1

2

4

6

7

chair	cupboard	fridge	lamp	sink	sofa	washing machine

2 Look at the home activities. Mark each one *A* (using my hands) or *B* (using technology). Compare your answers with your partner. Talk about the technology you use for activities you marked *B*.

open your front door	turn off the TV	turn on the computer	lock the car
turn on the lights	close the windows	close the garage door	

LISTENING

3 ▶1.31 Listen to a radio show interview about homes of the future. Write down all the 'home' words you hear.

4 ▶1.31 Listen to the radio programme again. Number the information in the order you hear it.

a The outside of houses will change a lot. ....

b Tables will have computers in them for playing games. ....

c People will use more technology in their homes. ....

d Chairs and things like that won't look very different. ....

e People won't need to turn machines on and off by hand. ....

EP Get talking! → page 131

... or something like that
Why not?
Finally
First of all

VOCABULARY

5 Read the descriptions of some words for things in the house. What is the word for each one? The first letter is already there. There is one space for each other letter in the word.

0 You can see your own face in this. m *i r r o r*
1 You stand under the water and wash yourself in this. s _ _ _ _ _
2 This is a kind of table where you can study or use a computer. d _ _ _
3 People use these to put their books and photos on. s _ _ _ _ _ _
4 A room usually has four of these and you can paint them. w _ _ _ _
5 This is a large comfortable seat for one person. a _ _ _ _ _ _ _

GRAMMAR Future with *will*

6 Look at these examples from the recording.

We use *will* when we think something is possible in the future.
We often use *think* before *will*.
I think they'll (will) be very different from today's homes.
You won't (will not) have to use your hands to do it.
Will it work for the heating and the lights too? Yes, it will.
Will furniture change very much? No, it won't (will not).

Choose the correct words to complete the rules.

1 We use *will* and the main verb *with* / *without* *to*.
2 To make questions we *use* / *don't use* 'do' or 'does'.
3 In questions the *subject* / *verb* and *will* change places.
4 We *do* / *don't* add *s* to *will* for 'he', 'she' and 'it'.
5 The negative of *will* is ....

→ Grammar reference **page 154**

Corpus challenge

Can you correct the mistake in this sentence?

I see you in front of the museum at 3 pm.

PRONUNCIATION *will* and *won't*

7 1.33 Listen and repeat.

Houses will be smaller.
People won't use door keys.
I'll live in a big house.
I won't walk anywhere.

8 Work with a partner. Use *will* and *won't* to talk about your family and friends five years from now.

My sister will have a lot of money in five years.

SPEAKING

9 Do the quiz. Put a tick (✓) in one of the columns.

	in the next five years	within 30 years	never
1 There will be wars about water.			
2 During the summer, there won't be any ice at the North Pole.			
3 Space travel will get cheaper and cost the same as a plane ticket.			
4 People will travel to Mars and live there.			
5 There will be cars without drivers.			
6 People will be able to communicate with technology by thinking.			
7 Most people will live to be 100 and their bodies won't get old.			

10 Discuss your answers in groups of three.

Number 1. I don't think there will ever be wars about water. What do you think?

What will we write?

READING

1 **Look at the pictures of time capsules. What do you think a time capsule is?**

2 **Read about three time capsules. Which two time capsules can you see in the pictures? Match them to two of the paragraphs.**

THREE AMAZING TIME CAPSULES

A Harold Davisson lived in a town in Nebraska in the USA in the last century. He didn't want his grandchildren just to look at pictures of what his life was like, so he decided to build a time capsule. He put more than 5,000 real things inside the capsule, including clothes and even a new car, and buried it in 1975 in front of his shop. His grandchildren will open it on July 4th 2025. It is the biggest time capsule in the world.

B There is a little bag on the Moon with a time capsule inside it. The capsule is tiny, about the size of a small coin. At the top, it says: "Goodwill messages from around the world brought to the Moon by the astronauts of Apollo 11." Astronauts left it there in 1969. There are 73 messages from different countries written on the time capsule in tiny letters. Each letter is smaller than a human hair. The messages are to anyone who finds the time capsule in the future.

C Two Japanese companies, Panasonic and The Mainichi Newspapers, buried time capsules next to Osaka Castle in 1970. No one will open the lower capsule until the year 6970. There are 2,090 things inside the capsule to show people in the future what life was like in the 1970s. These include written and recorded messages and examples of art, music and literature. There is also a letter from a Japanese school student to people living in the future.

3 **Read the texts again and answer the questions. Which time capsule, A, B or C, …**

1 … is the oldest?
2 … will people open after 5,000 years?
3 … will people probably open first?
4 … is the smallest?
5 … is for someone's family?
6 … has something for people to listen to?

4 **Work with a partner. Which time capsule do you think is the most interesting? Why?**

5 **What do you think the Japanese student said to people living in the future? Discuss with your partner. Read the letter on page 136 to check your ideas.**

About you

6 Imagine your school is going to bury a time capsule. Choose three things to put in it. They have to be things to show people in the future what life is like now.

Discuss your ideas in groups of four and choose eight objects to put in the final time capsule. Explain why each thing is important. Tell the class.

A: I'll put a smartphone in the time capsule because everyone has them and we use them for so many things.
B: I agree, that's important.
C: Yes, but it won't work because people won't have the right batteries.

VOCABULARY

7 All these words have two meanings. Do you know what they are?

book	kind	letter	picture	ring	watch

There are 73 messages written on the time capsule in tiny letters.
There is also a letter from a Japanese school student.

8 Complete the sentences with words from Exercise 7. Use some words twice.

1 Sorry, I'm busy now. I'll .... you later.
2 You can draw a .... of your time capsule, if you like.
3 She's really .... She lent me her favourite jacket for the party.
4 I don't want to .... TV. I'd prefer to listen to some music.
5 When you phone the cinema, can you .... me a ticket, too, please?
6 What .... of soup would you like? Vegetable or chicken?
7 That's a beautiful .... you've got on your finger.
8 Can I borrow your maths .... ? I left mine at home.
9 I'll take a .... of it with my phone.
10 I'm sorry, I don't know what the time is. My .... is broken.

WRITING

Prepare to write – too, also, as well

GET READY 50 years ago, some children buried a time capsule in their town. This year people in the town opened it. Read one of the messages in it. How many predictions does Liliana make? How many of them are true now?

> Hello,
>
> I'm writing this in 1965. Here are my predictions for 2015. There will be cities under the sea and cities on Mars, too. There won't be any teachers because robots will teach the students. Many doctors will be robots as well. Also, I think there will be all kinds of flying cars.
>
> Are my predictions true?
>
> Liliana

Look at the words in blue.
We use *too*, *as well* and *also* to add more information to our writing.
Choose the right words to complete the sentences.

1 *Too* comes at *the beginning / the middle / the end* of a sentence.
2 *As well* comes at *the beginning / the middle / the end* of a sentence.
3 At the beginning of a sentence, '*Also*' *has / doesn't have* a comma (,) after it.

PLAN What do you think the world will be like in 50 years? Write some ideas. Plan your message for your town's time capsule.

WRITE Write your message for the time capsule. Use Liliana's message to help you. Write 40–60 words. Use *also*, *too* and *as well* to join your ideas.

IMPROVE Read your message and your partner's. Check for mistakes and try to make your message better.

Video extra

Science

The birth and death of stars

1 Complete the sentences with the words in the box.

explosion	galaxy	gravity	moon	planet	space	star	universe

1. The .... is everything around us and everything we can see.
2. The Sun is an example of a ....
3. .... pulls things towards each other.
4. A .... goes around a star.
5. A .... goes around a planet.
6. You must travel through .... to get to the moon and the stars.
7. In a big .... , things fly apart very suddenly.
8. A .... is a group of hundreds of millions of stars.

2 Answer the questions about stars. Then read the text quickly and check your ideas.

1. How many stars are there in our galaxy?
2. How and where are they made?
3. What different colours can they be?
4. What happens when they die?

3 Read the text again. What is the difference between …

1. … red stars and blue stars?
2. … a supernova and a nebula?
3. … a white dwarf and a neutron star?

Project research black holes

Use the internet or books to find the answers to these questions.

- What is a black hole?
- How is a black hole made?
- What is special about black holes and light?
- How big are the biggest black holes?
- Where are they?

Write five or six sentences about black holes. Look at some pictures of black holes.
Then draw and colour your own picture of a black hole.
Work in groups and compare your sentences and pictures.

THE BIRTH AND DEATH OF STARS

1 No one knows exactly how big our Universe is, but it is very, very large. It contains billions of galaxies and each galaxy contains millions or billions of stars. Our own star, the Sun, is one of about 100 billion in a galaxy called the Milky Way. When you look at the sky at night, most of the stars you see belong to the Milky Way.

2 A star is born in a cloud called a nebula. Gravity pulls the gas and dust into a ball. This ball gets hotter and hotter. When it is hot enough, it begins to burn, and a star is born.

3 After they are born, stars burn for a long time before they die. They can be large or small, and they can be blue, white, yellow, orange or red.

4 Red stars are the smallest and coolest. There are many more small red stars than any other kind. They live for about 100 billion years.

5 Blue stars are the hottest and the largest. Very large blue stars live for about 10 million years.

6 Our Sun is a yellow star.

7 When small stars begin to die, they change. First, they become bigger and hotter. These are called red giants.

8 Then they lose most of their gas and become a white dwarf. These are not burning any more, so they are not very bright, but they are still hot.

9 Large stars end their lives in a very big explosion called a supernova. Supernovas are often called the factories of the universe, because this is where heavy materials (such as iron) are made. A supernova throws these elements into space, where they form a nebula. From this, new stars can be born. A supernova may leave behind a black hole or a neutron star. A neutron star is much heavier, smaller and hotter than a white dwarf.

Review 2
Units 5–8

VOCABULARY

1 Choose the right word to complete the sentences.

1 Those earrings are *rich* / *pretty*. Your mum will love them.
2 I'm going out for a *special* / *famous* meal on my birthday.
3 It's *possible* / *popular* to study at home if your parents teach you.
4 Tom's always very *useful* / *careful*. He never breaks anything.
5 My dad doesn't like our sofa. He says it's much too *fine* / *soft*.
6 We had a *famous* / *wonderful* holiday in the States last summer.
7 My *little* / *last* sister's name is Hannah. She's two years old.
8 Thank you for the *lovely* / *dear* chocolates. They are delicious!

2 Put the words in the right group. Some words can go into more than one group.

diploma fridge furniture helicopter paper parent
passenger scooter seat sink tram underground

Home	School	Travel

3 What's the name of the school subject? Write a school subject for each picture.

art biology chemistry geography history languages maths music physics

1 ....

2 ....

3 ....

4 ....

5 ....

6 ....

7 ....

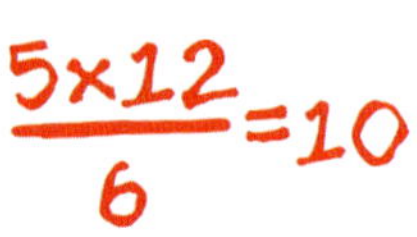

8 ....

9 ....

GRAMMAR

4 **Choose the right word to complete the sentences.**

1 She is very *good* / *well* at climbing.
2 You have to bring a pencil and an *art's* / *art* book.
3 I *go* / *am going* to visit you in the holidays.
4 How was *you* / *your* dinner yesterday?

Correct the mistakes in these sentences.

5 I went to the beach and swam with parents then we flew a kite.
6 I want to be a friend of him because he is funny.
7 I going to Mexico to visit Manuela, a friend.
8 We are meeting at the park at two o'clock because before that I will go to the dentist's.

5 **Complete the sentences. Use the future with *will*.**

1 .... (My brother study) drama when he's older.
2 .... (It not snow) tomorrow.
3 .... (We not get) lost if we follow the path.
4 .... (you visit) your grandparents at the weekend?
5 What time .... (they get) back?
6 .... (I not take) my camera on the school trip.
7 .... (People share) cars in the future.
8 What .... (we learn) in today's English lesson?

6 **Complete the sentences with the correct adverb form of the adjective in brackets.**

1 Please write your name .... (clear) on the exam paper.
2 Our team didn't win on Saturday. I played .... (bad) of all!
3 You have to speak .... (loud) than that. No one can hear you.
4 Usain Bolt ran .... (fast) of all the runners in the 2012 Olympic Games.
5 Our new television works .... (good).
6 My dad had an accident last year. Now he drives .... (careful) than before.
7 My baby brother smiles .... (happy) of all the babies I know.
8 Fred usually gets up .... (early) than his twin brother.

READING

7 **Read the sentences about Susie's trip. Choose the best word (A, B or C) for each space.**

0 Suzie is ....A.... to London next week with her family.
A going
B visiting
C coming

1 Suzie is a bit sad because she'll .... her best friend.
A break B lose C miss

2 The family are going by train. Suzie thinks trains are the best .... to travel.
A way B thing C place

3 Suzie's got a new camera, so she wants to .... lots of photos when she's there.
A take B make C do

4 Last year Suzie won a .... with one of her photos.
A race B present C competition

5 Suzie hopes she'll win .... this year with a picture of the London Eye.
A also B again C too

LISTENING

8 **1.34 Listen to the message and complete the notes.**

Message for:	*0* ......Paula......
Message from:	*1* ....
Message about:	*2* ....
Address:	*3* ....
Phone number:	*4* ....

SPEAKING

9 **Make questions.**

1 How many people / be / family?
2 Where / live?
3 What school subject / like / best?
4 Where / usually go / holiday?
5 Where / would like / go on holiday?
6 What / favourite way of travelling?

10 **Ask and answer the questions with your partner. Take turns to speak.**

9 Sport and games

They must do it for three months

VOCABULARY

1 **Match the words in the box to the activities. Which of the activities are sports? Which ones will help you get fit?**

> badminton chess climbing cricket dance classes diving fishing fitness classes golf karate puzzles skateboarding skiing video games

About you

2 What activities do you do to keep fit?
How often do you do them?
Do you enjoy team sports?
Do you prefer playing sport or watching it?

GRAMMAR *must, mustn't, have to, don't have to*

3 **Read the information about the Merrydown Award. Answer the questions.**

1 Which of the activities in Exercise 1 *can't* you do for the Merrydown Award?
2 Do you have to start a new activity?
3 How long do you have to do the activity for?
4 What does the coach or teacher have to do?

- For the Fitness part of the Merrydown Award you must choose an activity to make you fitter and stronger.
- You don't have to do a sport. You can choose another activity, for example dance or fitness classes.
- You don't have to do a new activity, it can be one you already do.
- You must do your activity for three months.
- You must ask your coach or teacher to write about how you are doing on the award website. You mustn't forget to do this, or you won't get your Merrydown Award.

4 **Find the examples of *must, mustn't, have to* and *don't have to* in the text. Match sentences 1–4 to meanings a–c. Use one meaning twice.**

1 You must do this.
2 You have to do this.
3 You mustn't (must not) do this.
4 You don't have to do this.

a Do not do this.
b It's not necessary to do this.
c It's necessary to do this.

Underline the main verb after *must* and *have to*. Is it the infinitive with *to* or without *to*?

The past of *must* and *have to* is *had to*.	Yesterday I had to do my homework.
The past of *don't have to* is *didn't have to*.	I didn't have to do any homework yesterday.

→ Grammar reference page 155

5 **Dylan is learning to climb for the Award. Read the climbing centre rules. Re-write them using *must*, *mustn't* and *don't have to*.**

Not necessary to join the club to climb here.
You don't have to join the club to climb here.

1 Fill in the form at reception.
2 Not necessary to bring your own ropes.
3 Don't talk to people when they are climbing.
4 Under-13s cannot climb without an adult.
5 Climb with a partner if you are a beginner.
6 Not necessary to book on a weekday.
7 Don't stand under people when they are climbing.

6 **Finn is doing swimming for his award. Last week he was in a competition. Write about what he had to do and what he didn't have to do.**

0 Cost: £5.00 to enter the competition.
He had to pay £5.00 to enter the competition.
1 Arrive at the pool at 8.30 am.
2 Wear a swimming hat.
3 You can wear goggles if you want.
4 Bring sandwiches for lunch.
5 Prizes at 6 pm. Not necessary to stay until 6 pm.

7 **Think of eight things you had to / didn't have to do last week. Compare with a partner.**

I had to clean my room.
I had to finish my geography project.
Did you have to … ? Yes, I did. / No, I didn't.

Corpus challenge

Can you correct the mistake here?
When I was younger I must live far away from my grandparents.

PRONUNCIATION *must* and *mustn't*

8 **1.35 Listen and repeat.**

You must listen carefully. /məs/
You mustn't talk now. /mʌsnt/

9 **1.36 Listen. Write m if you hear /məs/ and mx if you hear /mʌsnt/. Listen again and repeat.**

1 .... 2 .... 3 .... 4 ....
5 .... 6 .... 7 ....

LISTENING

10 **1.37 Look at the pictures and read the questions. What activity does Gabby want to do for her award?**
Listen to Gabby talking to Juliana. For each question, choose the right answer (A, B or C).

0 At Juliana's Dance School, Latin American dance classes are on
A Thursdays. ✔
B Fridays.
C Saturdays.

1 The beginners' class starts at
A 6.00 p.m.
B 7.30 p.m.
C 9.00 p.m.

2 The latest date for Gabby to book is
A July 31.
B September 3.
C December 16.

3 If Gabby pays for three terms together, the price will be
A £46.
B £75.
C £120.

4 What must Gabby bring to each lesson?
A dancing shoes
B a drink
C special clothes

5 What happens at the end of every term?
A There's a meeting for parents.
B There's a show.
C There are dance exams.

Are they really sports?

VOCABULARY

1 Match these things to the pictures in Exercise 4.

board game   card game   chess set   gold medal

2 Match the descriptions to the words.

1	This person comes first in a competition.	a	puzzle
2	This person loves a sports star or team.	b	prize
3	You have to think hard when you do one of these.	c	fan
4	This is a competition between two people or teams.	d	winner
5	You sometimes get this if you do well in a competition.	e	match

About you

3 Talk in groups. Ask and answer these questions.

What board games do you have at home? Which are your favourites?
Can you play chess? Are you good at it?
How many card games do you know? How often do you play them?
When was the last time you played cards?
Do you enjoy doing puzzles? What puzzles do you like? Which do you prefer, number puzzles or word puzzles?

READING

4 Look at the title of the article and the pictures. What do you think *mind sports* are? Read the first paragraph to check your ideas.

Mind Sports

At the moment, there are 28 sports in the Summer Olympics and seven in the Winter Olympics. Some people want to add another kind of sport to the Olympics – mind sport. Mind sports are thinking games. They include word and number puzzles, some card games, and also board games that make you think, like chess.

There are competitions around the world for a variety of mind sports. You can watch the larger ones on the internet, and these have millions of fans. Winners get big prizes, and matches are often very exciting. Some take hours, but others finish in just 10 minutes.

One of the newest competitions is the World Mind Sports Games. These happen every four years, just like the Olympics. There are five mind sports in the competition, including Go, one of the oldest board games in the world. Around 140 countries enter, and there are 35 gold medals to win.

16-year-old Vanessa Wong from Hong Kong is one of the best Go players in the world. She did very well in the last World Mind Sports Games. 'My dad first showed me how to play when I was about six,' she says. 'I plan to be a professional player when I leave university, and I'd love to be in the real Olympics one day.'

5 Read the article again. Are sentences 1–7 'Right' (A) or 'Wrong' (B)? If there is not enough information to answer 'Right' (A) or 'Wrong' (B), choose 'Doesn't say' (C).

0 There are more than 30 sports in the Summer Olympics.
A Right (**B**) Wrong **C** Doesn't say

1 All card and board games are examples of mind sports.
A Right **B** Wrong **C** Doesn't say

2 Mind sports competitions are popular with many people.
A Right **B** Wrong **C** Doesn't say

3 Matches in mind sports competitions always take a long time.
A Right **B** Wrong **C** Doesn't say

4 The World Mind Sports Games happen as often as the Olympics.
A Right **B** Wrong **C** Doesn't say

5 Some countries want to add extra games to the World Mind Sports Games.
A Right **B** Wrong **C** Doesn't say

6 Vanessa Wong won a gold medal in the last World Mind Sports Games.
A Right **B** Wrong **C** Doesn't say

7 Vanessa taught herself to play Go.
A Right **B** Wrong **C** Doesn't say

LISTENING

6 1.38 **You will hear Mark and Lily talking about the article. Read the sentences before you listen. Choose A or B for each sentence.**

	Yes	No
1 Lily thinks it's a good idea to have games like chess in the Olympics.	A	B
2 Mark thinks that some chess competitions are more famous than the Olympics.	A	B
3 Lily thinks it's wrong to call chess a sport.	A	B
4 Lily agrees that thinking is important in many sports.	A	B
5 Mark and Lily agree that chess will be in the Olympics one day.	A	B

SPEAKING

7 **Work in groups. Talk about the sentences. Say if you agree with them, or if you don't. Use the useful language to help you.**

Games like chess already have lots of competitions. They don't need to be in the Olympics.

It's a good idea to have mind sports in the Olympics.

Thinking and using your brain is important in every sport.

Mind sports will be in the Olympics in 10 years' time.

Useful language

I think / I don't think … That's true.
I agree / I don't agree … I'm not sure.

8 **Do these puzzles as fast as you can!**

1 NUMBER PUZZLE

Each line of the puzzle, and each box, must contain the numbers 1–4. You must only use each number once in each line or box.

	4	3	
2			1
4			3
	1	2	

2 ALPHABET PUZZLE

Q I E F Z
V G J L N S
X T H W K Y
M

Which letters of the alphabet are missing? Use the missing letters to make a word for a piece of furniture.

3 THINKING PUZZLE

Jake, Mary, Bob and Jane are aged 11, 12, 13 and 14. Each person likes a different sport: skiing, basketball, volleyball and tennis.

Read the sentences and match each person with their age and sport.

Jane is older than Bob and she likes basketball.
The oldest person is called Mary and she doesn't like tennis or skiing.
Jake is 13 and needs a ball for his sport.

Name	Age	Sport
	11	
	12	
	13	
	14	

10 Useful websites
Problems, problems!

VOCABULARY

1 Match the people and the descriptions.

1 guest	a you live near this person
2 old friend	b this person is a visitor in your home
3 neighbour	c you have this person's details in your phone or online
4 close friend	d this person belongs to a club
5 member	e you like this person very much
6 contact	f you met this person a long time ago

2 Choose the correct verb to complete each sentence.

1 I'm going to *invite* / *join* lots of people to my party.
2 I *make* / *miss* my dad when he goes away on business trips.
3 Give me your number so I can *contact* / *join* you by phone.
4 My brother loves *making* / *meeting* new people.
5 I *made* / *missed* lots of new friends when I went on holiday.

About you

3 How many contacts do you have online?
Are you friendly with your neighbours?
Are you a member of any clubs? Which ones?
Do your friends or family ever have problems? What kind?

READING

4 Read the website. Talk to your partner and think of some advice for each person.

Teen Troubles

Got a problem and not sure who to ask for advice? Write to us and we will help! When you see this click to hear some advice from Dr Mandy, our top teen expert!

1 I go to dance lessons with some close friends of mine. The teacher wants me to go into a higher level group, but she says my friends have to stay in the lower level. I'm worried about moving to a new class without them. I'll really miss seeing them! What should I do? **Andrea, 13**

2 I am home-schooled and I don't spend much time with people my age. I am friends with some of my neighbours, and I have old friends from primary school, but they often forget to invite me when they go out. **Ben, 15**

3 My best friend won't stop copying me! I love wearing bright clothes and looking different from everyone else. But last month my friend started buying all the same things as me. Now we look exactly the same as each other! **Katy, 14**

LISTENING

5 1.39 **Listen to Dr Mandy giving advice to the three teenagers. Match the advice to the people.**

6 1.39 **Listen again and make notes about the advice for each person. Was any of the advice the same as yours?**

EP Get talking! → page 132

After all, …
Good luck!
Make sure …
a bit more

GRAMMAR Verb patterns – gerunds and infinitives

7 Look at the examples of problems and advice. Complete the rules.

Try to talk to her about how you feel.
If you decide to do this, you can give her advice.
They often forget to invite me when they go out.
I'm worried about moving to a new class.
You'll get better at dancing.
Thank you for writing to the website.
My best friend won't stop copying me!
I'll really miss seeing them.
What activities do you enjoy doing?

1 Use the gerund (*-ing* form) after prepositions: ...at... , ... , ... (also *by*, *of*, *with*, etc.)
2 Use the infinitive + *to* after some verbs: ...try... , ... , ... (also *choose*, *learn*, *hope*, *plan*, *need*, *want*)
3 Use the gerund after some verbs: ..stop... , ... , ... (also *finish*, *don't mind*)
4 Use the gerund or infinitive after these verbs: *start*, *begin*, *like*, *love*, *prefer*

→ Grammar reference page 156

8 Choose the correct form of the verb.

1 My friend decided *buy* / *to buy* a new pair of sunglasses.
2 I helped the teacher by *carry* / *carrying* her books.
3 One day, I hope *to be* / *being* a doctor.
4 I don't mind *to wait* / *waiting* for you if you are nearly ready.
5 My older brother is learning *to drive* / *driving* at the moment.

Corpus challenge

Correct the sentences.
1 I hope see you very soon and I hope that you like my mobile phone.
2 I want write about my life.

READING

9 Complete the five conversations. Choose A, B or C.

1 The coach never chooses me for the team!
A He hopes to have enough soon.
B Well, you need to practise more.
C Maybe they'll stop playing at eight o'clock.

2 I need to improve the marks I get in maths.
A I don't mind helping you.
B I finished making mine yesterday.
C I thought it was right.

3 My neighbour's really noisy.
A Do you need to do that?
B She decided to ask me.
C You should tell her to be quiet.

4 Jack didn't come to my party last night.
A He probably just forgot about it.
B Are you sure that's a good idea?
C I prefer staying at home to going out.

5 My best friend spends all her time with the new girl in the class.
A She's trying to find another one.
B Why don't you talk to her about it?
C Thanks very much for doing that.

PRONUNCIATION *gh*

10 1.41 Listen to the sounds. Put the words into the right column.

bright caught daughter enough flight
neighbour right straight thought

/aɪ/ night	/eɪ/ eight	/ʌf/ rough	/ɔː/ bought

1.42 Listen and check. Then repeat the words.

SPEAKING

11 Work in groups of three. Each person chooses a problem. Listen to each other's problems and give advice. Try to use some words from Exercise 9. Who has the most interesting problem? Who gives the best advice?

I love using this website

READING

1 What are your three favourite websites? Tick (✓) the things you use websites for. Compare with a partner. Do you like the same websites? Why? / Why not?

playing games	☐	watching videos	☐	chatting to friends	☐
finding information	☐	doing school work	☐	reading articles	☐
listening to music	☐	sharing photos/stories etc.	☐		

2 Read what the people say. Which of the activities in Exercise 1 do they want to do?

I'm working on a project about the human body at the moment and I'm interested in learning about animals. I like having fun online too.

1

I'm hoping to become a writer one day. I'd like to put my stories online and discuss ideas with people my age.

2

I like to know what is happening in the world. I'm also interested in music and would like to learn more about my favourite stars.

3

I'm interested in nature and wildlife, and want to learn about ways to help the planet. I like making short films and want to share them with others.

4

3 Read about six websites and decide which is best for each person. Compare your answers.

SIX GREAT WEBSITES FOR TEENAGERS

A EcoCentral

This website is all about looking after the Earth. There are facts about different animals, as well as information about forests, deserts and oceans. You can upload your own videos onto the site for everyone to see.

B TeenPress

This is one of the best sites on the web for teenagers who love writing. You can share your work with others, and there are message boards where you can chat about things that are important to you.

C ChannelTwenty

On this site you can watch a daily news programme and search for information about big news stories. There are also videos on different subjects, articles about famous bands, games and competitions.

D ScienceZone

There's lots of information on this site about maths, chemistry and biology. You can 'visit' some of the world's most famous museums, and watch wildlife via webcams. There are also some very cool games, such as Save the Planet.

E Tune-in

There are millions of songs on this website for you to download or listen to online. You can save your favourite songs in your own list. If you're in a band, you can record your music and upload it. The website is large, but the menus are easy to use.

F Inside-the-cover

Finding out about your favourite writers is easy on this site. There are lots of interesting articles and information about the latest books. You can read blogs by well-known writers and post questions and messages to them. There are links to other sites too.

VOCABULARY

4 Find these nouns in the texts. Match them to their meanings.

1 menu	**a** all the pages online that you can visit
2 site	**b** a place to write things for others to read on a web page
3 the web	**c** an address to click on to go to another website
4 message board	**d** another way of saying website
5 blog	**e** a kind of online diary
6 link	**f** a list of pages on a website

5 Find these verbs in the texts. Make correct sentences.

	save	for information online by typing a word into a box.
You can	post	music, video or pictures so you can watch or listen to them again.
	record	a file from your computer onto a website.
	search	a document or other file on your computer so you don't lose it.
	upload	a file from the internet to your computer.
	download	a message or question on the internet for others to read.

6 Read the sentences about a website. Choose the best word (A, B or C) for each space.

0 Catherine Cook was only 15 when she .... myYearbook.com. *Answer A*
A started **B** arrived **C** decided

1 The website is now called meetme.com and is .... for making new friends.
A perfect **B** favourite **C** pleased

2 When you join, you have to fill in a form and .... a photo of yourself.
A record **B** describe **C** upload

3 After that, you can start .... for friends to add.
A finding **B** searching **C** missing

4 It's not difficult to explore the site and .... people.
A make **B** talk **C** contact

5 You can play games, post .... , do quizzes and more.
A messages **B** menus **C** screens

WRITING

Prepare to write – a description of a website

GET READY Count how many times these phrases are used to start sentences in the texts in Exercise 3. Then find three other ways of starting sentences in the texts.

1 There is / There are …
2 You can …
3 This …

PLAN Either (a) think about your favourite website or (b) imagine your perfect website. Make notes on:

- what it's about
- what you can do on it
- why it's useful/fun
- why you like it

WRITE Write a paragraph about your website. Use the descriptions of the websites in Exercise 3 to help you. Try to begin each sentence with a different phrase.

IMPROVE Read your paragraph and your partner's. Check that you included all the information from your plan, and that you started each sentence with a different phrase.

Culture

Football (The beautiful game)

1 **Look at the pictures from the Football for Hope Festival. What do you think happens at the festival? Do you think the people only play football?**

2 **Read about the Football for Hope Festival and check your ideas from Exercise 1.**

1 ....

The Football for Hope Festival is a festival of education, culture and, of course, football. It celebrates the power of football for social change. FIFA and Streetfootballworld organise the festival together and it happens every four years at the same time as the World Cup.

2 ....

During the World Cup in Brazil, 32 teams of young people from all round the world came to Rio for the Football for Hope Festival. These 192 young people were between the ages of 15 and 18. In the first week they got to know each other and learned about each other's countries. They also exchanged ideas and experiences through samba and other fun activities as well as a visit to Rio's famous Sugar Loaf Mountain.

3 ....

The football matches were in the second week. But it was a little different from the big World Cup tournament. The teams were a mixture of boys and girls and also of different nationalities. Also, there were no referees. When the players disagreed about anything, they had to find an answer by talking to each other. Often this meant talking through action and using a lot of eye contact. It helped the players understand each other better.

3 **Read the text again. Match the title to each paragraph.**

Playing the game	Meeting the teams	What is Football for Hope?

4 **Work in groups. Discuss the questions.**

1. Have you heard of the Football for Hope Festival before?
2. Think about what the young people did in the first week. Why was it important for them to do these things before they played the football matches?
3. Think about the football matches in the second week. In what three ways were these matches different from normal football matches?
4. Have you ever played football matches like this? Would you like to try? Why? / Why not?

5 Work with a partner. How much do you know about The World Cup? Take the quiz!

THE WORLD CUP QUIZ

1 Who or what is FIFA?
2 How many teams complete in the World Cup?
3 How often is the World Cup?
4 What is goal-line technology?
5 How long does the World Cup last?
6 Which country's team has won the most times?
7 Who receives the Adidas Golden Boot award each year?
8 Which team's nickname is *Orange*?
9 Where is the next World Cup going to be?
10 Is there a Women's World Cup?

6 Compare your answers with another pair. Can you answer all the questions? Which group in the class got the most questions right?

7 ▶1.43 Listen to the interview. What is it about?

8 ▶1.43 Listen again. Are the sentences right (✔) or wrong (✘)?

1 The first Women's World Cup was in 1995.
2 The USA were the first winners.
3 The Womens' World Cup is every four years.
4 20 teams play in the Women's World Cup.
5 Brazil have won twice.
6 Japan have won once.
7 The trophy is the same as for the Men's World Cup.

Project research a World Cup country

Work in pairs. Choose a country that held either a Men's or Women's World Cup. Find out:

- which year they hosted the World Cup
- the teams which played and who won
- its World Cup stadiums
- what the World Cup mascot was
- the most famous players from that World Cup
- what other sports the country is famous for.

Make a poster, or a PowerPoint Presentation to show your information to the rest of the class.

11 City living

It's a great place for tourists

VOCABULARY

1 Match each word with a picture.

cathedral mosque museum palace
stadium statue temple theatre

a

b

c

d

e

f

g

h

2 What can you do at these places? Write five questions to test your partner.

bridge hospital library park police station
post office restaurant shop sports centre
train station university

What can you do at a post office? *Buy a stamp, post a letter …*

LISTENING

3 What countries are these cities in? Which are capitals?

Beijing Cairo London Madrid Mexico City
Mumbai New Delhi New York Paris
Rio de Janeiro Rome San Francisco Seoul
Shanghai Tokyo

4 1.44 Listen to the quiz and write the name of the cities.

1 .... 3 .... 5 ....
2 .... 4 .... 6 ....

5 1.44 Listen again. Write the name of the city.

a It's the largest city in the world.
b Every year there's a big carnival here.
c The Olympic Games were in this city.
d It's a great place for tourists.
e The city has a lot of bridges.
f It has a famous bridge.
g It's the second biggest city in China.
h Its cathedral is on an island.

GRAMMAR Determiners

6 Read the sentences in Exercise 5 again and read the examples below. Choose the correct word to complete the rules.

All the questions are about cities.
Are you all ready?
There are many other great places to visit.
The city has both beaches and museums.
Alcatraz and Chinatown are both popular.
There's another beautiful church in the city.

1 We use *the* / *a* to introduce something for the first time and when we talk about things in general.
2 We use *the* / *a* to talk about something already mentioned / with superlatives / if there is only one in the world / in front of 'first', 'second' etc.
3 We use *all* / *both* to talk about two things.
4 We use *all* / *both* to talk about a total number of things.
5 *Another* / *Other* means 'one more'.

→ Grammar reference page 157

7 **Complete the email with the words in the box.**

a x2	all	an	another
both	other	the x5	

From: Rosa
To: Camilla

I had (**1**) .... great holiday in Rome with my family! We went to (**2**) .... the famous places. On (**3**) .... first day we visited (**4**) .... Colosseum and we went to (**5**) .... fantastic museum. There were lots of (**6**) .... tourists there, but we didn't mind. The next day we went to (**7**) .... museum, and afterwards my brother and I each had (**8**) .... ice cream in (**9**) .... city centre. We (**10**) .... said it was (**11**) .... best ice cream in (**12**) .... world!

Corpus challenge

Can you correct the mistake in this sentence?
It's a biggest zoo in my town.

PRONUNCIATION *the*

8 **1.45 Listen and repeat. When do we say /ðiː/ and when do we say /ðə/?**

/ðiː/ **the**	/ðə/ **the**
the oldest	the youngest
the east	the north
the Atlantic Ocean	the Pacific Ocean
the Olympic Games	the World Cup

1.46 Put the phrases into the right column in the table. Then listen, check, and repeat.

the apple	the North Sea
the Arctic	the orange
the dog	the River Nile
the Earth	the Statue of Liberty
the Indian Ocean	the umbrella

READING AND GRAMMAR

9 **Read the text about Australian cities. Choose the best word (A, B or C) for each space.**

Australian cities

Australian cities have a lot to offer visitors to (0) .... country. Among the (1) .... popular are Sydney, Melbourne and Cairns. (2) .... visitor to Australia should go to Sydney. Its Opera House and Harbour Bridge are famous (3) .... the world. Melbourne is (4) .... great Australian city. It has excellent museums and (5) .... a modern arts centre. Phillip Island is not (6) .... from Melbourne, and here you can see koalas, penguins and kangaroos.
Cairns is in Queensland, in the north west of Australia. Here you can enjoy (7) .... the rainforest and the ocean, with its wonderful fish. Cairns is a great place to (8) .... about the culture of the Aboriginal people of Australia.

	A	B	C
0	a	one	(**C**) the
1	most	more	many
2	All	Every	Some
3	along	around	about
4	each	other	another
5	also	anyway	instead
6	long	far	over
7	both	several	some
8	learned	learning	learn

WRITING

10 **Work with a partner. Write a city quiz.**

- Choose three cities.
- Write a short description of each one.
- Read the descriptions to another pair of students.
- Can they guess your cities? Can you guess theirs?

Do you mind if I sit here?

READING

1 Read the signs and notices. Where would you see them? Match each one to a place in the box.

by a river	on a poster	in a museum
in a clothes shop	at a sports centre	
in a park	at a train station	in a café

A
NO DOGS
in children's playground

B
The Silver Fish
Great coffee and free internet for all customers!

C
Boat Trips
10 am and 2 pm
Tickets available from Tourist Information Office

D
SWIMMING POOL
now open every afternoon
Adults – £5.00
Under 16s – £2.50

E
ROCK CONCERTS
in City Stadium
For details, visit www.stadium.co.uk

F
Winter Wildlife Exhibition
Wait here for tour guide.
Last tour begins 4 pm

G
JEANS FOR ALL
Need a bigger or smaller pair? Ask the assistant!

H
LEFT LUGGAGE
Large bag – £10.00 per day
Small bag – £5.00 per day

2 Which notice (A–H) says this (1–5)?

0 You can leave your suitcases here. H
1 Go online to get more information about these.
2 Staff here will help you find the right clothes.
3 Children pay less to use this.
4 You must keep these animals out of here.
5 There's one of these in the morning and another in the afternoon.

VOCABULARY

3 Match the words and phrases with similar meanings.

1 dogs	a visit the website
2 go online	b the right size
3 staff	c children
4 suitcases	d you can get it
5 information	e luggage
6 Under 16s	f shop assistants
7 available	g details
8 a bigger or smaller pair	h animals

GRAMMAR Uncountable nouns

Luggage, *staff* and *information* are uncountable nouns. We can't use these words with a number and they have no plural form. With them we use *much*, **not** *many*:

How much water have you got?
There isn't much water in the river.

We can also use words like *a bit of, a piece of, two slices of, three bottles of, a lot of …* etc. with uncountable nouns.

I've got a bottle of water.
Can we have two glasses of water?

4 Choose the correct word to complete each sentence. Check if you need to make it plural.

	Countable	Uncountable	
1	desk	furniture	I haven't got much .... in my room – just a bed and a chair.
2	project	homework	I've got two science .... to finish this weekend!
3	article	news	There's an interesting .... about RIhanna in this magazine.
4	car	traffic	There's too much .... on the streets in my town.
5	coin	money	Have you got a 50p .... ? I need it for the drinks machine.
6	meal	food	Mum prepared a lot of .... for our picnic.
7	battery	electricity	Dad says my new radio doesn't use much ....
8	necklace	jewellery	My grandmother gave me a lovely piece of .... for my birthday.

READING AND LISTENING

5 ▶1.47 **Read and listen to six conversations. Match each conversation to a picture.**

a

b

c

d

e

f

1 **A:** Hi. Can I help you?
B: (**1**) .... go bowling this afternoon.
A: Ah, (**2**) .... we're closing in ten minutes. Come back tomorrow morning.
B: Oh, OK. Thanks.

2 **A:** Excuse me. (**3**) .... open the door for me?
B: (**4**) .... There you are.
A: Thanks!

3 **A:** (**5**) .... leave my guitar here while I have a swim?
B: (**6**) .... You need to put it in the cloakroom. It's over there, next to the shop.
A: Thank you.

4 **A:** Excuse me. (**7**) .... open the window? It's really hot in here.
B: (**8**) .... I'm hot too!

5 **A:** Excuse me. (**9**) .... the way to the sports centre?
B: (**10**) .... Walk along this road for about 100 metres, then turn left. You'll see the centre on your right.
A: Great! Thanks very much.

6 **A:** Excuse me. (**11**) .... have a can of lemonade, please?
B: (**12**) .... That's £1.50, please.

6 ▶1.47 **Complete the conversations with the words from the box. Then listen again to check. Practise the conversations with a partner.**

Sure	I'd like to	That's fine
I'm sorry, but	Do you mind if I	Could you
Can you tell me	Could I	Is it OK if I
I'm afraid not	No problem	Of course

7 **Look at the sentence pairs. Which sentence in each pair is more formal? Write F next to the more formal phrase.**

1 Can you help me? ....
Could you help me? ....
2 Is it OK if I sit here? ....
Do you mind if I sit here? ....
3 Can I have a drink? ....
Could I have a drink? ....

8 **Work with a partner. Which of these replies mean *yes* and which mean *no*?**

Sure	I'm sorry, but …	Certainly
I'm afraid not	No problem	
That's fine	Of course	

SPEAKING

9 **Write three new conversations with your partner. For each conversation choose a different place and a different request. Use the conversations in Exercise 7 to help you.**

10 **Perform your conversations for the class. Can they guess where you are?**

Video extra

12 Festivals and films

It's a festival that everyone loves

VOCABULARY

1 Are these words 'Instruments' or 'Types of music'? Can you add any other words to each group?

blues classical drum folk guitar
jazz keyboards pop rap rock
soul trumpet violin

About you

2 What kind of music do you like?
Do you play an instrument?
If not, which would you like to play?

READING

3 Look at the photos and the title of the article. Where are the people? What are they doing? Read the texts. Which festival sounds the most fun?

Three great music festivals to go to this summer

Moon Fest

This is one of the biggest music festivals and one of the oldest. There are six stages with all kinds of music from dance to rock, pop, soul and jazz. As well as music, there are theatre shows, an outdoor cinema and even circus classes. In one tent there are musical instruments that you can play, and in another a silent disco. Everyone that comes has a great time.

Dynamics

Dynamics happens every year in a pretty town which is perfect for a summer holiday. It's near the sea. Between bands you can sail or windsurf, or just lie in the sun. Paul Jones started this festival just five years ago, and says it's one of the best places to listen to new music. 'If you want big names, try one of the other festivals,' he explains. 'I want to introduce people to music that's a bit different.'

Sounds

Sounds is a great place to see famous pop groups who don't usually play at summer festivals. It's in a beautiful park that has woods, lakes and gardens. There's even a 15th century castle that's often in films and TV shows. The festival goes on for three days, and there are fields where you can camp. When you want a break from the music, go down to the lake and enjoy the lovely views.

4 Read the article again. For questions 1–7, choose A, B or C.

0 Where can you see a building that's several hundred years old?
A Moon Fest **B** Dynamics **(C)** Sounds

1 Where can you make music yourself?
A Moon Fest **B** Dynamics **C** Sounds

2 Where can you hear music that most people don't know about?
A Moon Fest **B** Dynamics **C** Sounds

3 Which festival has a place that shows films?
A Moon Fest **B** Dynamics **C** Sounds

4 Which festival should you choose if you enjoy water sports?
A Moon Fest **B** Dynamics **C** Sounds

5 Which festival has a place that you can put your tent in?
A Moon Fest **B** Dynamics **C** Sounds

6 Which festival is good for people that like different types of music?
A Moon Fest **B** Dynamics **C** Sounds

7 Which festival has well-known bands that you can't see at other festivals?
A Moon Fest **B** Dynamics **C** Sounds

GRAMMAR Relative pronouns *who, which, that*

5 Study these sentences from the texts.

There's even a 15th century castle that's often in films and TV shows.
Everyone that comes has a great time.
Dynamics happens every year in a pretty town which is perfect for a summer holiday.
I want to introduce people to music that's a bit different.
Sounds is a great place to see famous pop groups who don't usually play at summer festivals.

Choose two words to complete each sentence.

1 We use *who* / *that* / *which* when we talk about people.
2 We use *who* / *that* / *which* when we talk about things.

→ Grammar reference **page 158**

Look at the questions in Exercise 4 again. Replace all the examples of *that* with *which* or *who*.

6 Match the two halves of the sentences and join them with *who* or *which*.

0 The Underage Festival is only for people who are aged between 14 and 18.

0 The Underage Festival is only for people
1 Tickets are cheap, so teenagers
2 There are shops
3 Sam Kilcoyne is the man
4 There are some famous bands
5 It's a festival

a always play at the festival.
b started the festival.
c parents think is safe for their children.
d ~~are aged between 14 and 18.~~
e sell clothes and food.
f haven't got much money can go.

Corpus challenge

Which of these sentences is NOT correct?

A My favourite colour is blue so I bought a mobile phone that was blue.
B My favourite colour is blue so I bought a mobile phone who was blue.
C My favourite colour is blue so I bought a mobile phone which was blue.

PRONUNCIATION Sounds and spelling

7 1.48 Listen and repeat the words. How many letters does each word have? How many sounds?

cheap children clothes festivals
great phone place which who

cheap – 5 letters, 3 sounds

SPEAKING

8 Work in groups of three or four. Plan your own festival. Think about:

- where your festival will be
- the kind of bands you will invite
- extra activities you will offer
- what you will sell
- the kind of people who will come.

Choose one person from your group to present your ideas to the class.

We'll have shops that sell …
We'll invite bands that …
People who come to our festival will …
Our festival will be in a place which …

This film looks exciting!

Showing today at STAR CINEMA

A The Drake Adventures

Tom Drake is on holiday with his family. They visit a castle where Tom sees two men stealing a painting. He is in big trouble when the men come after him. If he can't find a safe place to hide, he's dead!

21.30 23.30

B Game, Set, Match

Carly James is a brilliant young tennis player, but has lots of problems in her life. Nobody understands her except her coach. He knows that she can be a big star if she listens to him and works hard.

14.00 17.15 20.00

C A Forest of Dreams

Max goes to live with his grandmother while his parents are away on business. At first he's bored and unhappy, but things change when he meets a boy in the forest who shows him a world of magic and adventure.

16.45 19.35

D Body Swap

Hannah and her brother were good friends when they were little but now they fight all the time. Then one morning they wake up in each other's bodies. They have to learn to understand each other better, or they'll never return to their own body!

15.00 17.30 19.45

E New Boy

Leon comes from a small town where life is very quiet. When he moves to a new school in a big city, he wears the wrong clothes and likes the wrong bands. No one wants to be his friend except Alyssa, who teaches him how to be cool.

16.20 18.45

About you

1 What kind of films do you like?
What was the last film you saw?
Do you prefer watching films at home or at the cinema?

READING

2 Read the webpage and answer the questions.

Which film(s) …

1 … can you see at quarter past five?
2 … will finish after midnight?
3 … are on three times a day?
4 … is about someone in danger?
5 … is about sport?
6 … is about someone who isn't very popular?
7 … is about two people in the same family?
8 … are about someone who makes a new friend?

Which of these films would you like to see? Why?

GRAMMAR Conjunctions

A conjunction is a word like *or*, *but* or *and* that joins two parts of a sentence. *If*, *that*, *when*, *where* and *while* are also conjunctions. Find and underline the conjunctions in the cinema webpage.

3 **Match the sentence halves.**

1 My friends and I go to the cinema if
2 My friend says that
3 I like eating popcorn while
4 We usually sit at the back, where
5 I don't like it when

a we get the best view of the screen.
b we have enough money and there is a good film on.
c *Gravity* is a really good film.
d people talk during the film.
e I'm watching a film in the cinema.

4 **Complete the sentences so that they are true for you. Then compare your answers in groups.**

I often listen to music while I'm …
I'd like to live in a place where …
In the future I am sure that …
I'm happiest when …
I only get angry if …

LISTENING

5 **You will hear a boy, Gabriel, inviting a friend to the cinema. Before you listen, look at the notes. What kind of information do you need to complete each question?**

Cinema trip for Gabriel's birthday

Name of cinema:	**(0)** Star Cinema
Day we'll go:	**(1)** ....
Which film:	**(2)** ....
Time film begins:	**(3)** .... pm
Price of ticket:	**(4)** £ ....
How we'll get there:	**(5)** by ....

6 **1.49** **Listen to the conversation and complete questions 1–5.**

EP Get talking! → page 132

That sounds exciting.
I hope that's OK?
No problem!

WRITING

Prepare to write – an invitation to the cinema

GET READY Read the invitation to the cinema.

- Who is Jake inviting?
- What film does he want to see?
- When does he want to go?

Look at the prepositions in blue. Which preposition do we use with a) times b) days c) streets d) places where you do something e) if you are moving to a place?

> Hi Leo,
> Would you like to come to the cinema with me and a few friends on Saturday? We want to see *Now You See Me*. It's about a group of people who steal money from banks while they are doing magic shows. It sounds really good! It's on at Galaxy Cinema and it starts at 6.45 pm. We're meeting at the bus stop on Friar Road at 6 pm. Let me know if you can come!
> Jake

PLAN Plan your own invitation to the cinema. Make notes.

- What day are you going?
- Which film are you going to see?
- What's it about?
- Which cinema are you going to?
- What time does it start?
- How are you getting there?

WRITE Write your invitation. Begin with *Hi/Dear* and your friend's name. End with your name. Use some conjunctions and prepositions in your invitation. Write 50–80 words.

IMPROVE Check your invitation and your partner's for mistakes with prepositions and conjunctions.

History
The history of writing

1 Work in groups. Answer the questions.

1 When did writing first begin?
2 Why did people need to start writing?
3 Where in the world did it begin?
4 What did early writing look like?
5 What is the name of the alphabet you use in your language? What about English?

2 Read the text and check your ideas.

Writing

Writing is one of the most important things humans have ever invented. With it, we can learn, study and communicate. It's hard to imagine the world without writing, but in fact it only began around five thousand years ago, when people began to farm and do business together. At first it was only used for counting, and writing numbers for buying and selling animals and food, but later people used it for writing stories and other texts.

Different people around the world invented writing at about the same time. The Sumerians (from what is now Iraq) and the Egyptians were probably the first. Early writing began with small pictures for words. However, names and ideas are difficult to show as pictures, so people began putting the pictures together to make new words with their sounds. For example in Sumerian, *man* was *lu* and *mouth* was *ka*. The two pictures together made the new word *luka*, which means *speech* or *talk*. Over the centuries, this became 'syllabic' writing, where each sound in the language has its own sign. Chinese is an example of this kind of writing.

Finally, alphabets were used. Early alphabets only had consonants and no vowels. Today many different kinds of alphabet are used: the Roman alphabet, which you are reading now; Arabic – the language of the Koran; Cyrillic, used to write Russian and other languages; and Devanagari, which is used in India and Nepal. You read most Western languages from left to right, but Arabic is read from right to left. You can read Chinese and Japanese from top to bottom, or from right to left.

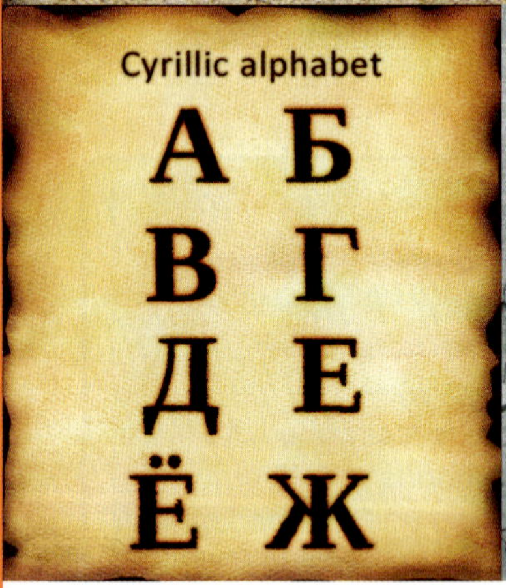

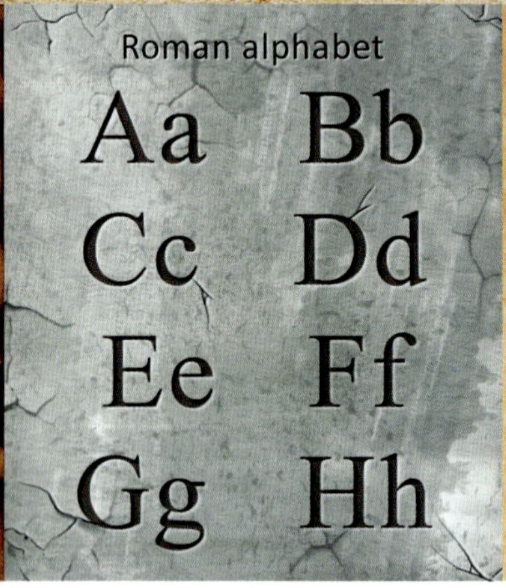

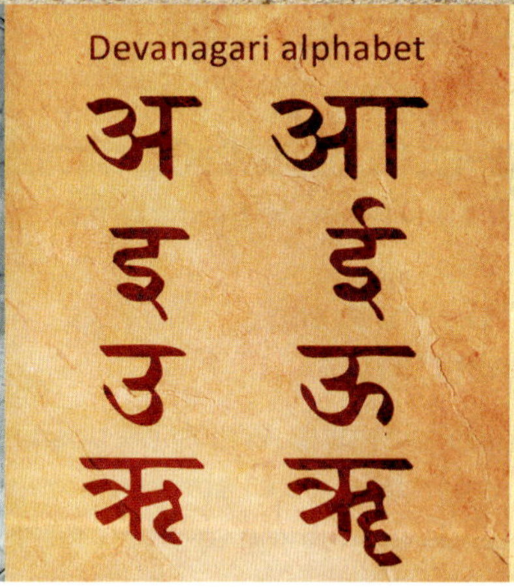

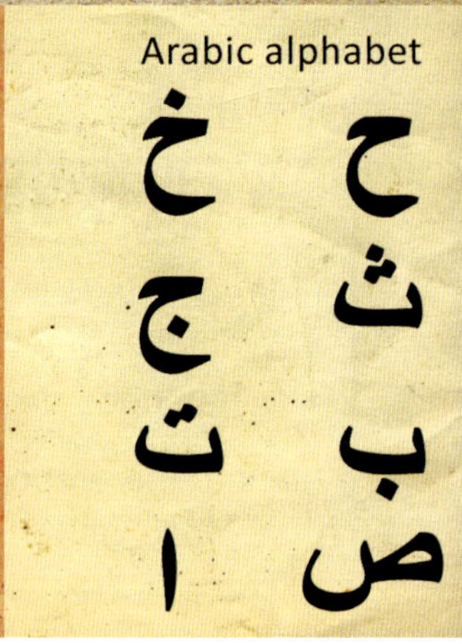

3 Read the information about alphabets on the opposite page and answer the questions.

1 Which alphabet(s) look most difficult to learn and use? Why?
2 Which look the easiest?

4 Can you read the sentences? Which words are easy to read? Which are difficult? Why?

1 my fvrt sprt s ftbll
2 cn y cm t wth m ths aftrnn?
3 whn s yr brthdy?

5 Write some sentences with only consonants for your partner. Can they understand your sentences? Why? / Why not?

ALPHABETS

early	late

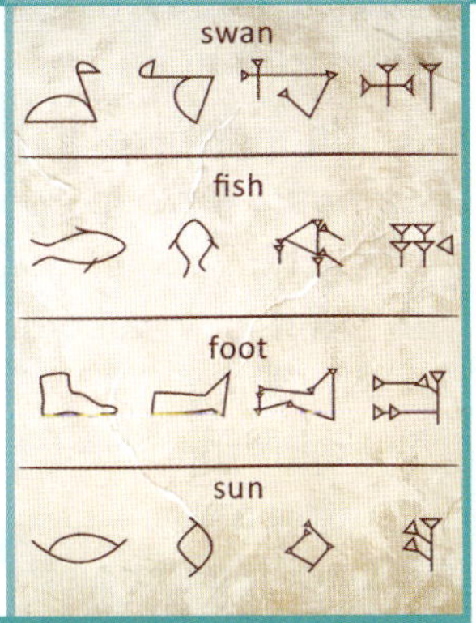

Cuneiform
Used by Sumerians from 3000 BCE. People wrote onto clay tablets, using a special wooden stick. It was used for thousands of years.

early	late

Hieroglyphs
Used in Egypt from 3000 BCE. Hieroglyphs were a mixed alphabet, with some pictures for whole words and some pictures for consonants.

early	late

The Phoenician alphabet
Used from around 1000 BCE. It had 22 letters and all of them were consonants. The Greek, Roman and Arabic alphabets all came from this alphabet.

early	late

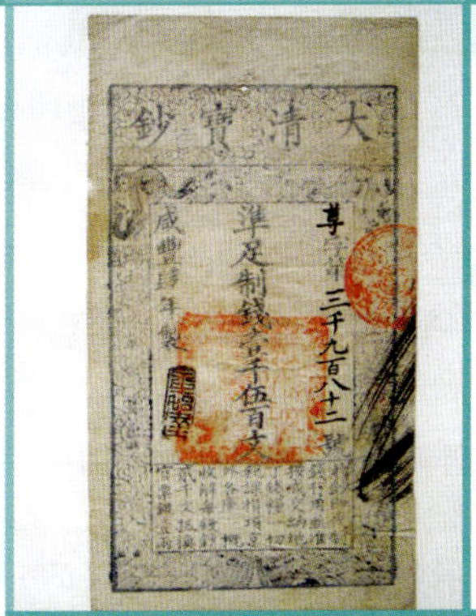

Chinese
Used from around 1500 BCE. It is the oldest writing system still used today. Chinese schoolchildren learn to write about 3000 different characters, but there are thousands more.

6 **We still use pictures instead of words today. Look at pictures 1–4. What do they mean?**

Project **research the history of an alphabet**

Work in groups.
Research the history of an alphabet. You could choose the Roman, Cyrillic or Greek alphabet, or another of your choice. Use the internet or books to find out:

- the history of the alphabet
- who used the alphabet
- pictures of the alphabet
- some important words in the alphabet.

In your groups, tell the class what you learned.

Review 3

Units 9–12

VOCABULARY

1 Match the words to make nouns. Use each word once only.

1	police	a	class
2	card	b	office
3	chess	c	game
4	fitness	d	centre
5	gold	e	festival
6	post	f	station
7	sports	g	medal
8	music	h	set

2 Find the odd word out in each set. Say why it does not fit.

0	laptop	chat	match	screen
1	speaker	stadium	cricket	fan
2	blues	golf	classical	soul
3	university	school	cathedral	college
4	guest	member	club	winner
5	climbing	diving	fishing	surfing
6	park	museum	zoo	theatre
7	prize	competition	race	neighbour

3 Write the missing letters to complete the word in each sentence.

1 Ben loves all kinds of sport. He's starting k _ _ _ _ _ lessons on Saturday.
2 I was really sad when my mum was in hospital. I m _ _ _ _ _ her a lot.
3 The best way to c _ _ _ _ _ _ the school is by email. They never answer the phone.
4 I don't want to play cards. Let's do a p _ _ _ _ _ instead.
5 People say that the v _ _ _ _ _ is one of the most difficult instruments to learn.
6 Who did you i _ _ _ _ _ to your party?
7 I found a great new website for teens. You don't have to pay. It's free to j _ _ _ .
8 My brother plays k _ _ _ _ _ _ _ _ in a band and my sister plays the drums.

GRAMMAR

4 Choose the right word to complete the sentences.

1 When you get to the library you only *must* / *have to* go right and then you see my house.
2 I'm happy with your idea about *go* / *going* shopping.
3 I think that I lost it on *the* /*a* sofa in the living room.
4 I bought three shirts *who* / *which* cost £10, £17 and £25.

Correct the mistakes in these sentences.

5 Oh and we must forget to take our video and camera.
6 I will try call to you on Wednesday
7 And here we have a good weather.
8 My favourite meal is pizza. I love them! I always eat it! And especially the pizza who my mom cooks!

5 Put the words in the right order to make sentences.

1 lots / I / to / listening / of / kinds / of / enjoy / music / different / .
2 for / contact / Could / to / school / you / try / the / me / ?
3 anyone / speak / exam / The / mustn't / to / before / students / the / .
4 The / of / the / comes / who / skiing / Klas / my / competition / town / was / winner / from / .
5 I / this / is / than / interesting / think / film / the / one / more / other / .
6 dad / is / a / buy / birthday / me / new / My / laptop / to / for / my / going / .
7 worried / was / about / another / Frank / dance / joining / class /.
8 caught / bus / outside / hospital / that / Elsa / stops / the / the / .

6 Read the email about a music festival. Choose the best word (A, B or C) for each space.

From: Sam
To: Laura

Hi Laura,

I'm back – but I'm really tired. I had (**1**) .... fantastic time at the music festival. The music was amazing! But I (**2**) .... you! I was so sad that you couldn't come. Are you feeling better now? I hope (**3**) .... We (**4**) .... go together next year.

It was so funny. Dad forgot (**5**) .... the big tent – so mum and dad and I (**6**) .... had to sleep in the same small tent! You know – the one (**7**) .... I got for my birthday. But we (**8**) .... cook our own food. There were lots of places to buy (**9**) .... food. I liked the Star Café. They have the best burgers!

Sorry, I've got to stop (**10**) .... now. I need to finish my maths homework!

See you tomorrow.

Sam

	A	B	C
1	**A** so	**B** such a	**C** some
2	**A** lost	**B** missed	**C** thought
3	**A** it	**B** not	**C** so
4	**A** have	**B** must	**C** will have
5	**A** bring	**B** to bring	**C** bringing
6	**A** all	**B** both	**C** each
7	**A** that	**B** who	**C** where
8	**A** can't	**B** mustn't	**C** didn't have to
9	**A** great	**B** a great	**C** the great
10	**A** write	**B** writing	**C** written

LISTENING

7 1.51 **Listen and tick the places the boy and the girl are going to visit.**

museum	☐	theatre	☐
park	☐	library	☐
sports centre	☐	café	☐
post office	☐	book shop	☐

READING

8 Read the theatre poster and the email and complete Monique's notes.

Admit 1

City Theatre

The Door:
Sundays to Wednesdays: 3 pm, 7 pm

Dance!
Thursdays to Saturdays: 4 pm, 8 pm

Tickets:

Daytime:	£8.00, under 16s £5.50
Evenings:	£9.50, under 16s £7.00

Phone: 0291467

Hi Monique

Can you get tickets for the theatre? Everyone says *The Door* is boring, so let's see the other show. I prefer the weekend. I've got basketball at 7 pm so we'll have to go to the early show. Lucky we're both 13! Call me on 0562889 if there's a problem.

Jim

Monique's notes

Trip to the cinema with Jim
Day: 1 ....
Time: 2 ....
Cost of my ticket: 3 ....
Show: 4 ....
Jim's mobile: 5 ....

SPEAKING

9 Talk about your favourite music, singers and songs. Which ones do you like? Why do you like them? Take turns to speak.

Tell me about … your favourite music / singers / songs. What is it / are they? Why do you like it / them?

My favourite music / singers / songs are … I like it / them because …

13 Life experiences

Have you ever wanted to be a chef?

LISTENING

1 1.52 **Read the fact files. Then listen to Dylan, Finn and Gabby talking about the 'skills' part of the Merrydown Award. Who do they each decide to interview?**

Have you ever interviewed a famous person?

No? Well, choose one of these people to interview!

Name: Clark Stevens
Job: Wildlife Photographer
I've travelled to Africa and South America.

Name: Hannah Stone
Job: Artist
I've painted pictures of the Royal Family.

Name: William Foster
Job: Model
I've worked for famous fashion magazines.

2 1.52 **Listen again. Why did they decide to interview the people they chose?**

GRAMMAR Present perfect with *ever* and *never*

3 Read the sentences and questions. Then choose the correct words to complete the rules.

Statements	Questions	Short answers
I've never talked to a real artist.	Have you ever interviewed a	Yes, I have.
I've travelled to Africa and South America.	famous person?	No, I haven't.
Maybe she's painted a picture of the Queen!	Have you decided, Finn?	

1 We use the *auxiliary verb* / *main verb* *have* plus the past participle of the *auxiliary verb* / *main verb* to form the present perfect.
2 We use the present perfect to talk about experiences in the *past* / *present* / *future*.
3 We *can* / *can't* use words like *last week* or *ago* with the present perfect.
4 We can use *ever* in present perfect *questions* / *statements*.
5 We can use *never* in present perfect *questions* / *statements*.

→ Grammar reference page 159

4 Make sentences in the present perfect.

1 My mum / never visit / Antarctica.
2 I / never camp / in the winter.
3 you / ever work / in a factory?
4 Tony / ever repair / a computer?
5 We / never return / to our old school.

Corpus challenge

Can you correct this sentence?
I don't never travelled there and I want to visit.

VOCABULARY

5 Match the jobs to the definitions.

1 An artist
2 A chef
3 A dentist
4 A tour guide
5 A mechanic
6 A model
7 A nurse
8 A photographer
9 A pilot
10 A receptionist

a shows interesting places to visitors.
b flies planes.
c shows clothes and make up by wearing them.
d takes pictures.
e paints or draws pictures.
f checks and repairs teeth.
g works at the welcome desk in a hotel or office.
h repairs car engines and other machines.
i cooks food in a restaurant.
j looks after sick people.

About you

6 Which job would you like to do? Which job wouldn't you like to do?

7 Read the sentences about Tanya's summer job. Choose the best word (A, B or C) for each space.

0 Tanya .....B..... a summer job last week.
  A was B got C came

1 Tanya starts at 8 am and .... at 5 pm, five days a week.
  A closes B completes C finishes

2 Tanya .... the bus to work.
  A goes B catches C travels

3 Tanya often plays games and .... sports with the children.
  A does B makes C gives

4 Tanya thinks it's very .... working with young children.
  A tired B friendly C exciting

5 In the future, Tanya .... to be a teacher.
  A thinks B knows C wants

PRONUNCIATION Past participles

8 1.53 Listen to three *-ed* endings. How do you say the past participles of the verbs in the box? Put them into the right column.

ask call climb fail help play point push record text visit wash

/ɪd/ **decided**	/d/ **arrived**	/t/ **hoped**
		asked

1.54 Listen and check. Then repeat.

SPEAKING

9 Make questions using the present perfect.

0 you / ever / interview / a famous person?
  Have you ever interviewed a famous person?
1 you / ever / want / climb / a mountain?
2 you / ever / help / a neighbour?
3 you / ever / cook / meal / for your family?
4 you / ever / join / drama club?
5 you / ever / work / as a DJ?
6 you / ever / repair / anything?

10 Work in pairs. Ask and answer the questions from Exercise 10. Add questions of your own to ask your partner.

No, I've never done that

READING AND VOCABULARY

1 Match each picture to a question in the Life Quiz.

LIFE QUIZ

WHAT HAVE AND HAVEN'T YOU DONE IN YOUR LIFE?

1 Have you ever lent anyone your phone?
2 Have you ever broken something expensive?
3 Have you ever met a famous person?
4 Have you ever worn your parents' clothes?
5 Have you ever eaten snake?
6 Have you ever been in a play?
7 Have you ever sold anything on the internet?
8 Have you ever dreamed that you were flying?
9 Have you ever grown vegetables to eat?
10 Have you ever ridden on an elephant?
11 Have you ever fallen asleep in class?
12 Have you ever forgotten your door key?

a

b

c

d

e

f

g

h

i

j

k

l

2 Do the Life Quiz with your partner. How many *yes* and *no* answers does your partner have?

A: *Have you ever lent anyone your phone?*
B: *No, I've never done that. I've never lent my phone to anyone.*
A: *Yes, I have. I've lent my phone to my brother.*

3 Talk about your answers in groups of four. Did you all have the same answer for any of the questions?

4 **Match each verb in the box to a past participle in the quiz. What is the past simple form of each verb?**

be	break	dream	eat	fall	forget
grow	lend	meet	ride	sell	wear

5 **Think of six things you've done in your life. Write sentences.**

I've swum with dolphins.
I've flown in a hot air balloon.

6 **Work with a partner. Ask and answer about the things you have done in Exercise 5.**

A: Have you ever swum with dolphins?
B: Yes, I have.

B: Have you ever flown in a hot air balloon?
A: No, I haven't.

Decide together which is the most exciting thing you have both done. Tell the class.

7 **Complete the five conversations.**

0 I've won first prize in a competition.
  A Certainly!
  (B) Congratulations!
  C Good idea!

1 I went to an awesome concert last night!
  A You're so lucky!
  B I'm sorry.
  C Are you OK?

2 Can I borrow your English textbook?
  A How do you know?
  B Sure.
  C No, I haven't.

3 I've never learned to swim.
  A Yes, I have.
  B Where was it?
  C That's a pity.

4 Do you want to watch the film now or later?
  A Of course not.
  B I do.
  C I don't mind.

5 Shall we meet at six o'clock tomorrow?
  A See you later.
  B Great idea!
  C I had a good time.

1.55 Listen and check. Then repeat.

SPEAKING

8 **Work in pairs. Choose a pair of people from the top box and a situation from the bottom box.**

Two friends
Two sisters **Two brothers**
A brother and sister

Situation 1

Person A: You have passed an important exam. You are phoning B to tell him/her. You are very excited.
Person B: You are playing a computer game and don't really want to talk to A at the moment. Be polite to A!

Situation 2

Person A: B has arrived late at the cinema. You have waited a long time and you have missed the start of the film. What do you say to B?
Person B: You left home late and missed the bus. You ran all the way from the bus stop in the rain and you're tired and wet. What do you say to A?

Situation 3

Person A: You have bought a new jacket. It was very expensive and no one else has one. You tell B about it when you meet.
Person B: You have got a new jacket, too and want to show it to A. It's the same as A's jacket. You thought no one else had one.

Write a short conversation using some of the phrases from Exercise 7. Practise your conversation in pairs. Then perform it for the class.

A: Ah, here you are. We've missed the beginning of the film. Are you OK?
B: Yes, I'm fine.
A: What happened?
B: I'm sorry. I forgot the time and then I missed the bus.
A: What can we do now? Let's have a hot coffee and go to the next show.
B: Good idea! I'm cold and really wet. I can get dry.

Video extra

14 Spending money

It's just opened

VOCABULARY

About you

1 Discuss with your partner.

Do you like shopping? Why? / Why not?
What shops do you go to the most?
Use the words in the box below to help you.

bookshop	café	chemist
clothes shop	department store	
market	shoe shop	sweet shop
supermarket		

READING

2 Read the magazine advertisements. What does each shop sell?

3 Read the advertisements again and answer the questions.

1 When does *Eat Me* open?
2 When does *Drinks and Things* open?
3 When does *Shop and Try* open?

Where can you …
4 … surf the internet?
5 … buy a belt?
6 … sit down comfortably?
7 … have some free food?
8 … shop from home?

4 – 11 October

Businesses and Shops in Cardiff

eat me

NEW!

52 Main Street

Do you like sweets and chocolates?
Come and choose from the hundreds we have in our shop.
You can even try before you buy!
Opening 3 October.

Drinks and Things

13 River Avenue

NEW!

A large variety of juices available.
Delicious sandwiches and cakes, freshly made every day.
Comfortable sofas and chairs.
Free wifi.
Our first day is 15 October.
10% discount with this advertisement.

Shop and Try

NEW!

www.shopandtry.net

All the latest fashions in clothes.
Order online, collect from our shop in Cardiff.
Try your clothes on in store.
Make sure they're right for you!
Open from 20 September.

GRAMMAR Present perfect with *just, yet* and *already*

4 **Look at the date of the free magazine. Answer *yes* or *no* for each of these questions.**

Has *Drinks and Things* opened yet?
Has *Shop and Try* opened yet?
Has *Eat Me* opened yet?

5 **Study the examples and the words in red. Then match 1–3 with a–c to make sentences about the present perfect.**

Shop and Try opened on 20 September. It has **already** opened.
Eat Me opened on 3 October. It has **just** opened.
Drinks and Things opens on 15 October. It hasn't opened **yet**.

1 To talk about something which happened a very short time ago,
2 To talk about something which will happen very soon,
3 To talk about something which happened not long ago, or sooner than someone expected,

a we use the present perfect with *yet*.
b we use the present perfect with *already*.
c we use the present perfect with *just*.

→ Grammar reference page 160

6 **Study the examples in Exercises 4 and 5 and complete the table.**

	Present perfect positive	Present perfect negative	Present perfect questions
yet	✘	✔	✔
just			
already			

Corpus challenge

Which sentence is correct? Correct the other two sentences.

A I have already bought a mobile phone.
B Actually, my classes haven't finish yet, so perhaps I won't go with you.
C Hi, Arnold I just see a football match with my father.

7 **Look at the things Jacob has just bought for a camping trip. Then look at his shopping list. Which things has he already bought? Which things hasn't he bought yet? Make sentences using *yet* and *already*.**

8 **Make a list of the ten things you do every day. Then ask and answer in pairs about today.**

A: Have you done your homework yet?
B: Yes, I've already done my homework.
B: Have you used the computer yet?
A: Yes, I've just used the computer.

PRONUNCIATION Questions with question words

9 ▶ 2.02 **Listen and repeat.**

Where's the shop?
What can you buy there?
Why do you like it?
How expensive is it?
When does it close?

SPEAKING

10 **Student A. Look at page 136. Student B. Look at page 137.**

Let's have three slices each

VOCABULARY

About you

1 What types of food do you like to eat on a picnic or at a barbecue?

2 Complete the sentences.

kilograms **millilitres** **grams** **pounds and pence** **euros and cents** **metres** **kilometres** **litres** **centimetres**

1 You buy food in .... or ....
2 You buy drink in .... or ....
3 You use .... and .... to buy things.
4 You find out how far away something is in .... , ... and ....

3 Put the numbers in the box into the right column.

225 g   €19.22   200 ml   22 cm   15 l   57p   £15.00   5 kg   99c   1.65 m

How heavy?	How much liquid?	How long / tall?	How much money?

▶ 2.03 **Check with your partner. Then listen, check and repeat the numbers.**

LISTENING

4 What do you like to do on your birthday or your name day? Tell your partner.

5 ▶ 2.04 **Greg and Ruth are planning a birthday picnic for their friend Sonya. Listen and tick (✓) the things they have already got.**

Things for Sonya's Picnic

pizzas	fruit juice
crisps	water
apples	PLUS
cake	blanket
lemonade	presents!

6 ▶ 2.04 **Listen again. How much of each food and drink have they got or do they want?**

7 Look at these things from the conversation. Match the words to the pictures.

1 

2 

3 

4 

5 

a variety of drinks
a pair of sunglasses
a bit of water
a slice of pizza
a set of watercolour paints

8 Complete the sentences with the words in blue from Exercise 7.

1. I've just bought a new .... of shoes. Do you like them?
2. Let's have a .... of music at the party. We can have rock, blues and rap.
3. I want a .... of CDs of all the band's music. That's five CDs altogether!
4. Could I have a .... of chocolate, please? I'm hungry.
5. Can you pass me the knife? I'll cut you a .... of cake.
6. Our teacher has got a .... of keys for the school.
7. There are a .... of books in the library so everyone can find something they like.

SPEAKING

9 Read the next part of Ruth and Greg's conversation and answer the questions.

Ruth: Hey, just a minute, we forgot about music. We can't have a party without music. What shall we do?
Greg: I could bring my guitar, I suppose.
Ruth: Yes, and I can text everyone who's coming, if you like, and ask them to bring instruments, too. Right. Is that all?
Greg: Oh, I nearly forgot. The biscuits! I'll try and make them this afternoon. If not, I'll make them in the morning.
Ruth: OK.

1. Which two underlined phrases make suggestions?
2. Which underlined phrase says what the situation will be when something does not happen?

EP Get talking! → page 133

I suppose ...
If you like
if not

10 Work with a partner. Write conversations using these ideas. Use Exercise 9 to help you. Then practise the conversation with your partner.

1. You're planning a visit to a festival with your friend. You forgot about the food.
2. You're planning a visit to a new shopping mall. You forgot how you're going to get there.

WRITING

Prepare to write – a note

GET READY Read the note from Greg to his dad. Correct the punctuation. Add full stops, capital letters, apostrophes and question marks.

dear dad
Ruth and i need to get some things for Sonya's party please can you take us to the supermarket this morning thanks
see you later
Greg

Compare your corrected note in pairs.

PLAN You have just bought a birthday present for your sister. Write a note about it to your English friend. Make notes about:

- what you have bought for your sister
- why you chose it
- which shop you bought it in.

WRITE Write your note. Use 25–35 words. Make sure you include information about all three ideas in your answer. Think carefully about punctuation.

IMPROVE Read your note and look for mistakes. Check that you have included all the necessary information and that you used punctuation correctly.

Culture

Instrument families

1 **Look at the phrases in the box. Which ones describe the pictures a–d?**

hit the drums	blow air into a bag	blow air into a hole	squeeze the bag
cover holes (with your fingers)	move the strings		

2 **2.07 Listen to the instruments. Do they know what they are called or where they come from? Do any of them come from your country?**

3 **Read and check. Match the texts to the pictures from Exercise 1.**

1

This Taiko drum is from Japan. Its body is made of wood, and the skin, which players hit with big sticks, is made from animal skin. Usually a group of drummers play the taiko drums. Their body movements are an important part of taiko drumming. Sometimes two drummers play one drum at the same time, one at each end.

2

Bagpipe players blow air into a bag made of animal skin which is under one arm. Then they gently squeeze the bag with their arm and the air goes into pipes to make a sound. Pipers can change the sound by covering holes in the pipes with their fingers. This is a picture of a Scottish piper.

3

There are many types of guitar all over the world. The guitar in the picture is a Spanish Flamenco guitar. Flamenco guitars are acoustic and the body of the guitar is made of wood. They have six strings. The height of the strings above the fingerboard is lower than in classical guitars. This means the guitarist can play faster.

4

You can find flutes in most countries around the world. However, they are often made of different materials and you play them differently. The flute in the picture is a Chinese flute and is made of wood. Players hold the flute at an angle and blow into a hole near the top. Like the bagpipes, players can change the sound by covering holes with their fingers.

4 Read the texts again. What is each instrument made of? Show your partner how you play each one.

5 Look at the pictures. Which instrument family from Exercise 2 is missing?

Uilleann pipes ☐

....

Cajon ☐

....

Banjo ☐

....

Talking drum ☐

....

Bagpipes ☐

....

Balalaika ☐

....

6 ▶2.08 Listen to the interview. Number the instruments in the order the speaker talks about them.

7 ▶2.08 Listen again. Write the name of the country under each instrument.

8 ▶2.09 Listen to some of the instruments from Exercise 5. Do you know which one is which? Check with your partner.

Project research a musical instrument family

Work in a group. Choose one of the instruments below.

piano maracas violin trumpet

Use the internet or books to find out:

- where it comes from
- how it is played
- the names of one or two other instruments in the same family
- pictures of your instruments
- recordings of your instruments on the internet.

Tell the rest of the class what you found out. Show your pictures and play the recordings of the instruments.

15 Free time
I've had a guitar since I was ten

VOCABULARY

1 Work with a partner. Match the pictures to an activity from the questionnaire.
What free-time activities in the questionnaire do you like doing, or are you interested in?

a

b

c

d

Activities	Boys	Girls
playing computer games		
playing sport		
watching TV		
chatting		
reading books		
going shopping		
cooking		
singing/acting/dancing		
photography		
listening to music		
playing an instrument		
spending time online		
going out with friends		
collecting things		
making things		

e

SPEAKING

2 Do the questionnaire in your class. Walk around the room and ask people which activities they like doing in their free time. Write your results for each activity or hobby like this. ~~||||~~ ||

3 Work in groups of four or five. Put your information together and complete the results below. Were you surprised by any of your results? Why?

In our class these activities are more popular with girls: ...., ..., ...,
In our class these activities are more popular with boys: ...., ..., ...,
In our class both boys and girls like these activities: ...., ..., ...,
In our class no one likes these activities: ...., ..., ...,

LISTENING

4 ▶2.10 **Listen to three young people talking about what they do in their free time. Write the activity/activities from the questionnaire below each speaker.**

Owen	Kyle	Erin
....	....	....
....	....	....
....	....	....

5 ▶2.10 **Listen again. Are the sentences right (✔) or wrong (✘)?**

1 Owen keeps his computer in his bedroom.
2 Owen thinks he uses his computer too much.
3 Kyle still collects pins and badges.
4 Kyle does two different sports.
5 Erin has got a new guitar.
6 Erin has her own camera.

GRAMMAR Present perfect with *since/for*

6 Look at these examples. Then complete the rules below with *for* or *since*.

I've had my own computer for three years.
I haven't bought any football cards for a long time.
I've played the guitar for two years.
I've had this guitar since January.
I've had one of them since I was ten.
My Dad's had his camera since he was a teenager.

1 We use .... with an amount of time, such as a number of hours/months/years.
2 We use .... with the time when the action started, such as a day/date/age.

→ Grammar reference page 161

7 Complete the phrases with *for* or *since*.

1 .... I was three years old
2 .... four hours
3 .... last month
4 .... three days
5 .... October 31
6 .... Monday
7 .... six months
8 .... yesterday
9 .... a long time

8 Complete the sentences so they are true for you. Then compare with a partner.

1 I haven't read a comic since ....
2 I haven't watched a cartoon for ....
3 I've played .... for ....
4 I've been able to .... since I was ....
5 I've lived in my home since ....
6 I've had this pen for ....
7 I've known my best friend since ....
8 I've wanted to .... since I was ....

Corpus challenge

Can you correct the mistake in this sentence?
It's been my hobby from I was ten years old.

PRONUNCIATION Weak forms

9 ▶2.11 **Listen to the sentences and notice the pronunciation of the underlined words.**

I've had this since I <u>was</u> three.
I've played basketball <u>for</u> two years.
I've just walked home <u>from</u> school.
I haven't been <u>to</u> your house since Saturday.
I've bought <u>some</u> nice shoes.

Listen again and repeat.

SPEAKING AND WRITING

About you

10 Ask and answer with your partner.

Do you have a hobby?
Yes → What is it?
No → What do you do in your free time?
How long have you enjoyed doing it?
Do you need anything special to do it?
Yes → What do you need? How long have you had it?
No

11 Write some sentences about your partner. In groups read out your sentences. How much did your partner remember about you?

Andrei has done karate since he was seven. He has a special white jacket and trousers called a 'gi'. He has a blue belt. He's had it for six months and hopes to get a purple one soon.

Birthday challenges

VOCABULARY

1 Join the verbs and nouns to make phrases. Then match each phrase to a picture.

1	do	a bill
2	clean	a pizza
3	book	a broken shelf
4	pay	the car
5	repair	a 15-km run
6	order	a hotel

2 Which of the phrases above are 'jobs around the home'? Can you think of any more jobs?

About you

3 What do you do to help around the house? Which of the things in Exercise 1 have you done alone? Which haven't you done yet? Do you ever go out alone? What's the most frightening thing you have ever done?

LISTENING

4 Read the information about a podcast. Can you guess what Sarah's challenges were?

9.00 am Morning Chat

On today's show, presenter Gary talks to a girl called Sarah who has just had her 15th birthday. Her mother gave her 15 challenges to do. Sarah's challenges are about growing up, becoming an adult, and doing things she hasn't done before.

5 2.12 **Listen to the podcast. Which things in Exercise 1 does Sarah talk about?**

6 2.12 **Listen again and answer the questions.**

1. What was Sarah's first challenge?
2. How does Sarah get her challenges?
3. How did Sarah feel about her second challenge?
4. What has been Sarah's worst challenge?
5. What did Sarah have to do for the trip to London?
6. What's Sarah's next challenge?

7 Here are some more of Sarah's challenges.

paint a picture of yourself
learn Chinese
work in an office for a day
make £150 for charity

In groups, talk about which challenges you would like to do and which you have already done. Think of three more ideas for birthday challenges and tell the class.

READING

A *special* birthday

For her 101st birthday, Mary Hardison, from Utah in the USA, wanted to do something a bit different. So, instead of having a party and inviting her friends and family to her home, she decided to go paragliding. She is now in the *Guinness Book of World Records* as the oldest person in the world to do this. She got the idea from her 75-year-old son, who started doing the sport a few years ago. After the jump, she spoke to journalists, and told them: "I don't want my son to do something that I can't."

Mary did her flight with an instructor called Kevin Hintze. He said she was not afraid, even when they were turning over in the air. While she was coming down, Mary says she looked all around, at the buildings and at the mountains. On the ground below, she could see her children, grandchildren, great-grandchildren and even a few great-great-grandchildren. They cheered and held up signs that said HAPPY BIRTHDAY GRANDMA!

This isn't the first time Mary has done something exciting. On her 90th birthday, she went to Disneyland. A few of the rides were shut for repairs, but she went on all the ones that were open. For her next adventure, she's planning to go down the Alpine Slide at Utah's Park City Mountain Resort. It is 1,000 metres from the top to the bottom, and very fast, but Mary isn't afraid at all. In fact, she can't wait.

8 **Read the article about an old lady who did something special on her 101st birthday. Are sentences 1–7 'Right' (A) or 'Wrong' (B)? If there is not enough information to answer 'Right' (A) or 'Wrong' (B), choose 'Doesn't say' (C).**

0 Mary Hardison had a party for her 101st birthday.
A Right **B** Wrong **C** Doesn't Say

1 Mary's son tried paragliding before his mother did it.
A Right **B** Wrong **C** Doesn't Say

2 Mary spent more than an hour talking to journalists after her flight.
A Right **B** Wrong **C** Doesn't Say

3 Kevin said Mary was worried during some parts of the flight.
A Right **B** Wrong **C** Doesn't Say

4 Mary was able to enjoy the view during her flight.
A Right **B** Wrong **C** Doesn't Say

5 Some members of Mary's family travelled a long way to watch her.
A Right **B** Wrong **C** Doesn't Say

6 When Mary went to Disneyland, some of the rides were closed.
A Right **B** Wrong **C** Doesn't Say

7 Mary thinks she has done enough exciting activities now.
A Right **B** Wrong **C** Doesn't Say

SPEAKING

9 **Work in pairs to write an interview. One of you is a journalist. The other is Mary Hardison. Look at at page 137.**
Prepare and practise together. Then perform your interview in groups of four.

16 So many languages!

He has learned 11 languages

READING

1 **Look at the title, picture and first sentence of the text about Alex Rawlings. Match the languages Alex speaks with the speech bubbles.**

AN AMAZING LANGUAGE LEARNER

Alex Rawlings is a student at Oxford University and has learned to speak 11 languages: English, Greek, German, Spanish, Russian, Dutch, Afrikaans, French, Hebrew, Catalan and Italian. Last year, he won a competition to find the student who speaks the most languages in Britain. Since then, Alex has been on radio stations around the world and the BBC has made a video of him speaking all 11 of his languages for their website.

On the video Alex explains that he's been interested in languages all his life. Greek is his favourite, because his mother is half Greek and he has spoken the language since he was a young child. He became interested in other languages after he travelled to different countries for holidays and his father's job. He wanted to be able to talk to people, but couldn't.

When he was 14, he went on a trip to Holland with his family. Afterwards, he bought some Dutch language books and CDs, and the next time he went he was able to speak to the people there. That was the beginning of his language learning adventure, and he says he has not finished yet. He plans to start learning Arabic next. Alex says that he has already made many new friends through his languages and that learning new ones gets easier each time you do it. He started a blog a few months ago where he shares his ideas about language learning and gives advice to people who send in questions.

2 **Read the text. Imagine you are Alex and answer the questions that people have sent you.**

1 What has happened to you since you won the competition?
2 Which is your favourite language and why do you like it?
3 How did your interest in languages begin?
4 How did you learn Dutch?
5 What language do you want to learn next?
6 Is each new language as difficult as the last?

GRAMMAR Present perfect and past simple

3 **Look at the sentences from the text. Which are present perfect and which are past simple? Write PP or PS.**

1 He has learned to speak 11 languages.
2 Last year, he won a competition.
3 He has spoken the language since he was a young child.
4 When he was 14 he went on a trip to Holland.
5 He has already made many new friends.
6 He started a blog a few months ago.

4 **Complete the rules with 'present perfect' or 'past simple'.**

1 We use the .... with words like *yesterday*, *ago*, *last year*, *when he was little*.
2 We use the .... with words like *since*, *already*, *yet*, *just*, *ever*.
3 We use the .... to talk about:
– an action that finished in the past. (**a**)
4 We use the .... to talk about:
– an action that began in the past but continues into the present (**b**)
– someone's general life experiences (**c**)
– an action that finished in the past, but the result is important now. (**d**)

Corpus challenge

Can you correct the mistake in this sentence?

Yesterday I have watched a swimming competition with my brother.

→ Grammar reference **page 162**

5 **Find more examples of the past simple and present perfect in the text. Match them to uses a–d in the box.**

6 **Complete the conversations by putting the verbs into the present perfect or past simple.**

1 **A:** (do) .... your homework yet, Tania? **B:** Yes, I (finish) .... it an hour ago.
2 **A:** Where (you go) .... on holiday last summer, Robin?
B: We (go) .... to New York to visit my sister. She (live) .... there since 2014.
3 **A:** (you ever eat) .... curry? **B:** Yes, I (have) .... some yesterday. Delicious!
4 **A:** (you enjoy) .... the *Toy Story* films when you were little, Sergio?
B: I (never see) .... any of the *Toy Story* films. But I (like) .... *The Incredibles*.

VOCABULARY AND SPEAKING

7 **Complete the quiz with the words in the box.**

articles chat dictionary exercises guess interesting list mistakes spell

1 When do you use English outside the classroom?
A when I study on the internet
B when I'm on holiday
C to (**1**) .... to tourists
D to watch English language movies/TV shows
E to sing pop songs
F never

2 What do you do when you find a new word in a text?
A find it in a (**2**) ....
B try to (**3**) .... what it means
C ask your teacher what it means
D ask your little brother what it means

3 What's the best way to learn vocabulary?
A from a (**4**) .... of words
B by doing vocabulary (**5**) ....
C by reading books and (**6**) ....
D five minutes before a test

4 Which of these sentences do you agree with?
A It's important to be able to (**7**) .... correctly.
B Making (**8**) .... is an important part of learning.
C Pronunciation doesn't matter as much as grammar.
D I only learn if the topic of the lesson is (**9**) .... to me.

8 **Now do the quiz. Choose only one answer for each question. Turn to page 137 to see your results. Compare them with a partner.**

PRONUNCIATION Word stress

9 **Say these words with a partner and underline the stressed syllable.**

1 adjectives
2 article
3 dictionary
4 exercises
5 important
6 interesting
7 mistakes
8 sentence
9 vocabulary

▶ 2.13 **Listen, check and repeat.**

Languages of the world

READING

1 **How many languages do you think there are in the world? Read the text once. Find three things you already knew and three new facts. Compare with a partner.**

LANGUAGES *of the* WORLD

There are around 7,000 different languages in the world today. Languages that are similar to each other are in groups or 'families'. Some languages have a lot of speakers and others have very few. Many of the smaller languages have no writing, so when the last speaker dies, the language dies too.

Europe

Europe has 284 different languages. One language family here is Romance languages, which includes Spanish, Portuguese and Italian. Another is Slavic languages such as Russian, Polish and Czech. English is the third largest language in the world, with 335 million speakers, and belongs in the Germanic group. The Basque language from France and Spain is very unusual. It doesn't belong to any language family!

Asia

Asia has 2,303 languages. Chinese has a billion speakers – more than any other language in the world. Hindi is the world's fourth largest language, and Arabic comes fifth. Some parts of Asia have a very large number of languages.

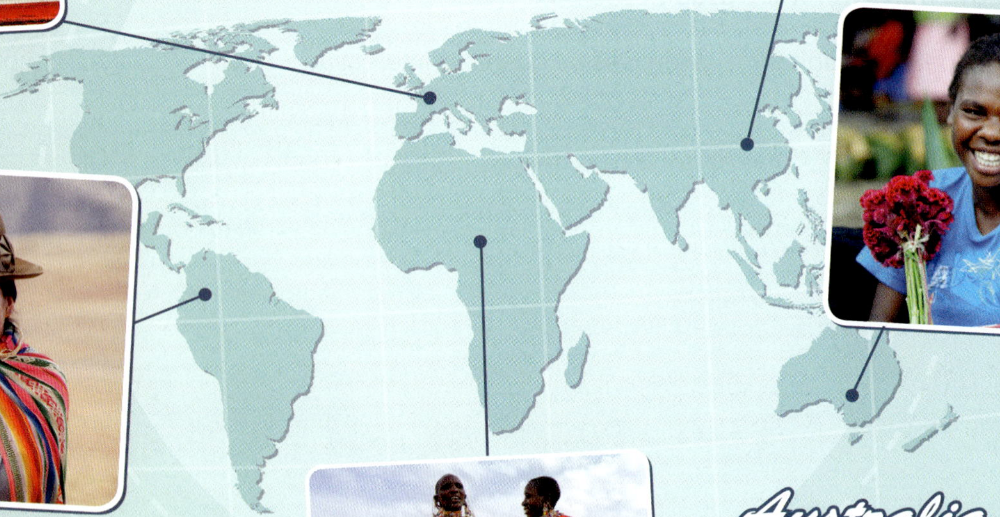

Americas

This area has 1,060 languages. English and Spanish are the largest. Spanish, with 406 million speakers, is the world's second largest language. Portuguese is spoken in Brazil, and mainly English and French in Canada. There are also many other native languages, for example Mam, a Mayan language which people speak in parts of Mexico and Guatemala.

Africa

Human language probably began on this continent. There are 2,146 languages here. Many people in Africa can speak more than one language, because, as well as their own language, they also speak English, French or Portuguese.

Australia and Oceania

This area has 1,311 languages in total. The main language of Australia and New Zealand is English but there are a lot of smaller languages too. Papua New Guinea has only 4 million people but it has 832 languages – more than any other country! Unfortunately some aboriginal languages are very small now and have only one or two speakers.

2 Read the text again and answer the questions.

1 What are the three biggest languages in the world? How many speakers do they have?
2 Which continent has the most languages?
3 What language family does Polish belong to?
4 What is special about the Basque language?
5 What are the main languages in Canada?
6 Where do people speak Mam?
7 Which country has the largest number of languages?

About you

3 Work in groups of three. Talk about:

- where you come from
- what language(s) you speak
- other languages in your country
- what languages you are studying
- what languages other people in your family can speak.

LISTENING

4 ▶ 2.14 You will hear a woman giving some information about different languages. Can you answer any questions before you listen?

1 How many colour words are there in Russian and Greek? How many in English?
2 How many number words does the Pirahã language of Brazil have?
3 Some languages have two sets of vocabulary. Why?
4 Some languages have no words for *left* / *right* / *in front of* / *behind*. How do they say where things are?
5 How is modern technology helping small languages?

EP Get talking! → page 133

unfortunately
at least
quite a few
these days …

VOCABULARY

5 Read the descriptions of the words about reading and writing. What is the word for each one? The first letter is already there. There is one space for each other letter in the word.

0 When you are learning a language you often study from this. t e x t b o o k
1 You look in this to find out what a word means and how to say it. d _ _ _ _ _ _ _ _ _
2 You can write this on a piece of paper or send it from your phone. m _ _ _ _ _ _
3 This place has books and computers for people to use. l _ _ _ _ _ _
4 This is at the front of the class and the teacher writes on it. b _ _ _ _
5 This has articles and photographs in it and you can buy it monthly or weekly. m _ _ _ _ _ _ _

WRITING

Prepare to write – information about your English class

GET READY Read what a Spanish student wrote about her English class.

My name is Maria and I come from Spain. Most of the people in my English class are from Spain too, but two of us are from Poland and three are from Morocco. The languages people speak in my class are Spanish, Catalan, Polish, Arabic, French and English. I like speaking in English but I find listening difficult. I plan to spend more time learning vocabulary in the future.

Look at how she uses capital letters. Find examples of these uses:

- after a full stop
- for peoples' names
- for countries
- for nationalities
- for languages
- for 'I'

PLAN Plan a paragraph about your English class. Make notes about:

- peoples' nationalities
- languages people speak
- languages people in the class are learning
- your likes/dislikes/plans about learning English

WRITE Write 50–70 words, using all your notes.

Video extra

Design and Technology

Materials from nature

1 Work in groups. People developed the design of airplanes by looking at the shape of birds. Can you think of other design ideas we have taken from nature?

2 Match pictures 1–4 with the close-ups a–d. What part of the animal or plant do you think it is?

3 Read the text quickly and check your answers.

4 Work in groups of four. What materials did scientists develop from these animals and plants? Each student read one part of the text (a–d). Make notes in the chart on page 95.

Ideas from Nature

a **Have you ever** seen geckos running up walls? Do you know how they do it? Well, their feet have millions of tiny hairs, which means that they can walk on or stick to almost anything, even if they are upside down!

Scientists have used this idea to develop super-strong and super-sticky glues. It's possible to re-use these glues over and over again. They work in space and under water, we use them to repair planes, and at home they can even stick your TV to the wall!

b **Lotus leaves** look beautiful when they float on water. But have you ever noticed how the water just falls off the leaves? Scientists have looked closely at the leaves and found that they have a very smooth surface. Water doesn't stick to this surface, and even more amazing, the water cleans the leaf as it moves over it.

Scientists have now developed materials which can do the same thing. We use them on wind turbine blades, roofs and even snowboards. You can even get paint for the outside of houses which doesn't get dirty!

c **Sharks are** the most successful predators in the sea. Why? Well, one reason is that they can move very fast through the water because they have extraordinary skin. If you look at sharkskin through a microscope, you can see hundreds of little 'teeth'. These have lines on them which help the water to flow over the shark more quickly so they move very smoothly and fast. Scientists have used the shape of sharkskin to develop material for super-fast swimsuits and the bottom of boats.

d **Velcro is** something you probably use every day, for example when you put on your trainers. Have you ever thought about where the idea for this material came from? Well, George de Mestral invented it in 1948 after a walk with his dog. He was pulling some seeds from a burdock plant from his dog's fur when he saw that there were little hooks all over the seeds. The hooks made the seeds stick to the dog. So the idea for Velcro was born and now it's difficult to imagine a world without it!

Name of animal or plant:	
Which part of the animal/plant the design idea came from:	
The new material:	
Examples of its use:	

5 **Tell the other students about your material. Use your notes from Exercise 4 to help you. Which do you think is the most interesting material? Which do you think is the most useful idea? Why?**

Project design a new material or product

Work in pairs.

Choose a topic you are both interested in: sports equipment, music, clothes, games, furniture, cars, etc. Discuss these questions:

- What animals or other things from nature do you think of when you think about your topic?
- Why do you think about those animals or things from nature?
- What is special about them?
- How can you use that special quality to design a material or product for your topic?

Create a new material or product for your topic. Tell the rest of the class which animals or things from nature your idea came from.

We designed a new material for making clothes. The idea came from butterflies' wings. Butterflies' wings are made of many tiny, smooth shapes that change colour in the light. With our material we can make clothes that change colour in the light.

Review 4
Units 13–16

VOCABULARY

1 Complete the sentences with a word from the box.

euros	grams	litres	metres	pair	pounds	set	slices

1 I've lost my .... of coloured pens. Can I borrow yours?
2 There are ten of us, so let's cut the melon into ten ....
3 I think I've lost my new .... of gloves. My mum won't be pleased!
4 The jacket was on sale for thirty .... and ninety-nine pence.
5 We need 250 .... of flour to make the cake.
6 My dad's nearly two .... tall. That's much taller than me.
7 In our family, we drink four .... of milk a day. We all have it on our cereal.
8 I haven't got any money for the bus. Can you lend me two .... and fifty cents, please?

2 Find ten job words in the word snake.

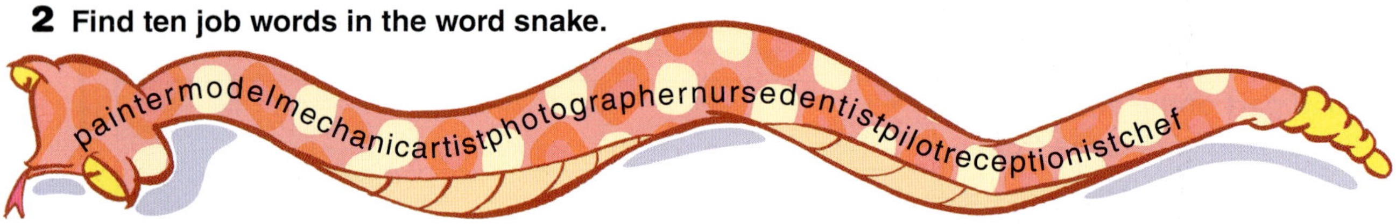

3 Look at the pictures and complete the phrases. The first letter is already there.

1 c............................ a meal

2 r............................ a bike

3 p............................ a bill

4 c............................ football cards

5 o............................ a pizza

6 c............................ the car

GRAMMAR

4 Choose the right words to complete the sentences.

1 I *have never seen* / *never don't see a* city like it.
2 I *have already bought* / *already buy* the paint.
3 I have had it *since* / *for* one year.
4 Last night I *left* / *have left* my bag in your house.

Correct the mistakes in these sentences.

5 I never been to a wedding and I want to come.
6 Yesterday, I left a book at your house and I need it because I don't do my homework yet.
7 I have had them when I was six.
8 I have telephoned you an hour ago but you weren't at home.

5 Write the questions for the answers. Then answer the questions about yourself. Use *never, just, yet, already* in your answers.

0 Have you ever done a Saturday job?
No, I've never done a Saturday job.

1 ....
Yes, I've just finished my homework.

2 ....
I've lived in this town for five years.

3 ....
Yes, I have. I visited Brazil in 2014 for the World Cup!

4 ....
Yes, I've already read three English books this year.

5 ....
No, I've never cooked a pizza.

6 ....
I've known my best friend since I was three years old.

6 Complete the text with the verbs in brackets. Use the past simple or present perfect.

I (1) .... (love) languages since I (2) .... (be) a little boy. My dad is English and my mum is Spanish and they (3) .... (speak) both languages to me at home. So I (4) .... (begin) learning English and Spanish as a baby. Then we (5) .... (move) to Turkey for my dad's work and I (6) .... (go) to primary school there. I (7) .... (learn) to speak Turkish quite quickly in school. Now we live in Japan. I (8) .... (not start) learning Japanese yet. But I'm going to learn it soon.

READING

7 Read the article about bananas. Choose the best word (A, B or C) for each space.

	A	B	C
0	A to	B from	C in
1	A but	B so	C because
2	A All	B Most	C Each
3	A since	B when	C for
4	A finds	B found	C finding
5	A any	B most	C some
6	A the	B a	C one
7	A which	B where	C who
8	A more	B other	C both

Billy's Gone BANANAS!

Billy Jones goes into the supermarket on his way home **0** ....B..... school. He always goes straight to the bananas **1** .... he's not interested in eating them. He's interested in the labels.
Billy collects the small colourful labels. 'They're amazing. **2** .... one is like a piece of art,' he says. He's collected the labels **3** .... five years, and has **4** .... more than 4,000.
Billy remembers his first label. 'There were **5** .... bananas on the table and I saw there were two different labels on them. I put **6** .... labels in a little notebook.'
But Billy isn't the only person **7** .... collects them. He has seen on the internet that there are lots of **8** .... people with the same hobby.

LISTENING

8 2.16 Listen to the phone conversation and complete the notes about the tablet.

Name of the tablet: **1** ....
Model number: **2** ....
Price: **3** £ ....
Name of shop: **4** ....
Phone number of shop: **5** ....
Contact person: **6** ....

SPEAKING

9 Make questions.

1 How many languages / you speak?
2 your mum / dad / speak / same language?
3 What language(s) / they speak?
3 Which languages / would / like / learn? Why?
4 like / learn / English?
5 What / most difficult / about English?
6 What / best thing / about learning English?

10 Ask and answer the questions with your partner. Take turns to speak.

17 Staying healthy
I've hurt myself

VOCABULARY

1 **How many body parts do you know? Match the words in the box to parts 1–9.**

back	blood	brain	ear	finger
heart	neck	stomach	toe	

2.17 Can you also name parts a–h? Listen and check.

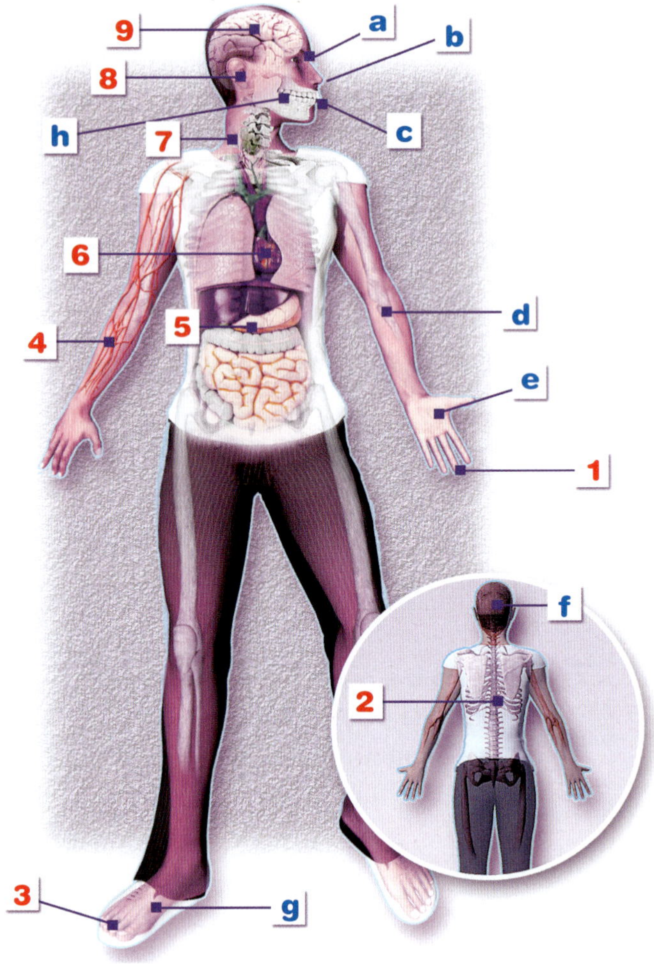

About you

2 Have you ever had an accident?
Have you ever broken a bone in your leg, foot, toe, arm, hand or finger?
Have you ever hurt your back or your neck?
Have you ever had toothache?

Choose two questions you answered 'yes' to. Tell your partner about what happened.

LISTENING

3 **Look at the pictures (1–3). What is happening? Try and tell the story in pairs. Use the words in the box to help you. How do you think the story ends?**

actor	ambulance	cyclist	fall off	poster

4 **2.18 Listen and check your ideas to Exercise 3.**

5 ▶ 2.18 **Listen again and choose the right word(s) to complete the sentences.**

1 Klara saw an accident on *Tuesday* / *Friday*.
2 Klara *read* / *heard* information about the play.
3 The play is about things happening *today* / *in the past*.
4 When Klara got to the theatre it was very *busy* / *quiet*.
5 The director was the *ambulance driver* / *cyclist* from the accident.
6 Klara *is* / *isn't* in the new play at the theatre.

GRAMMAR Pronouns *myself, yourself, herself, himself, ourselves, yourselves, themselves*

6 Look at the examples from the recording.

Have you hurt yourself?
I went to the audition by myself.
We use *-self* when the subject and the object of the verb are the same person.
We use the expression *by* .... *self* to mean (**a**) *alone* or (**b**) *without any help*.

Match 1 and 2 to meanings a and b.
1 I can cook a meal by myself.
2 I like to watch television by myself.

I	myself
you	yourself
he	himself
she	herself
we	ourselves
you	yourselves
they	themselves

→ Grammar reference **page 163**

7 Complete the sentences.

1 Peter wasn't badly hurt and drove .... to the hospital.
2 Simon and I really enjoyed .... at the party.
3 I hurt .... when I fell off the chair.
4 Zoë told .... that she wasn't ill.
5 Ben and Sara prepared all the food by ....
6 'Be careful you don't cut .... ,' the mother said to her son.
7 'You can help .... to paper and pens,' the teacher said to the students.

Corpus challenge

Correct the sentences.
a I went to Chile and I enjoyed a lot.
b Now I'll talk about me.
c Take care of you.

READING AND SPEAKING

8 Complete the phone conversation between two friends.
What does Katya say to Harry? Write the correct letter A–H.

Harry: Hi, Katya. It's Harry.
Katya: 0 ....D....
Harry: But it's twelve o'clock! Were you up late last night?
Katya: 1 ....
Harry: Oh dear. What's the matter?
Katya: 2 ....
Harry: Oh, that's horrible. Have you told your mum?
Katya: 3 ....
Harry: To ask you to come round to my house later to meet my cousin.
Katya: 4 ....
Harry: Never mind. Maybe you'll feel better tomorrow.
Katya: 5 ....
Harry: OK. Take care, Katya. Bye.

A I've got a terrible stomach ache and a headache.
B What a shame! But I don't feel well enough to go out today.
C I'm really sorry. When did she leave?
D Hello. I'm still in bed.
E I hope so! I'll text you and let you know.
F She's been at the doctor's since this morning.
G It's not that – I'm afraid I'm not feeling well.
H Yes, before she went to work. Why did you call me?

9 ▶ 2.19 **Listen and check your answers. Then practise the conversation with a partner.**

10 Work with a partner. Make short conversations using the ideas on page 137.

If you want to talk, I'll listen

a I'm not in the first team.

b I failed an exam.

c Someone in my school doesn't like me.

d I hate my hair.

e My parents don't understand me.

VOCABULARY AND READING

1 **Look at the pictures. All the students are worrying about something. Match what they're saying to the kind of problem.**

body and health	family	friends
schoolwork	sport	

2 **Work with a partner. Think of two more examples for each kind of problem in the box.**

About you

3 Do you worry about any of these things? What do people your age usually worry about? What do you worry about? Why?

4 **Look at the questions on the Teen Health website. Match them to the paragraphs.**

Teen HEALTH

Today's Topics

- How much exercise should I do?
- Are some foods healthier than others?
- Can it be dangerous to listen to loud music?
- Is it OK to feel sad sometimes?

1 ....
Yes! But how do you know? Can someone sitting next to you on the train hear the music on your earphones? They can? Well, then you need to make it quieter. Remember, if you do this to your ears now, you won't be able to hear well when you're older.

2 ....
Everyone tells you it's not healthy to sit at the computer all day. But doing too much sport can also be bad for you. Your body is still young. Don't do too much sport. You can easily hurt something. And think about when you do sports too. For example, you'll get a stomach ache if you play tennis just after you've eaten.

3 ....
Everyone feels unhappy sometimes, so you're not alone. It's normal for your feelings to change. Talk to a friend or to a parent about how you feel, or even a teacher. If you talk about your problems, they won't seem so bad.

4 ....
The answer to this is yes! I'm sure you know that a plate of fruit is healthier than a plate of chips! But what your growing body, your heart and your brain need is variety. If you are careful and eat a bit of everything, then you'll be healthier. Don't forget fresh fruit, vegetables and eggs! These types of food are good for your blood.

5 **Work with a partner. Read the texts again. Tell your partner what they say about:**

1 earphones
2 hearing well
3 too much sport
4 playing sport after meals
5 feelings
6 a friend, parent or teacher
7 a plate of chips
8 variety

PRONUNCIATION /uː/ and /ʊ/

6 **2.20 Listen and repeat the sentence. Do the 'oo' words have the same sound?**

These types of food are good for you.

How many words can you think of which sound like:

a *food*? **b** *good*?

GRAMMAR First conditional

7 **Look at the sentences from Exercise 4 and answer the questions.**

> If you do this to your ears now, you won't be able to hear well when you're older.
> You'll get a stomach ache if you play tennis just after you've eaten.

1 Which part of the sentence has *will (not)* plus *infinitive*?
2 Which part of the sentence has the present simple?
3 Where in the sentence is *if*?
4 Do the sentences talk about the past, the present or the future?

Now find two more examples of conditional sentences in the text.

8 **Match the two halves of the sentences.**

1 We'll miss the film
2 If I find your book,
3 I won't tell anyone
4 If you don't eat fast food every day,
5 I'll lend you my earphones
6 If I pass the exam,

a I'll give it to the teacher.
b my mum will be very surprised.
c if you don't hurry.
d if you can't find yours.
e you'll be healthier.
f if you don't want me to.

Corpus challenge

Can you correct the mistake in this sentence?

If I will go I will play with my brother and my friends.

LISTENING

9 **2.21 You will hear five short conversations. There is one question for each conversation. For each question, choose the right answer (A, B or C).**

1 What time is basketball practice today?

2 Which food does the girl choose?

3 Which earphones does the boy buy?

4 What's the weather like?

5 What are they going to do?

WRITING

10 **Choose an *If …* sentence below and complete it. Then start a new sentence with the second part of your first sentence. Then write five more sentences.**

If I have enough money, I'll buy …
If I pass all my exams, I'll …
If my birthday is on a Saturday this year, I'll …
If I move to a new class next year, I'll …

Here's an example.

If my birthday is on a Saturday this year, I'll have a big party.
If I have a big party, I'll ask all my friends.
If I ask all my friends …

Now compare what you've written with a partner.

18 Expedition!

It may rain on Sunday

The MERRYDOWN AWARD EXPEDITION

KIT LIST

We are going to the Brecon Beacons in Wales for our expedition. The whole expedition is 25 kilometres long. We will walk for two days and camp for one night. You will be in groups of three or four. You have to carry everything you need for camping and cooking between you. Check what the weather will be like before you pack!

CLOTHES
- walking boots
- waterproof trousers
- walking socks
- underwear
- T-shirts
- pyjamas
- sweaters (or fleece tops)
- trainers (for the evening)
- walking trousers (not jeans!)
- waterproof jacket

KIT FOR EACH GROUP
- tent
- map and compass
- food

OTHER KIT
- backpack
- towel
- sleeping bag
- torch
- wash bag with soap and toothpaste
- first-aid kit
- plate/bowl/mug/knife/fork/spoon
- water bottle

YOU MAY ALSO WANT:
- warm hat or sun hat
- gloves
- sun cream
- sunglasses
- playing cards
- snacks

READING AND VOCABULARY

1 Read the information. Answer the questions.

1 Where are the friends going for their expedition?
2 How many kilometres will they walk?
3 How many nights will they camp for?
4 Why do you think they are going?
5 What will they learn?

2 Match the pictures with a word from the kit list.

1

2

3

4
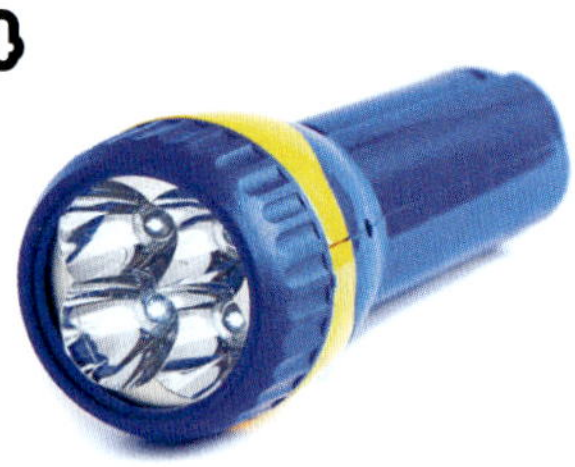
5
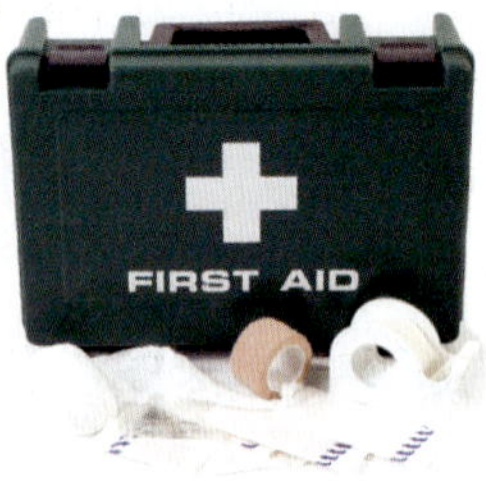

6

7

8

9

3 Which of the things on the list do the students need for:

wet weather?
sunny weather?
cold weather?
having fun?
eating and drinking?
sleeping?
keeping themselves clean?
finding the way?

LISTENING

4 2.22 **Gabby, Finn and Dylan are talking about the expedition. Listen and tick the items on the kit list you hear.**

5 2.22 **Listen again. Are these sentences right (✔) or wrong (✘)?**

1 Gabby bought a sleeping bag last weekend.
2 Dylan wants to get another pair of socks.
3 Gabby is taking two pairs of trousers.
4 The weather will be dry on Saturday.
5 Gabby wants to take fresh food with them.

GRAMMAR *may/might*

6 Match the sentences from the recording.

1 Our backpacks are going to be very heavy!
2 I just need to get another fleece top.
3 I'm taking two pairs of walking trousers.
4 It's going to be warm and dry on Saturday.
5 Let's not take any fresh food.
6 I'm going to take lots of snacks too.

a But it may rain a bit on Sunday morning.
b One pair might get dirty or wet.
c It might go bad in our backpacks.
d We might not be able to carry them!
e I might get hungry when I'm walking.
f I've only got one, and it may not be enough.

7 Choose the correct words to complete the rules.

1 In these sentences *may* and *might* mean the same thing.
We use them to say that something is *possible* / *impossible*.
2 After *may* and *might*, we use the infinitive *with to* / *without to*.
3 We *do* / *do not* use third person 's' with *may* and *might*.
4 To make a negative, we put 'not' *before* / *after* *may* or *might*.

→ Grammar reference **page 164**

8 Complete the sentences with words from the box.

might be	might not go	might not finish
might take	might invite	

1 I .... my homework tonight. Can I give it to you on Tuesday?
2 I .... my coat. I don't want to be cold later.
3 I .... Sam to my party. Do you think it's a good idea?
4 'I can't find my keys!' 'They .... in your school bag.'
5 I .... to the cinema tonight. I feel really tired.

Corpus challenge

Which sentence is correct? Can you correct the other two?

1 I think you might wear a raincoat because tomorrow we will have rain.
2 You can think it is expensive but the park is very good!
3 The book may be on the table in your room.

Pronunciation Sentence stress

9 2.23 **Listen to the sentences. Mark the stressed words.**

They might come later.
He may miss the bus.
It might start raining.
She may not agree.
We might go sailing.
I might have a drink.

SPEAKING

10 Work in groups. You are going on an expedition. Decide:

- where you are going
- how you will get there
- how far you will travel
- what you will need
- what you might need
- what might happen.

Then tell the class.

It was hard to wake Dylan up

LISTENING

1 **Gabby, Finn and Dylan are looking at photos of their expedition. Describe the photos. Can you guess what happened?**

2 **▶ 2.24 Listen and number the photos in the order the friends talk about them.**

3 **▶ 2.24 Listen again. Are these sentences right (✔) or wrong (✘)?**

1 Finn's dad drove the friends home after the expedition.
2 As soon as Dylan arrived home he got in the shower.
3 Gabby took the photo of Dylan in his sleeping bag.
4 Dylan was taking photos while the others were washing the dishes.
5 Someone helped the friends when they got lost.
6 Finn bought his waterproof trousers in a shop.

Have you been on an expedition like this? If not, would you like to? Why? / Why not?

EP Get talking! → page 134

Me too.
What about you?
the same

VOCABULARY Phrasal verbs

4 **Match the phrasal verbs to the meanings.**

1 pick up
2 get back
3 take off
4 lie down
5 wake up
6 get up
7 wash up
8 put on
9 try on
10 give back

a return something to a a person
b when you open your eyes and stop sleeping
c when you want to wear something you do this
d return to a place
e you do this when you go to bed
f go and collect someone in a car
g put on clothes to see if they are the right size
h remove clothes
i get out of bed
j clean the dishes

5 Complete each sentence with a phrasal verb from Exercise 4.

1 If you don't feel well, why don't you go and .... ?
2 My mum will .... us .... at 8 pm after the film finishes.
3 Everybody must .... their dirty boots before they come inside.
4 There are birds outside my window that .... me .... early every day.
5 Please .... your hat. The sun is very strong.
6 Thanks for lending me some money! I'll .... it .... to you tomorrow.
7 I can't wait to .... to school and see all my friends after the summer holidays.
8 When we are camping, my mum cooks and my brother and I ....
9 I usually .... at about ten o' clock at the weekends.
10 I think you should .... those jeans before you buy them.

6 Choose one of the situations on page 137 and write a short conversation with your partner. Use at least five phrasal verbs. Then perform it for the class.

READING

7 Read Gabby's description of her expedition for the school website. Number the four paragraphs in the correct order.

A ....
It rained a bit on Sunday morning, but we had waterproof clothes with us, so we put those on. The rest of the day was dry, which was lucky. I took lots of photos during the trip. I'm going to put them on the website.

B ....
On Saturday we walked 17 km and on Sunday we did 9 km. We were all good at map reading, except Finn. When it was his turn, we got lost! Camping was great fun. We cooked, ate and washed up. After that we sang songs around the fire.

C ....
The expedition was hard work but I really enjoyed it. I learned a lot about myself and about what I can do. It was my first camping trip without my family, and I am happy to say I didn't miss them at all! I can't wait to do another expedition with my friends next year.

D ....
Last weekend I did my Merrydown Award expedition in the Brecon Beacons in Wales. We had to carry our tents and food ourselves. Our backpacks were really heavy! The countryside was beautiful, and we camped between a mountain and a river.

the Brecon Beacons

WRITING

Prepare to write – a description of an expedition

GET READY Look at the prepositions in red in Exercise 7. Use them to complete the sentences below.
1 We put our tent .... two trees, next to the river.
2 I woke up a few times .... the night.
3 I remembered to pack everything .... my toothbrush.
4 On Sunday we walked for three hours .... a break.

PLAN Work in groups of three or four. Plan a description of an expedition. Make notes.
First paragraph: when you went, where you went, how you travelled there
Middle paragraph(s): what you did, what happened, what the weather was like
Last paragraph: how you felt about it, your plans for future trips

WRITE Write your description. Each person in the group should write one paragraph.

IMPROVE Check each other's paragraphs for mistakes with prepositions. Do the paragraphs fit together well? Make any changes you need. Then read your story to the class.

Culture

Mumbai, India

1 **Work with a partner. Describe the map and pictures.**

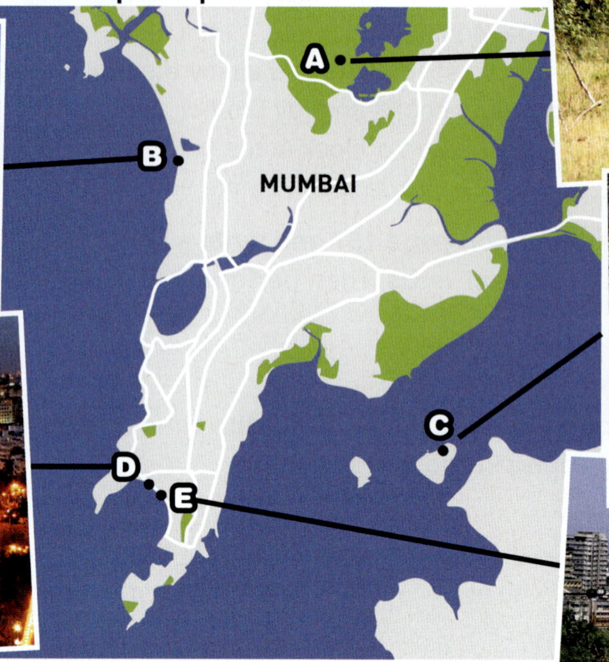

2 **Read the blog about Mumbai and name places A–E on the map.**

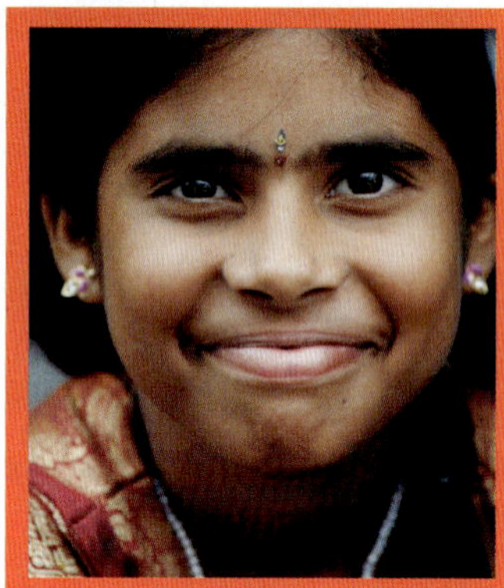

Some facts about

Mumbai

By Ameya, aged 14

Thanks for visiting my webpage! I'm Ameya and I come from Mumbai, India's largest city and its business capital. I love my city and I'd like to tell you a bit about it.

- Mumbai is a very busy city. It has a population of over 15 million people and it is still growing. There are people from many different cultures and all parts of India living in Mumbai. This means there are lots of celebrations and festivals in the city.
- The most famous street in Mumbai is **Marine Drive**. It is also called The Queen's Necklace because at night, when all the lights are on, it looks like a diamond necklace. It goes along the coast for about 3 km and passes the popular **Chowpatty Beach**. Juhu Beach, **further north**, is another popular beach in Mumbai. I love going to these beaches with my friends.
- The **Sanjay Gandhi National Park** is a 104 square km forest in the north of the city. It has crocodiles, leopards, deer, snakes and monkeys as well as many different kinds of birds and insects. No other city in the world has a national park inside it! It's a great place to relax and enjoy nature.
- The **Elephanta Caves** are on an island to the east of Mumbai. Here there are wonderful sculptures of Hindu gods and goddesses that are over 1000 years old.
- Hindi is the most popular language in Mumbai, but you will hear people speaking many other languages too. Most people also speak English. Hinglish (a mix of Hindi and English) is popular with young people. Can you guess what these Hinglish words in red mean?

I'm feeling glassy – can I have a drink?
That movie was just a timepass – it wasn't very interesting.
Last week my Dad had a problem at work so he airdashed to Chennai.

3 Read the blog again. Are the sentences right (✔) or wrong (✘)?

1 Mumbai is India's most important city for business.
2 The population of Mumbai is getting smaller.
3 People come to live in Mumbai from different places in India.
4 Marine Drive goes through the centre of Mumbai.
5 There are some dangerous animals in the Sanjay Gandhi National Park.
6 Hinglish has words in it from two different languages.

4 Work with a partner. Draw a map of your city or another important city in your country. Write about the most famous places in the city. Compare maps with another pair.

5 You are going to listen to a radio interview about Bollywood. Before you listen, look at the posters and read the fact file. What do you think the films in the posters are about? Can you guess any answers in the fact file?

Bollywood fact file

Age of Indian film industry: [1] .... years

Date people first used name 'Bollywood': [2] ....

Number of Bollywood films made each year: [3] ....

How long most Bollywood films are: [4] .... hours

Countries where Bollywood films are popular: Britain, Egypt, Turkey and [5] ....

Date Bollywood films first came to Britain: [6] ....

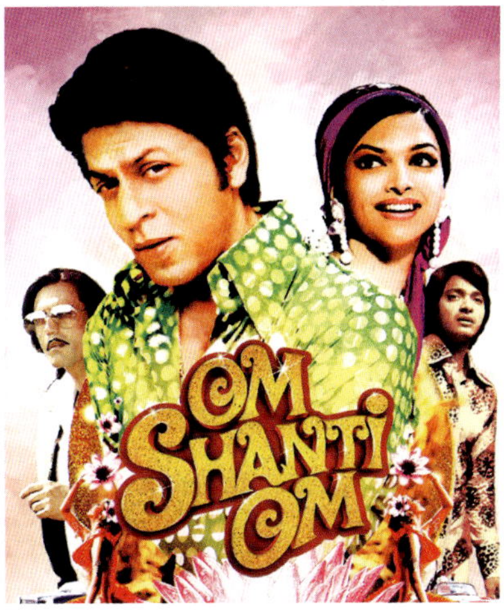

6 ▶ 2.26 Listen and complete the fact file.

7 Work in groups. Discuss the questions.

Do you watch foreign films in your country?
If yes, which country's films do you enjoy most?
What's your favourite film from your country?
Who are your favourite actors?

Project research an English-speaking country

Work with a partner.
This map shows countries where English is the official or main language. Choose one country and find out more about it. Use the internet or books to find out:

- the name of the country
- important cities in the country
- pictures and maps of the country
- special English words from the country

Tell the rest of the class what you found out.

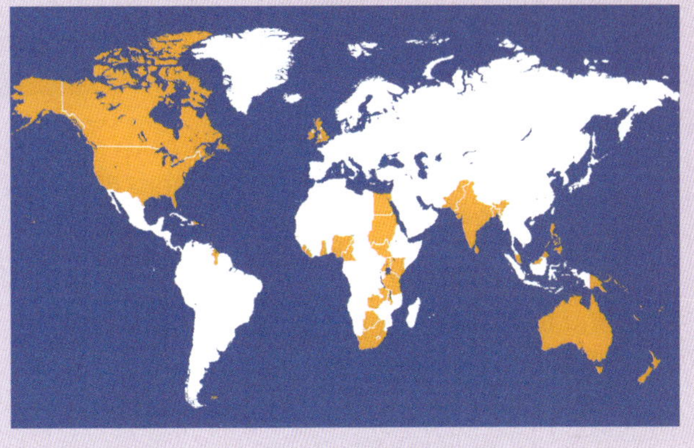

19 Different ingredients

They are eaten with milk

Do you eat breakfast cereals?

YES — **Describe the best breakfast you have ever had.**

NO — **What kinds of food do you eat for breakfast?**

How often do you eat them? What kinds do you like?

READING

1 **Discuss the questions with a partner.**

2 **Work with a partner. Read the sentences about breakfast cereals and say if you think they are right (✔) or wrong (✘)?**

1 Everyone in the USA eats breakfast cereal.
2 Doctors developed breakfast cereal as a health food.
3 The first breakfast cereals were very popular.
4 There were no sweet cereals until the 1930s.
5 Companies that made children's cereals became rich.

3 **Read the first part of the text and check your answers to Exercise 2.**

Breakfast cereals

Breakfast cereals

Breakfast cereals are popular in many countries, especially in the USA, where they are served in nine out of ten homes. They are made from grains such as corn, wheat and rice. They are usually eaten with milk, or with yogurt and fruit.

In the beginning, cereals were health foods. In the late 1800s, some doctors in the USA made them in hospitals and gave them to their patients. At first they used whole grains, without sugar or salt and they didn't taste good. However, this soon changed, and from the 1930s, some companies began to add sugar to their cereals and to advertise them to children. They made a lot of money this way, but it wasn't a healthy food any more. These days some children's cereals are 50% sugar and doctors say we shouldn't eat them too often.

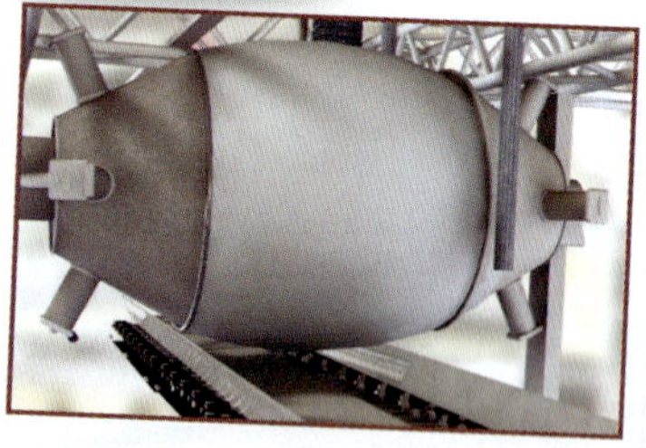

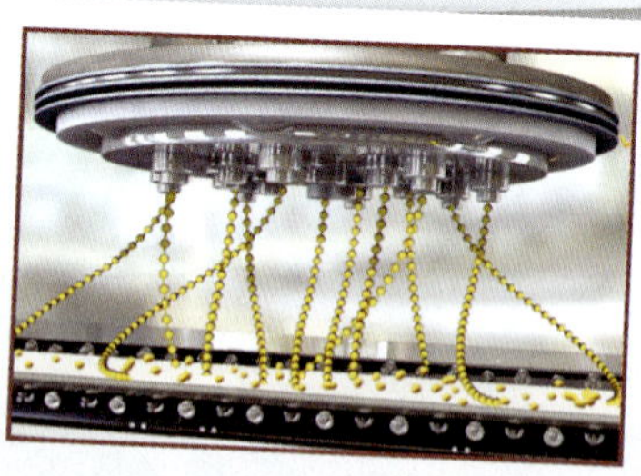

There are lots of kinds of cereal. This is how cereal in different shapes, like stars and balls, is made.

- First, the grain is taken to the factory, where it is cleaned and checked.
- Then it is prepared for cooking. It is made into flour, and mixed with other ingredients. Water is added and the mixture is boiled.
- When it is soft, it is put into special machines which make it into shapes like stars, circles, or even letters of the alphabet.
- The shapes are baked in an oven to dry them. Then they are 'puffed' in another machine to make them light and full of air.
- After that, they are covered with sugar or honey. Some are filled with chocolate. The cereal pieces are then dried in hot air.
- Finally, the cereal is packed into boxes, ready for the shops.

VOCABULARY

4 Find the verbs (0–7) in the text and complete the definitions with a word from the box.

~~another~~	cook	empty	oven
ready	spoon	top	water

0 add — put one thing with ....*another*.... thing

1 prepare — make something ....

2 dry — take the .... out of something

3 mix — join two or more things together using a .... or a machine

4 bake — cook something like a cake in an ....

5 boil — .... in water

6 cover — put something on .... of something else

7 fill — make an .... space full

GRAMMAR Present simple passive

5 Look at the sentence from the text. The verbs in red are in the *present simple passive.* Find other examples of the present simple passive in the text and complete the rules.

The grain is taken to the factory, where it is cleaned and checked.

1 To make the passive, we use the verb .... and the .... of the main verb.

2 When we use the passive, we *always have to / don't always have to* say who does the action.

→ Grammar reference page 165

Corpus challenge

Choose the correct verb form to complete the sentence.

My house .... red and blue.

A paints **B** painting **C** is painted

6 Rewrite the sentences in the passive. You don't need to say who does the action.

0 People throw away a lot of food these days.
A lot of food is thrown away these days.

1 They play loud rock music in my favourite café.

2 People often eat bread with butter and jam.

3 At my school they serve lunch at 12.30 every day.

4 Our teacher always puts our paintings on the classroom wall.

5 People in Britain eat a lot of sweets and chocolates.

PRONUNCIATION Ways to pronounce *ea*

7 2.27 Listen to the different ways to say the letters *ea*. Then say the words with a partner and put them into the right column.

/ɪə/ **ear**	/e/ **head**	/iː/ **seat**

beach bread breakfast cereal clean eat healthy meal near ready teacher wheat

2.28 Listen and check. Then repeat the words.

SPEAKING AND WRITING

8 Work with a partner. Invent a snack, for example a new kind of ice cream, cake or biscuit. Draw a picture of it and describe what it is like and how it is made. Read your description to the class.

While you listen to the other students' descriptions, imagine you are the manager of a food company. Which new snack are you going to make in your factory?

I hope you like my blog

About me | Ingredients | Meals I've made | Contact me | Links

Extra Stuff!

Other great food blogs

Competitions

The Taste Test

About me | Ingredients | Meals I've made | Contact me | Links

The Taste Test

About me | Ingredients | Meals I've made | Contact me | Links

a

b

c

d

e

About me

Hello everyone!

Thank **(0)** ......you...... for visiting my blog. I hope you enjoy reading **(1)** .... My name is Caitlin and I'm 14 years **(2)** .... I've always loved cooking. **(3)** .... I was nine, I told my parents I wanted to be **(4)** .... chef and that's still my plan today. I especially love making cakes and baking.

On this blog I want to show people **(5)** .... much fun it is to cook. I also want to show them that cooking a meal can **(6)** .... quick and easy, and that it tastes better **(7)** .... food that is made in a factory.

And remember, if you do the cooking, you don't have **(8)** .... do the dishes! So you can make **(9)** .... much mess as you want. I always do!

Don't forget **(10)** .... leave me a message if you like anything on my website. Happy reading!

READING

1 **Look at the website. Whose blog is this? What is it about? What information can you find on the website?**

2 **Complete the *About me* text on the webpage. Write one word for each space.**

VOCABULARY

3 **Match the words in the box to the ingredients (1–8) on the website.**

beans carrots garlic melon pears
potatoes salt and pepper steak

Now write them in a table under these headings: Meat, Fruit, Vegetables, Other. Can you add more words to each column?

4 **Check the meaning of these words in a dictionary. Can you find pictures of foods cooked like this on the webpage?**

1 boiled **3** grilled **5** baked
2 fried **4** roast

5 **Speak to your partner. What is the difference in meaning between these words? What do you use each thing for?**

1 knife/fork/spoon
You use a knife to cut food. You use fork to pick food up. You use a spoon to …
2 mug/glass/cup
3 bowl/plate/dish

6 **Put the words and phrases with *make* and *do* in the right column in the table.**

the bed a cake ~~the cleaning~~
~~a cup of tea~~ the dishes your homework
a mess a mistake the shopping
the washing

make	do
a cup of tea	the cleaning

About you

7 Which of the things in Exercise 6 do you do … sometimes / often / never?

LISTENING

8 2.29 **You will hear a woman giving information about a cooking competition. Read the questions carefully and think about the kind of information you will need to listen for. Then listen and complete each question.**

Young Chef Competition

Age of students who can enter: **(0)** 12–15
Last date to email recipe idea:
(1) *June* ……………
Number of teams that will cook:
(2) ……………
Place of cooking competition: **(3)** ……………
Name of chef who will choose winners:
(4) *John* ……………
Prizes for winners: **(5)** *T-shirts, cookbooks and* ……………

SPEAKING

9 **You are going to enter the Junior Chef cooking competition. Work in teams of three or four and decide on your recipe.**

- What ingredients will you need for your recipe?
- How you will cook it?
- Who will do the different jobs?
- Why is it a good meal to serve in a school café?

Useful language

Why don't we …?
Let's …
What about …?
I'll buy the ingredients.
Can you cut the vegetables?
I'd prefer not to do the dishes.
That sounds good!
I'm not sure about that.
That's a great idea.

10 **Present your ideas to the class. Choose the best dish for your school café.**

20 Changes
It was built by a prince

VOCABULARY

1 **How many different kinds of building can you name?**

castle, supermarket …

About you

2 Think about one or two buildings in your town or city which have changed their use.
What was their use before?
What are they used for now?

READING

3 **Look at the pictures. What do you think these buildings are used for now? What do you think they were before? Work with a partner and discuss your ideas.**

a

b

4 **Now read the article and check your ideas. Which two buildings are in the pictures? What are they called now?**

CHANGING BUILDINGS

We can reuse buildings in the same way as we can reuse things like cars, clothes and furniture. Do you ever think about what buildings were before? In this article you're going to read about three buildings which started their lives with very different uses from those they have today.

The Taj Lake Palace hotel in Udaipur, India, looks like it's floating in the middle of a lake. However, it started its life as a palace called Jag Niwas. Now it is a very comfortable hotel. Jag Niwas was built by Prince Maharana Jagat Singh II more than two hundred and fifty years ago. It has been a hotel for more than forty years now. Some of the James Bond movie *Octopussy* was made there!

In Rosario, Argentina, there is a busy restaurant called Don Ferro. It is especially famous for its meat and fish dishes. But a few years ago, it was a train station! The station was built in 1860 and was the first train station in Argentina. A lot of work was done to the building before it could open as Don Ferro. Now it is even possible to have dinner on one of the station platforms.

The Attendant, a very popular little café in Central London, serves drinks and local food. The Attendant is quite long and thin. Does it remind you of anything? Yes, this café started life as a men's public toilet! The toilets were closed in the 1960s and the building was unused for more than 50 years. After two years of planning and hard work, the old toilets were turned into a pleasant café.

5 **Read the article again. Are these sentences right (✔) or wrong (✘)?.**

1 Jag Niwas became a hotel more than a century ago.
2 Sometimes Jag Niwas is used for making films.
3 You can catch a train as well as eat at Don Ferro.
4 Argentina's first train station was in Rosario.
5 The shape of The Attendant café is still like that of a public toilet.
6 It took five years to change the toilets into The Attendant café.

GRAMMAR Past simple passive

6 **Look at the example sentences from the article.**

1 Jag Niwas was built by Prince Maharana Jagat Singh II.
2 The old toilets were turned into a pleasant café.

Choose the correct words to complete the rule.

The past simple passive is formed with the *present simple* / *past simple* of the verb 'be' plus the *past simple* / *past participle* of the main verb.

→ Grammar reference page 166

Corpus challenge

Can you find the mistake in this sentence?

I'm from Russia and my family born there.

7 **Find other examples of the past simple passive in the article. How many examples tell you who did the action? Is it always necessary to say who did the action? Why? / Why not?**

8 **Rewrite the text, changing the verbs in italics to the past simple passive. It isn't always necessary to say who did the action. You choose!**

The Summer Palace, Beijing, China

The Qing Emperor Quinlong (**1**) *designed* the Garden of Clear Ripples in the middle of the 16th century. But there was a war about one hundred years later and people (**2**) *destroyed* some of the garden. So the Emperor Guangxu (**3**) *built* the garden and the buildings again and he (**4**) *gave* them a new name: The Summer Palace. Empress Dowager Cixi (**5**) *used* the Summer Palace. In 1924 someone (**6**) *made* it into a public park.

SPEAKING

9 **Look at the picture of a room in the Lee Plaza Hotel, Detroit. Work with a partner. Decide how to reuse the building. Why would this be a good idea?**

10 **Share your ideas with two other pairs. How similar are their ideas to yours? Tell them what you think about their ideas. Will they work? Why? / Why not? Agree on the best idea in your group. Then present it to the class.**

A big change in my life

LISTENING

1 **Make a list of all the jobs you know. Compare with your partner. How many of your jobs are the same?**

2 **Look at your jobs in Exercise 1. What do the people do? Tell your partner.**

A farmer keeps animals or grows food in the country.

3 **2.30 Listen to an interview in the series *Changing Lives*. Which two jobs has Fiona Drayton done?**

detective	police officer	radio presenter
receptionist	taxi driver	waitress

4 **2.30 Listen again and answer the questions.**

1 How long ago was Fiona doing her office job?
2 What two reasons made her decide to leave?
3 What problem did a friend of hers have?
4 What did Fiona see when she was sitting in her car?
5 What was the answer to the problem?
6 What's the name of Fiona's company? What do you think she does?

5 **Work with a partner. Ask and answer the questions.**

1 How do you think Fiona's new life is different from her old life?
2 What do you think she does every day?
3 Do you think she prefers her new life to her old life? Why?

VOCABULARY

6 **Look at the uses of the word *change* (a–g) in the word maps and match them to 1–7.**

1 I'm sorry, I can't change a ten-pound note.
2 Remember to bring a change of shoes. It might be wet.
3 You've really changed your life.
4 It was such a big change in your life!
5 We had to change planes in San Francisco.
6 Please can I change this jacket? It's too small.
7 I'll email you my change of address.

CHANGE (verb)
- a to something different
- b shopping
- c money
- d transport

CHANGE (noun)
- e difference
- f something new
- g clothes

EP Get talking! → page 134

You're welcome.
not bad
all the time
one day

PRONUNCIATION Sounds and spelling quiz

7 **Choose the word in each group which has a different sound to the other words.**

1	buy	boy	by	6	meat	meet	met
2	fair	for	four	7	own	one	won
3	hear	hair	here	8	their	there	they
4	or	hour	our	9	toe	too	to
5	know	now	no	10	were	wear	where

2.32 Compare your answers in pairs. Then listen and check.

READING

8 **Read the fact file for Robert Smith and complete his biography.**

Fact File: Robert Smith

Born: Texas, April 27th 1965
April 27th 1973: got first pet
1982–85: studied maths at Harvard University
1986: joined Central High School in Boston
2009: left Central High School
2010: opened Zoo World near Boston

From Money to Animals

Robert Smith was born in **(1)** .... on the 27th of April, 1965. He loved animals and on his **(2)** .... birthday he was given his first pet.

Robert went to **(3)** .... in 1982 and studied **(4)** .... He wanted to be a teacher.

After leaving university, Robert got a job in a high school. He worked in the same school until **(5)** ....

Robert left teaching because he wanted to change his life. He wanted to work with his first love, animals, and in 2010 he bought a **(6)** .... ! He is very happy with the change he made to his life.

WRITING

Prepare to write – a biography

GET READY Look at the text about Robert Smith again.
How many paragraphs are there?
What are the topics of each paragraph?
When in each paragraph is Robert's name used?
When is his full name used?
When is the pronoun *he* used instead of *Robert*?

PLAN
Read the fact file for Victoria Beckham. You are going to write a short biography about her.
Think about:

- how many paragraphs you will write
- what the topic of each paragraph will be
- when you will use her full name, first name and the pronoun *she.*

WRITE Write your biography.

IMPROVE Read your biography and look for mistakes. Check that you have included all the necessary information and that you used paragraphs and pronouns correctly.

Fact File: Victoria Beckham

Born: 17 April 1974 in Harlow, England
Family: husband – David, three sons – Brooklyn, Romeo and Cruz, one daughter – Harper
1993: joined a new girl band called *The Spice Girls*
1996: *The Spice Girls'* first single, *Wannabe*, was released and was a big success!
1998: acted in movie *Spiceworld* with the other *Spice Girls*
1999: separated from *The Spice Girls*
2000: released her first solo single *Out of Your Mind*
2006: moved to Los Angeles, California and started working as a fashion designer with her own brand of sunglasses and jeans
2009: started modelling for Emporio Armani
2015: a very successful fashion designer

Literature
Michael Morpurgo

1 Have you heard of Michael Morpurgo? Have you read any of his books, or seen films of them? Read the text and complete the fact file.

Michael Morpurgo

Michael Morpurgo is a much-loved British author. He was born in 1943 and grew up in the south of England. French was his favourite subject at school and he studied it at university. After that, he became an officer in the army, but soon left and became a primary school teacher. This is when he began writing stories for children. 'I could see there was magic in it for them, and realised there was magic in it for me,' he said.

He left teaching after 10 years and bought a farm with his wife. Together they began a charity called Farms for City Children. They now own three farms where children from cities can come to spend time in the country looking after animals.

Michael Morpurgo has written over 100 books for children. He writes about children and their relationships with older people and animals. Many of them have won prizes and several are now films or plays, including War Horse, which is now well known around the world. Another popular book is Kensuke's Kingdom, which he wrote in 1999.

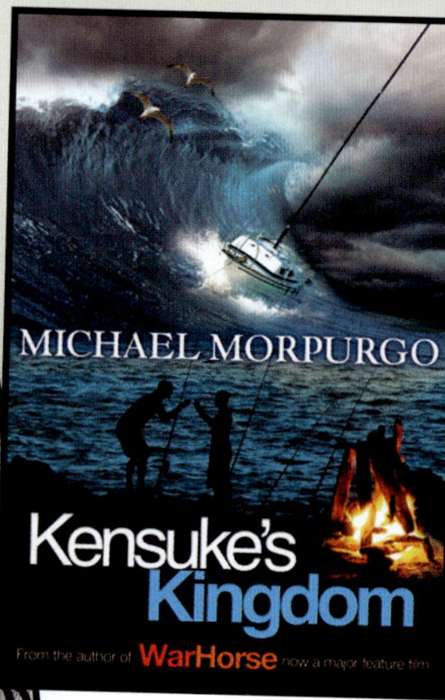

Fact File: Michael Morpurgo

1 Author's name: ....
2 Born: ....
3 Favourite school subject: ....
4 First two jobs: ....
5 Name of his charity: ....
6 Number of books written: ....
7 Most popular books: ....

2 Look at the cover of *Kensuke's Kingdom* and the words on the back cover. What do they tell you about …

1 … the story? **2** … the characters? **3** … how good the book is?

Would you like to read the book? Why? / Why not?

Washed up on an island in the Pacific, Michael struggles to survive on his own. With no food and no water, he curls up to die. When he wakes, there is a plate beside him of fish, of fruit, and a bowl of fresh water.
He is not alone …

'A dazzling adventure'
The Times

'This is a wonderful book, a modern day *Robinson Crusoe*'
Wendy Cooling

3 Put the sentences about *Kensuke's Kingdom* in the correct order.

a .... He never sees who is leaving this for him.
b .... He wakes up on an island in the Pacific ocean.
c .... Suddenly, he sees an old man running over to his fire.
d ..1.. Michael and his family decide to go on a round-the-world sailing trip.
e .... At first he thinks he is alone there, but then someone starts giving him food and water.
f .... Then one day Michael finds a piece of glass and uses it to start a fire.
g .... They have a wonderful time until one night Michael falls over the side of the boat in bad weather.
h .... He does this because he hopes a ship will see it and come to get him.

4 2.33 **Read and listen to part of Chapter 5 of *Kensuke's Kingdom*. Guess unknown words, or ignore them! Answer the questions.**

1 Why is the old man angry?
2 What language does Michael think he is speaking?
3 What do you think 'Dameda!' means?

Chapter 5

I, Kensuke

He was as old a man as I had ever seen. What little hair he had on his head and his chin was long and wispy and white. I could see at once that he was very angry. 'Dameda! Dameda!' he screeched. His whole body was shaking with fury. I backed away as he scuttled up the beach towards me. He was moving fast, running almost. 'Dameda! Dameda!' I had no idea what he was saying. It sounded Chinese or Japanese maybe.

He was no more than a few feet away from me when he stopped. We stood looking at each other in silence for a few moments. He was leaning on his stick, trying to catch his breath. 'Americajin? Americajin? American? Eikokujin? British?'

'Yes,' I said. 'English. I'm English.'

It seemed a struggle for him to get the words out. 'No good. Fire, no good. You understand? No fire.' He seemed less angry now.

'But my mother, my father, they might see it, see the smoke.' It was plain he didn't understand me. So I pointed out to sea. 'Out there. They're out there. They'll see the fire. They'll come and fetch me.'

Instantly he became aggressive again. 'Dameda!' he shrieked, waving his stick at me. 'No fire!'

He tapped his chest. 'Kensuke. I, Kensuke. My island. No fire. Dameda. No fire. You understand?'

I did not argue, but walked away at once.

5 Read the text again. How does Michael feel at the beginning, in the middle and at the end of the text? How does Kensuke feel? Use the words in the box to help you.

afraid	angry	confused	disappointed	happy
hopeful	lonely	sad	surprised	worried

6 Write sentences about *Kensuke's Kingdom*. Use the words in Exercise 5.

I think Michael / Kensuke felt/was .... when/before/after ....

I think Michael felt afraid when he fell off the boat.
I think Kensuke was surprised when he found Michael on the island.

Project – write a book blurb and author fact file

A blurb is a short description about a book on the back of its cover. It should make you want to read the book! Write a blurb of no more than 50 words about your favourite book. Include:

- an outline of what happens in the book
- why it is a good book.

Find out about the book's author and write a fact file to go with your blurb. Tell your class about your favourite author and read your blurb.

Review 5
Units 17–20

VOCABULARY

1 Put the letters in order to make words for parts of the body.

0 arthe ......heart......
1 osachtm ....
2 grinfse ....
3 cekn ....
4 esto ....
5 are ....
6 ranib ....
7 thumo ....

2 Complete the crossword.

Across
3 You can drink tea out of this.
4 You can cut your steak with this.
8 This person answers the phone in a hotel or office.
9 You find this with salt on the table at supper.
10 This is another name for a jumper.

Down
1 This takes you to hospital.
2 This is at the end of your arm.
5 You do this when you want to get fit.
6 You can borrow books from this place.
7 You wear these on your feet inside your shoes.

3 Complete the sentences with the words in the box.

back (x2)	down	off	on (x2)	up (x2)

1 Could you pick .... some milk for me when you go to the shops, please?
2 Finn was very tired and had to lie ....
3 I washed .... after supper last night.
4 Let me try .... your hat. It's so cool!
5 Take .... your dirty trainers, please.
6 Did you give me .... my backpack?
7 It always takes my little sister a long time to put .... her clothes in the morning.
8 Call me when you get .... from holiday.

GRAMMAR

4 Choose the right word to complete the sentences.

1 You must bring your pyjamas and clean clothes for *you* / *yourself*.
2 You *must* / *might* wear shorts, sneakers and a T-shirt.
3 After the film *finish* / *is finished*, *we* will go for a walk.
4 All the museum's paintings were lost *in* / *by* a fire.

Correct the mistakes in these sentences.

5 I bought a blue shirt for me which is very nice.
6 I think it can be in the living room.
7 The meal is started at one o'clock.
8 They were made by different kinds of materials.

5 **Complete the text with the verbs in brackets. Use the present simple active or present simple passive.**

How Orange Juice is Made

First the oranges (1) .... (pick) from the trees. Sometimes people (2) .... (do) this but these days it (3) .... (usually do) by machines. Then the oranges (4) .... (take) to a factory, where they (5) .... (wash). Next the oranges (6) .... (put) into a machine and squeezed to make all the juice come out. Someone (7) .... (check) the juice to make sure it is clean. After that, the juice (8) .... (heat) to make it safe to drink. Finally, the juice (9) .... (go) into cartons and (10) .... (send) to the shops for us to buy.

LISTENING

6 **2.34 William's granddad is telling him how the town they live in has changed. Listen and tick the places you hear.**

apartments ☐ art gallery ☐
cathedral ☐ cinema ☐ factory ☐
garage ☐ hospital ☐ museum ☐
post office ☐ restaurant ☐
shopping centre ☐ sports centre ☐

7 **2.34 Listen again. Complete the notes.**

The place was:	Now it's:
1	
2	
3	
4	

READING

8 **Which notice (A–H) says this (1–5)?**

0 You can visit in the evenings. F
1 You cannot usually choose where you want to sit.
2 You mustn't use this door to leave the museum.
3 You don't have to pay to go in.
4 If you want to buy something, you must follow the sign.
5 A member of staff will tell you what food is available.

SPEAKING

10 **Work in groups of four. Take turns to ask and answer the questions.**

1 What were your favourite topics in *Cambridge English Prepare! 3*? Why?
2 What new vocabulary did you learn when you were studying those topics?
3 Which topics would you like to learn more about?
4 What are you going to do now you have finished *Cambridge English Prepare! 3*?

Exam profile 1

Speaking Part 1 Talking about yourself

What is Part 1?

- Questions from the examiner about you

1 The examiner will ask you questions like these. Which need short answers and which need longer answers?

1 What's your name? How do you spell that?
2 Where do you come from?
3 What's your favourite subject at school?
4 What do you like doing in your free time?
5 Tell me something about your family.
6 Tell me something about your last holiday.

Now you try Speaking Part 1

- Ask the examiner to say the question again if you don't understand.
- When the examiner says 'Tell me about ...' try to answer in two or three sentences.

2 Ask and answer with a partner. Take turns to be the examiner.

Listening Part 1 Answering questions about short conversations

What is Part 1?

- Five short conversations with five multiple-choice questions based on pictures

1 ▶2.35 Look at the pictures for question 1. Write down some words you think you are going to hear in the conversation. Read the question carefully. Is it asking about what Ann has got, or what she wants? Now listen and answer the question. Listen again to check your answer.

1 What would Ann like to get for her room?

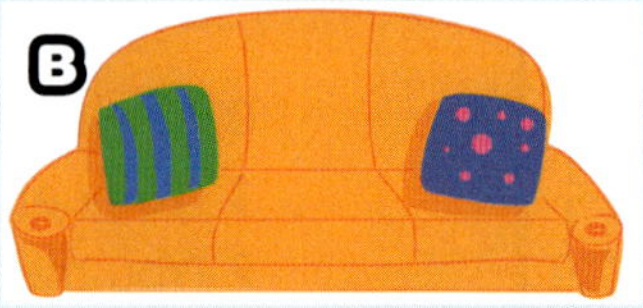

Now you try Listening Part 1

- You will hear something about each picture, but only one picture answers the question.
- You hear the conversation twice, so don't worry if you miss the answer the first time.

2 ▶2.36 Now answer questions 2 and 3. You will hear each conversation twice. There is one question for each conversation. For each question choose A, B or C.

2 Where did they go camping last year?

3 What are the boys going to do now?

Speaking Part 2 Talking to your partner

What is Part 2?

- You get some information from the examiner and answer five questions.
- You get some notes from the examiner and ask questions about prices, times, addresses, etc.

Now you try Speaking Part 2

- Use the prompts to make full questions.
- Listen carefully to your partner's questions and answer them in full sentences.

Now B, ask A your questions about the wild animal park and A, you answer them.

Candidate A, here is some information about a wild animal park.	Candidate B, you don't know anything about the wild animal park, so ask A some questions about it. Use these words to help you.
African Days Wild Animal Park Open daily 10 am to 5 pm (Winter 4.30 pm) Elephants, monkeys, birds and much more! Tickets: Over 16s £20 Under 16s £11.50 info@africananimals.com 	**Wild Animal Park** name / wild animal park? close? ? ? children's ticket ? £ ? elephants? email address? 

Reading and Writing Part 7 Completing a short text

What is Part 7?

- One or two short texts, such as emails or notes
- 10 spaces for you to fill in

1 **Read the two emails. Why is Shammi happy? What does he want Bart to do?**

To: Bart
From: Shammi

Guess what? Mum says I can paint the walls in **(0)** ......my...... bedroom. I'm really happy **(1)** .... I hate the colour it **(2)** .... now! **(3)** .... you want to come and help me do it **(4)** .... weekend? When can you come? I'm free **(5)** .... day on Saturday, and on Sunday afternoon too.

To: Shammi
From: Bart

That's great news! **(6)** .... course I can come and help. I know **(7)** .... much you hate your pink walls! Is it OK **(8)** .... I come at ten on Saturday morning? By the way, **(9)** .... colour are we going to use? I painted my room black a few weeks **(10)** .... and it looks fantastic!

2 **Now complete Shammi's email. Look at the spaces. What kinds of words are missing? Write ONE word for each space.**

Now you try Reading and Writing Part 7

- Only write one word in each space, or you will not get the mark.
- Spell each word perfectly, or you will not get the mark.

3 **Complete Bart's email to Shammi.**

CAMBRIDGE OFFICIAL PREPARATION MATERIAL

Exam profile 2

Reading and Writing Part 4 Answering multiple-choice questions about a text

What is Part 4?

- This kind of Part 4 has a text and seven multiple-choice questions.

1 **Read the travel blog by a girl who is going on a trip around the world. Study the first paragraph and the example. Can you see why *C, June* is the correct answer? Why are A and B wrong?**

ANNA'S TRAVEL BLOG

In September my family and I are leaving Britain to travel round the world. We started planning the trip last January, and we won't be back until June – that's 10 months of travelling! We're hoping to visit at least 20 countries in that time.

People often have to change their jobs or sell their home to do a trip like this, but Mum and Dad have their own business, and are going to find a manager for it until we get back. Unfortunately, I won't get a break from studying – Mum says we'll be able to go online most places, so I'll just email my school work to my teachers.

We have to pack much more carefully than usual. There won't be space for lots of nice clothes and different pairs of shoes, but I know I can't live without my travel pillow. If I have that, I can sleep anywhere. Of course we can't take our cat and I know I will miss her badly. But I'm sure she'll have lots of fun at my grandparent's house. I'll chat to my friends online often and will put photos on this blog.

Bye for now!

0 When will Anna and her family return from their trip?

A January
B September
(C) June

Now you try Reading and Writing Part 4

- The questions will always be in the same order as the information in the text.
- For each question, find the right bit of text and read it carefully before you choose the answer.

2 **Now answer questions 1–4. Choose A, B or C. Then compare answers with a partner. Say why you chose each answer.**

1 What will Anna's parents do about their business?

A They will close it until they return.
B They will ask someone to look after it.
C They will sell it before they leave.

2 What will happen about Anna's school work on the trip?

A She will take a break from it.
B Her mother will teach her.
C She will send work to the school.

3 What does Anna think is the most important thing for her to pack?

A nice clothes
B a travel pillow
C different pairs of shoes

4 Anna knows that she will feel sad to leave

A her pet.
B her friends.
C her grandparents.

Reading and Writing Part 8 Completing notes with words or numbers

What is Part 8?

- Two short texts and notes with five spaces to complete

1 **Read the advertisement and the email. Look at question 1. Underline the dates in the two texts. Which date is the correct answer in question 1? Why?**

Applewood Museum

10.00–17.30

Special exhibitions:

1–14 March *Space Travel*
15–31 March *19th Century Cars*

Adults: £12.50
Students: £5.00

Sorry – no large bags

To Sam
From Pete

It's great you can come to the museum with Dad and me on 10 March. The special exhibition on that date looks amazing! And our tickets are quite cheap as we're still at school. Dad and I'll be at your house at 9.30, so be ready. Don't forget your phone this time!

Sam's notes

Museum trip with Pete

Museum:	(0)	Applewood Museum
Date we'll go:	(1)	....
Exhibition we'll see:	(2)	....
Price of my ticket:	(3)	....
What to bring:	(4)	....
Time Pete will pick me up:	(5)	....

Now you try Reading and Writing Part 8

- There will be two or more dates, prices, etc. for you to choose from in the texts, but you must only write one.
- You must spell words correctly, so copy them very carefully.

2 **Now answer questions 1–5. Check your partner's answers. Is there just one answer to each question? Is the spelling correct?**

Reading and Writing Part 6 Finding the right word and spelling it

What is Part 6?

- Five descriptions of some words

1 **Read the descriptions of some words for things that you can find in a student's bag. What is the word for each one? The first letter is already there. There is one space for each other letter in the word.**

Now you try Reading and Writing Part 6

- Check the number of spaces carefully because you must spell the word correctly.
- If you see a word like *these* you must write the word in the plural.

0 This has dates in it and you can write in it. d i a r y
1 Some people carry a bottle of this to drink when they get thirsty. w _ _ _ _
2 You read these, and they usually have many pages. b _ _ _ _
3 You can put this up over your head when it rains. u _ _ _ _ _ _ _
4 Girls keep things like money and bus tickets in this. p _ _ _ _
5 This piece of fruit can be green or red and you may eat it in your break. a _ _ _ _

Exam profile 3

Reading and Writing Part 5 Multiple-choice cloze

What is Part 5?

- A short text with eight spaces with eight three-option multiple-choice questions

1 Read the article about a famous British music festival. In which month does the festival happen?

2 Look at the example. A is the correct answer. Can you see why B and C are not correct?

GLASTONBURY

The world famous Glastonbury Festival happens **(0)** ....A..... year on a farm in a little village in the English countryside. When it began **(1)** .... 1970, tickets cost just £1, and included **(2)** .... free bottle of milk. Only 1000 people went. These days, the Glastonbury Festival has 175,000 visitors, and tickets cost over £200. It is **(3)** .... famous for pop and rock music. However, it also has cinemas, a circus, dance shows, shops and theatres.

The festival happens in June, **(4)** .... work begins in February to get everything ready. The festival needs ten stages. One is **(5)** .... there – the famous Pyramid stage – and workers must build **(6)** .... nine. They also put in 300 showers and 4,500 toilets. After the festival, it **(7)** .... a month to clean the whole area **(8)** .... it can become a farm again – until the next time!

0 (**A**) every **B** all **C** both

Now you try Reading and Writing Part 5

- Read the whole text so you understand what it is about.
- Look at the words around the space carefully before choosing the best one.

3 Now answer questions 1–8. Choose the best word (A, B or C) for each space.

	A	B	C
1	**A** in	**B** on	**C** at
2	**A** the	**B** a	**C** any
3	**A** much	**B** most	**C** many
4	**A** but	**B** that	**C** if
5	**A** next	**B** early	**C** already
6	**A** another	**B** other	**C** enough
7	**A** take	**B** takes	**C** taking
8	**A** or	**B** if	**C** so

Reading and Writing Part 3a Multiple-choice

What is Part 3a?

- Five separate dialogues with three-option multiple-choice questions

1 Look at question 1. Complete the conversation by choosing A, B or C.

1 Don't forget to bring your tennis racket.

A Sorry, I'm not sure. **B** I don't remember her. **C** Don't worry, I won't.

Now you try Reading and Writing Part 3a

- Think about when and where the conversation is happening.
- Don't choose an answer just because it has the same words – think about the meaning.

2 Now complete conversations 2 and 3.

2 Are you going home now?

A It starts earlier than that. **B** I'm staying a bit longer. **C** Going by bus is quicker.

3 This magazine is really interesting!

A How much are they? **B** Can I do that? **C** What's it about?

Reading and Writing Part 2 Multiple-choice

What is Part 2?

- Five sentences that tell a story, or are about the same topic
- Five three-option multiple-choice questions

1 Read all the sentences. What are they about? (Don't worry about the spaces.) Look at the example. Why are B and C wrong?

0 Bao Yu is 14 and ....A.... playing chess when she was seven years old.
A started **B** decided **C** learned

Now you try Reading and Writing Part 2

- Try each word in the space before you choose the answer.
- The words will be similar in meaning, but only one will be correct in the sentence.

2 Now complete questions 1–4. Choose the best word (A, B or C) for each space.

1 Bao Yu was very good at it, so she .... a chess club in her town.
A moved **B** joined **C** took

2 She .... a lot of time practising at home and improved quickly.
A kept **B** got **C** spent

3 Sometimes it was .... for Bao Yu to find time to see her friends.
A terrible **B** difficult **C** unhappy

4 Bao Yu .... a lot of competitions and often wins.
A enters **B** makes **C** goes

Listening Part 3 Multiple-choice

What is Part 3?

- A long dialogue with five three-option multiple-choice questions

1 Read the questions 1–3 carefully. What is the conversation going to be about?

2 Read the first part of the audioscript and look at the example. Why is C the answer? Why are A and B wrong?

G: Shall we go to the new skate park tomorrow?
M: OK, George, but I didn't know there was a new one! Is it near your house?
G: It's opposite the swimming pool. It's much better than the one near the cinema.

0 The new skate park is close to
A the cinema. **B** George's house. **C** the swimming pool. ✓

Now you try Listening Part 3

- Read the questions before you listen so you know what information to listen for.
- You will hear something about all three options, so listen carefully.

3 ▶2.37 Now listen to the conversation. For questions 1–3, tick ✔ A, B or C.

1 What will the skate park have in the future?
A a shop **B** a roof **C** a café

2 How much does it cost to use the skate park at the moment?
A £7.00 **B** £5.00 **C** £3.00

3 The friends will see each other at the skate park at
A 1 o'clock. **B** 12 o'clock. **C** 10 o'clock.

Exam profile 4

Reading and Writing Part 4 Right / Wrong / Doesn't say

What is Part 4?

- This kind of Part 4 has a text and seven Right / Wrong / Doesn't say questions.

1 Look at the instructions and at the example. Why is B the answer to the example question?

Read the article about a boy who started his own business. Are sentences 1–7 *Right* (A) or *Wrong* (B)? If there is not enough information to answer *Right* (A) or *Wrong* (B), choose *Doesn't say* (C).

0 David Nderitu lived in a house until he was 16.
A Right **(B)** Wrong **C** Doesn't say

2 Look at question 1. Read the second and third sentences carefully. The text does not tell you which city David is from, or what its size is. So you must choose C – *Doesn't say*.

1 The home for young people that David lived in was in a large city.
A Right **B** Wrong **C** Doesn't say

Now you try Reading and Writing Part 4

- The questions are in the same order as the information in the text.
- Find the bit of text that has the information you need and study it carefully to find the answer.

3 Now answer questions 2–7.

A young businessman

WHEN HE WAS A CHILD, David Nderitu, from central Kenya, had to live on the streets, as he did not have a home of his own. Then, when he was 16, he got a place in a home for young people. He made friends there and was able to study. Teachers from Nairobi University and a university in the USA visited the home and talked to the young people about work and jobs, and gave them advice about how to start their own businesses.

After listening to the teachers, David had an idea. He went on a course and learned how to work with metal. Then he began making jewellery to sell. He used old computers and mobile phones that he found, and bought a few other things that he needed. Now, he makes 60 pairs of earrings in 15 days and is able to sell each pair for \$4. At first, he did not sell many, but now his jewellery is much more popular. He can continue with his studies as well as running his business.

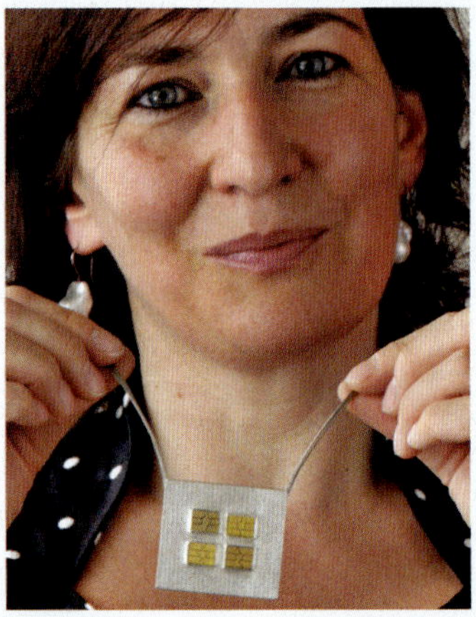

2 Teachers from two different universities visited the home where David lived.
A Right **B** Wrong **C** Doesn't say

3 The university teachers spoke to the young people about working for themselves.
A Right **B** Wrong **C** Doesn't say

4 David got everything he needed to make his jewellery for free.
A Right **B** Wrong **C** Doesn't say

5 It takes David two months to sell 60 pairs of earrings.
A Right **B** Wrong **C** Doesn't say

6 David sold more jewellery in the beginning than he does now.
A Right **B** Wrong **C** Doesn't say

7 David stopped studying as soon as he started his business.
A Right **B** Wrong **C** Doesn't say

Listening Part 2 Matching

What is Part 2?

- A long conversation between two people
- Five people, days, times, etc. for you to match to eight possible answers

1 Read the instructions and questions 1–5.

Listen to Jasmin telling her grandmother about her half-term holiday. What activity did each person do? For questions **1–5,** write a letter **A–H** next to each person. You will hear the conversation twice.

People

0 Jasmin ....C....
1 Sophie ....
2 Sam ....
3 Joe ....
4 Emily ....
5 Gemma ....

Activities

A cooking
B going online
C music practice
D photography
E shopping
F studying
G sport
H travelling

2 2.38 Listen to the first part of the dialogue and read the audioscript. Look at the example and question 1. The answer is G. Underline the part of the text that gives you the answer.

Grandma: How was your half-term holiday, Jasmin? What did you and your friends do?
Jasmin: Well, Grandma, I played the guitar a lot. I'm in the school concert next week and I need to get ready for it.
Grandma: Oh, yes, I remember. Did Sophie practise with you?
Jasmin: She played hockey all week with her team. She was lucky. No studying!

Now you try Listening Part 2

- Before you listen, read the list A–H carefully and think about the kinds of words you may hear.
- You will hear the conversation twice, so don't worry if you cannot answer all the questions the first time.

3 2.39 Now answer questions 2–5. Listen again to check your answers.

Reading and Writing Part 1 Matching

What is Part 1?

- Five sentences to match to eight notices

1 Look at the example (0). Underline the words that tell you C is the answer.

0 You can stay here later than usual this evening. C
1 You can get a two-course meal for this price.
2 Things here are cheaper for a short time.
3 This may be useful if you have things you don't need.

Now you try Reading Part 1

- Read the sentences carefully and find the notice with the same meaning.
- Don't choose a notice just because it has the same words in it as the sentence.

2 Now match 1–3 to the answers (A–E).

A
TEEN FASHION
Everything half price
This weekend only

B
Silver Star Café
Cheese and tomato pizza plus dessert
only £5.00

C
BRIDGETOWN SHOPPING CENTRE
Restaurants and shops open until ten!
Tonight only

D
Hill's Department Store
Café opening Saturday 24 July
Great food, great prices

E
STUDENTS!
Sell your old books and clothes on our new website.

Exam profile 5

Reading and Writing Part 4 Multiple-choice

What is Part 4?

- This kind of Part 4 has three short texts with seven three-option multiple-choice questions.

1 Read the article about three girls who live in unusual houses. Look at the example and underline the part of text that gives the answer – B.

0 Who says the weather is sometimes bad where she lives?
A Sarah **B** Andrea **C** Trudi

THREE UNUSUAL HOMES

SARAH

My home is a houseboat on a river. My parents and I have lived here since I was four, so I can't remember living anywhere else. Lots of my friends live on houseboats too, so it feels normal to me. We haven't got much space but we don't mind – it's enough for us. Visitors love coming here. They always sleep really well and love being on the water.

ANDREA

My friends at school think my lighthouse home is very cool. I like it, but it's not easy living here. My parents have to drive me everywhere, as we are so far from town. The sea is only about 10 metres away, so it gets very exciting when there is a storm. But the building is very strong, and I never feel afraid.

TRUDI

My dad built our house. It took him four years because he did most of it by himself. The front of the house is all glass, with big windows, but the sides and the top are covered with earth and grass. Lots of light comes in and it's lovely and quiet. There's always lots of fresh air too. When I am at my friends' houses, I often feel too hot and want to open a window.

Now you try Reading and Writing Part 4

- Underline the important words in the questions.
- Read the texts and find the information which matches the question.

2 Now answer questions 1–7.

1 Who knows other people who live in homes similar to hers?
A Sarah **B** Andrea **C** Trudi

2 Who says that she feels safe in her home?
A Sarah **B** Andrea **C** Trudi

3 Who is happy with the size of her home?
A Sarah **B** Andrea **C** Trudi

4 Who says that her house is bright?
A Sarah **B** Andrea **C** Trudi

5 Who says that guests enjoy spending the night in her home?
A Sarah **B** Andrea **C** Trudi

6 Who needs a lift when she wants to visit friends?
A Sarah **B** Andrea **C** Trudi

7 Who feels less comfortable when she is in other people's homes?
A Sarah **B** Andrea **C** Trudi

Listing Parts 4 and 5 Gap fill

What are Parts 4 and 5?

- Part 4 is a long conversation between two people and Part 5 is one person speaking.
- Five spaces to fill with a word or number

1 You will hear a boy asking a friend about a gym club for teenagers. Before you listen, read the notes.

Bodyfit Gym
CLUB FOR TEENAGERS

Day:	0 ....Saturday....	Teacher's name:	3 ....
Time:	1 .... am	What **not** to wear:	4 ....
Price:	2 £	What to bring:	5 ....

2 2.40 Listen to the first part and look at the example. You hear two days – Saturday and Friday. Why is Saturday correct and Friday wrong?

Now you try Listening Parts 4 and 5

- Before you listen, think about the kind of information you need for the space.
- Sometimes you will hear two possible answers. Listen carefully to understand which one is correct.

3 2.41 Now listen and complete questions 1–5. You will hear the conversation twice.

Reading and Writing Part 3b Matching

What is Part 3b?

- A dialogue • Five spaces in the dialogue and eight options to choose from

1 Read the conversation between two friends and all the options. What is the conversation about?

2 Look at the example. Can you see why B is the correct answer?

Nick: What are you doing after school today, Jake?
Jake: 0 ....B....

Now you try Reading and Writing Part 3b

- Make sure you read the whole conversation before you begin filling the spaces.
- Look carefully at what comes before AND after the space to see which option fits.

3 Now complete the rest of the dialogue.

Nick: Do you want to come to cooking club? It's really good.
Jake: **1** ....
Nick: Just some money. Miss Jones buys what we need – we give her £2.00 a week.
Jake: **2** ....
Nick: I'm afraid not – it's vegetable soup! It's good for you, you know.
Jake: **3** ....
Nick: I will!

A What are we making? I hope it's chocolate cake!

B Nothing much. Why?

C I'm busy then, sorry Nick.

D I'm sure it is, but I don't like it. Enjoy the club!

E Maybe. Do I have to bring anything?

F That's quite expensive!

CAMBRIDGE OFFICIAL PREPARATION MATERIAL

Get talking!

Units 1 and 2

EP Get talking!

You're so lucky! | Really? | What?? | Oh, right. | have fun / a good time | I do now! | It was great fun.

1 **1.10 You will hear three short conversations. Match each one to a photograph.**

2 **1.10 Match the sentences to the correct conversation. Then listen again and check.**

1 I do now. ....
2 Oh, right. I forgot about that. ....
3 It was great fun. ....
4 You're so lucky! ....
5 Really? Why? ....
6 What?? I didn't know you liked climbing. ....
7 We had a really good time. ....

3 **Work with a partner and practise the conversations. Use the pictures and the sentences in Exercise 2 to help you.**

4 **Work with a partner. Choose a situation from the box and write your own conversation. Use the words from the *Get talking* box to help you. Practise your conversation.**

you won a prize in a competition
you went to a party   you tried a new activity

Units 3 and 4

EP Get talking!

By the way | it's the best way to … | Have a good day. | sure | I don't agree. | I'm sorry | Yes, that's right. | Excuse me

1 **What do you think?**

The best way to keep fit is …

a … playing football.   **b** … running.
c … swimming.

2 **1.18 Listen. What is Sandra's answer to Exercise 1? What is Phil's answer?**

3 **1.18 Listen again and complete the conversation with words from the *Get talking* box.**

S: Hi, Phil. What are you doing here?
P: Hi, Sandra. I'm joining a swimming class.
S: I didn't think you liked swimming.
P: Well, I don't, but everyone says [1].............................. to keep fit.
S: Do they? Well, [2].............................. , [3].............................. ! I prefer team sports.
P: But I'm not very good at team sports!
S: True! [4].............................. , Phil, can I borrow your phone? I lost mine.
P: Yes, [5].............................. , Sandra.
A: [6].............................. , is your name Sandra?
S: [7].............................. .
A: Then I think this is your phone. It's got your name on it.
S: Yes, it is. Thanks very much.
P: I've got to go now, Sandra. [8]..............................
S: You too! Enjoy your swim. Bye.

4 **Work in a group of three. Choose your own topic and write a conversation. Use the words in Exercise 3 and the *Get talking* box.**

Units 5 and 6

EP Get talking!

Let's have …
Why don't we …
Shall we …
Why not …
Actually, it …
I think it's …
I don't know why …
That's not …

1 ▶ 1.24 **Listen to the conversations. Choose A, B or C.**

1 Who are going to the cinema?
 A Jack and Tom
 B Olivia and Tessa
 C Paula and Harry
2 Who decide to go and eat?
 A Jack and Tom
 B Olivia and Tessa
 C Paula and Harry
3 Who are going to catch a train?
 A Jack and Tom
 B Olivia and Tessa
 C Paula and Harry

2 ▶ 1.24 **Listen again and write the number of the conversation next to the café.**

Grand Café ☐ Mix and Match ☐
Oranges and Lemons ☐
Quick Bite ☐ Star Café ☐
American Café ☐

3 Complete the sentences with phrases from the *Get Talking* box. Then listen and check.

1 .... meet for a coffee first?
2 .... meet at the Star Café?
3 .... a bit expensive for us!
4 .... a look at the menu.
5 .... right!
6 .... *is* the right name.
7 .... catch the train in forty minutes?
8 .... it's called that, do you?

4 Work with a partner. Choose your topic and write a conversation in pairs. Use the phrases in the *Get talking* box to help you. Practise your conversation.

Units 7 and 8

EP Get talking!

Never mind. ☐
It's a shame that … ☐
including ☐
all kinds of / all sorts of ☐
First of all, ☐
Why not? ☐
… or something like that ☐
Finally, ☐

1 In pairs, write as many words as you can on the word map in one minute. Then compare your word map with another pair.

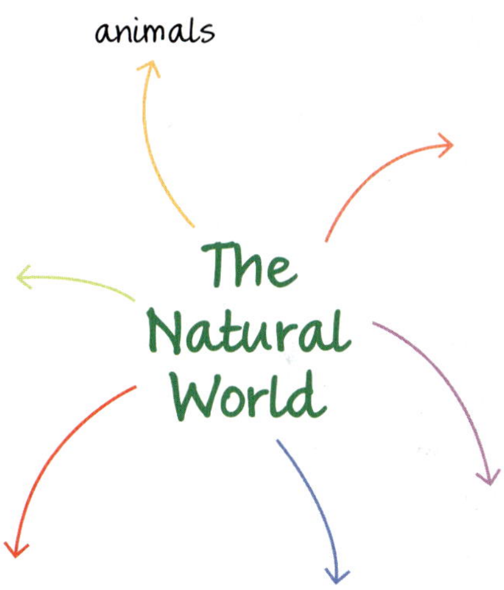

2 ▶ 1.32 **Listen to Carl and Gemma. What is the topic of their talk? Is it on your word map? Who has more ideas for the talk, Carl or Gemma?**

3 ▶ 1.32 **Listen again. Number the phrases in the *Get talking* box in the order you hear them. Then listen and repeat.**

4 Plan a talk on a topic of your choice. Use the words in the *Get talking* box to help you. Write a plan, then role play the talk with a partner.

Units 9 and 10

EP Get talking!

After all,
Good luck
make sure
a bit more
I can't wait
that's fine
Excellent!
I don't mind

1 ▶ **1.40 Listen to Emma and Stella. What do they decide to do this afternoon?**

2 ▶ **1.40 Listen again and answer the questions.**

1 What did Stella get for her birthday?
2 What does Emma think Stella should do?
3 What's the subject of the competition?
4 What's the closing date of the competition?

3 ▶ **1.40 Complete the sentences with words and phrases from the *Get talking* box. Then listen and check.**

1 .... , Stella. What do you want to do?
2 Sure, ...
3 .... to go out and use it again!
4 I'll just look online and find .... information for you.
5 .... , most of my photos are of streets and buildings.
6 .... ! Just .... you enter before June 5. That's the closing date.
7 .... in the competition!

4 Work with a partner. Try to remember the conversation. Use the words in Exercise 3 and the *Get talking* box to help you. It doesn't matter if it's not exactly the same! Compare your conversation with another pair.

Units 11 and 12

EP Get talking!

That sounds exciting!
I hope that's OK?
No problem!
the rest
Guess what?

1 ▶ **1.50 Listen to Tom talking to Hayley about the school show. What does he ask Hayley to do? Choose the correct picture.**

2 ▶ **1.50 Complete the conversation. What does Hayley say to Tom? There is one extra sentence.**

A Sure. No problem!
B Yeah, I'll be there. Is it in the hall?
C Yes! That sounds exciting Tom! What's it going to be about?
D I think so, but I'll need to check.
E Wow! Congratulations, Tom! So, what do you want me to do?

T: Do you want to be in the school show this year, Hayley?
H: [1] ....
T: It's a musical called *Bugsy Malone*. And guess what? I'm going to be Bugsy!
H: [2] ....
T: We need someone to play guitar in the band. I hope that's OK?
H: Sure. [3] ....
T: Great. There's a meeting about it in the hall after school today. Are you free?
H: [4] ....
T: Great. You can meet the rest of the band, and hear all the songs.

3 ▶ **1.50 Listen and check. Then practise the conversation.**

4 Work with a partner. Choose one of the sentences below and use it in a new conversation.

Guess what? Mr Clarke says I can play the violin in the concert.
I told the teacher you were a really good singer. I hope that's OK?
Let's ask the rest of the class what they think.

Units 13 and 14

EP Get talking!

Awesome! | Congratulations! | Cool! | it's a pity that … | I suppose | If you like | If not,

1 ▶2.05 **Listen to the conversation. What is Ruby going to do on Saturday? Who is going to ask Ruby's dad for the ticket?**

2 ▶2.05 **Listen again. Write *R* (Ruby) or *E* (Emily).**

1 Guess what? ....
2 How did you get it? ....
3 Please can I come instead? ....
4 I'll tell you all about it afterwards. ....
5 I just have to go. ....
6 No, it's OK. ....

3 Complete the sentences with the words from the *Get talking* box.

1 .... , Ruby!
2 .... But .... you don't have another ticket… for me!
3 I can ask Dad, ...
4 .... ! .... , maybe I can watch it on TV.
5 .... , I can ask your dad for his ticket.

4 ▶2.06 **Listen and check. Then repeat the sentences in Exercise 3.**

5 Work with a partner. Write a phone conversation between two friends. One of the friends is going somewhere. The other friend wants to go too but there's a problem. Use the words in the *Get talking* box and the conversation in Exercise 1 to help you. Practise your conversation.

Units 15 and 16

EP Get talking!

at least | quite a few | certainly | such a | these days | anyway | unfortunately

1 ▶2.15 **Listen and match the conversations to a topic in the box. There is one extra topic that you don't need.**

food	friends	shopping	sport	studying

Conversation 1 ....
Conversation 2 ....
Conversation 3 ....
Conversation 4 ....

2 ▶2.15 **Work with a partner. Listen again and complete the conversations with words from the *Get talking* box. Then listen and check. Practise the conversations with your partner.**

Conversation 1

A: How was the football match, Joe? Did you win?
B: No, ... Dominic was ill. He's .... good player! It's hard to win without him.

Conversation 2

A: Nice T-shirt Gina! Is it new?
B: Yes. I went to that new department store last weekend and got .... new things.

Conversation 3

A: The science teacher is giving us too many tests .... !
B: She .... is! And the last one was really hard!

Conversation 4

A: I'm really angry. I asked Sarah not to invite Chris to her party, but she did it .... !
B: Don't worry. She's invited .... 20 other people. You won't have to talk to him.

3 Work with a partner. Write three new conversations. Use the words in the *Get talking* box to help you. Practise your conversations.

Units 17 and 18

EP Get talking!

Me too. | What about you? | the same | it's not that | see you there | I'm not sure.

1 ▶2.25 **Listen to Mitch and Josh talking about going to the cinema. Are the sentences right (✔) or wrong (✘)?**

1 Mitch wants Josh to help him with his homework.
2 Mitch paid a lot of money for his cinema tickets.
3 Both Mitch and Josh like the idea of seeing *Sky Blue*.
4 The film begins at 2.30.
5 The boys decide to meet at the library.

2 ▶2.25 **Complete the conversation with words from the *Get talking* box. Then listen and check. Practise the conversation with your partner.**

Mitch: Hi, Josh. Are you busy this afternoon?
Josh: Not really, Mitch. Why? Do you need help with your maths homework again?
Mitch: No, [1]............................ ! I've got two free tickets for the cinema. Do you want to come?
Josh: Yeah, great! What's on?
Mitch: [2]............................ . Just a moment – I'll have a look on the website. Er ... *Sky Blue* is on. I haven't seen that yet. [3]............................
Josh: No, I haven't seen it. I've heard it's really good.
Mitch: [4]............................ OK, well that's on at three o'clock. I can catch a bus to the cinema from the library at two thirty.
Josh: I'll do [5]............................ .
Mitch: OK, [6]............................ . Bye.

3 **Work with a partner. Write a new conversation, inviting a friend to go somewhere with you. Use the words in the *Get talking* box to help you.**

4 **Act out your conversation to the class.**

Units 19 and 20

EP Get talking!

That's a great idea. | I'd prefer not to … | I'd prefer to … | just now | You're welcome. | not bad | all the time | one day

1 **Which of these subjects are you studying now? Which would you prefer to study in the future? Which would you prefer not to study in the future? Why? / Why not?**

languages	computer science	
history	geography	art
biology	chemistry	sport
maths	physics	

2 ▶2.31 **Listen to the conversation. Which subjects would Matthew prefer to study next year? Which subjects would he prefer not to study next year?**

3 ▶2.31 **Listen again. Answer the questions.**

1 What did Matthew want to do 'just now'?

....

2 What does Matthew have to do 'all the time'?

....

3 How did Mrs Green decide which job she wanted to do?

....

4 **Tell your partner about Mrs Green's decision in your own words.**

One day …

5 **Have you ever made a decision like Mrs Green did? Tell your partner.**

One day I …

6 **Work in pairs. One of you is a student and the other is a teacher. Write a conversation about your plans for the future. Use the conversation in Exercise 2 and the words in the *Get talking* box to help you. Practise your conversation.**

Unit 2, page 17, Exercise 6

Student A. Answer your partner's questions about the kakapo. Then ask your partner for information about the Siberian tiger. Make a note of the answers.

Kakapo

A kind of parrot
From: New Zealand
Lives: on two islands
Eats: plants/ fruit/ nuts
Adult weight: 2–4 kilos
About 127 kakapos left in the wild, 0 in zoos.
Kakapo babies called *chicks*. Females have 2–3 chicks every two years. The chicks stay with their mother for 10 weeks.

Student B. Ask your partner for information about the kakapo. Make a note of the answers. Then answer your partner's questions about the Siberian tiger.

Siberian tiger

A kind of cat
From: Russia, China, North Korea
Lives: in forest
Eats: meat (rabbits/deer/pigs)
Adult weight: 180–300 kilos
About 400–500 left in the wild, 500 in zoos.
Siberian tiger babies are called *cubs*. Females have 2–6 cubs every two years. The cubs stay with their mother for two years.

UNIT 3, page 23, Exercise 10

Student A

Look at number 1. Here is some information about a city tour. Student B is going to ask you some questions. Answer them using this information. Look at number 2. You don't know anything about the Rock Concert. Make five questions to ask Student B.

Student A: Answers

1 CITY TOUR

Every day except Monday
Tour takes one hour
Price: £1.50.
Children under five free
Meet at: the Town Hall
Visit www.visitourcity.com for more information.

Student A: Questions

UNIT 3, page 23, Exercise 10

Student B. Look at number 1. You don't know anything about City By Bike. Make five questions to ask Student A.

Look at number 2. Here is some information about a Rock Concert. Student A is going to ask you some questions. Answer them using this information.

Student B: Questions

1

CITY BY BIKE

- where / meet ?
- how long / tour?
- website ?
- when ?
- cost £ ?

Student B: Answers

2

ROCK CONCERT

In People's Park
Saturday 7th July
from 2 pm to 11 pm
Come and see the latest new bands.
Tickets: £15.00
Call us on
07231 37829

UNIT 8, page 48, Exercise 5

"How are you, people of 5,000 years from now? I want to live again in your age, but I am quite happy now. I have kind parents and also a sister who I don't always agree with. We have to do our best until the next age comes. Goodbye from 5,000 years in the past."

UNIT 14, page 81, Exercise 10

Student A

Look at Number 1. Here is some information about the Bicycle Show. Student B is going to ask you some questions. Use the information in Number 1 to answer the questions.

Look at Number 2. You don't know anything about the Star Music Shop so ask Student B some questions about it.

Your answers

1

Bicycle Show
Sunday 19 July 10 am – 6 pm
At Central Hall
30% discount on everything
Entry: £2.50 Children under 12 free
For information call Val on
06353 77092 after 6 pm

Your questions

2

Star Music Shop
what / sell?
address?
expensive?
open every day?
website?

Student B

Look at Number 1. You don't know anything about the Bicycle Show so ask Student A some questions about it.

Look at Number 2. Here is some information about the Star Music Shop. Student A is going to ask you some questions. Use the information in Number 2 to answer the questions.

Your questions

1

Bicycle Show

where / show?

date?

ticket £ ?

open? ? ?

phone number?

Your answers

2

Star Music Shop

15 Lion Street

Hours: 9 am – 6 pm Monday – Saturday

Great prices!

Get your guitars, drums and keyboards here.

Find us at: www.starmusic.com

UNIT 15, page 89, Ex 9

Journalists: you must ask at least five questions:

- Tell me about …
- How do you feel about … ?
- Why did you … ?
- How did you get the idea to … ?
- Are you glad you … ?
- Are you going to … again?

Mary Hardison: you must think about:

- how you felt about the jump
- why you did the jump
- how you got the idea
- if you were glad you did the jump
- if you would do another jump

UNIT 16, page 91, Exercise 8

Quiz scores: What kind of English language learner are you?

Add up your scores

A = 6 points
B = 5 points
C = 4 points
D = 3 points
E = 2 points
F = 1 point

20–24 You are a very serious language learner. You will do very well in your studies, but remember you can have fun when you are learning English! It's not all about getting the best mark in the class.

16–20 You enjoy learning English. You are happy to try new ways of learning and you are not afraid to make mistakes. You like using the language in real situations.

10–15 English probably isn't your favourite subject but if you work hard you can be good at it. Study a little but often and you'll soon see the difference!

UNIT 17, page 99, Exercise 10

1

A You phone B to say that you can't come to his/her party. Give reasons.

B You are unhappy that A can't come to your party. You think that A's reasons for not coming aren't very good!

2

B You phone A to say that you can't come and help with his/her homework this evening. Give reasons.

A You really need B's help and suggest other ways B might help you, e.g. internet/phone.

UNIT 18, page 105, Exercise 6

A You have nothing to wear to a party and want to borrow something from your friend, B.

B You are not sure about lending A your clothes!

A Your parents are out and have asked you to tidy up the house before they return. You want your brother/sister (B) to help.

B You are still in bed and don't want to help tidy up.

Vocabulary list

UNIT 1

busy /ˈbɪzi/ *adjective*
friendly /ˈfrendli/ *adjective*
funny /ˈfʌni/ *adjective*
kind /kaɪnd/ *adjective*
lazy /ˈleɪzi/ *adjective*
pleased /pliːzd/ *adjective*
polite /pəˈlaɪt/ *adjective*
popular /ˈpɒpjʊlə/ *adjective*

UNIT 2

desert /ˈdezət/ *noun*
dolphin /ˈdɒlfɪn/ *noun*
forest /ˈfɒrɪst/ *noun*
hill /hɪl/ *noun*
island /ˈaɪlənd/ *noun*
lake /leɪk/ *noun*
lion /ˈlaɪən/ *noun*
monkey /ˈmʌŋki/ *noun*
mountain /ˈmaʊntɪn/ *noun*
penguin /ˈpeŋgwɪn/ *noun*
river /ˈrɪvə/ *noun*
sea /siː/ *noun*
snake /sneɪk/ *noun*
valley /ˈvæli/ *noun*
volcano /vɒlˈkeɪnəʊ/ *noun*

UNIT 3

adventure /ədˈventʃə/ *noun*
aeroplane /ˈeərəpleɪn/ *noun*
engine /ˈendʒɪn/ *noun*
flight /flaɪt/ *noun*
fuel /fjʊəl/ *noun*
guest /gest/ *noun*
holiday /ˈhɒlɪdeɪ/ *noun*
luggage /ˈlʌgɪdʒ/ *noun*
map /mæp/ *noun*
passenger /ˈpæsəndʒə/ *noun*
pilot /ˈpaɪlət/ *noun*
radio /ˈreɪdiəʊ/ *noun*
receptionist /rɪˈsepʃənɪst/ *noun*
suitcase /ˈsuːtkeɪs/ *noun*
tourist /ˈtʊərɪst/ *noun*
visitor /ˈvɪzɪtə/ *noun*

UNIT 4

apartment /ə'pɑːtmənt/ *noun*

attractive /ə'træktɪv/ *adjective*

beach /biːtʃ/ *noun*

boat /bəʊt/ *noun*

cave /keɪv/ *noun*

cold /kəʊld/ *adjective*

dark /dɑːk/ *adjective*

electricity /elek'trɪsɪti/ *noun*

light /laɪt/ *noun*

lorry /'lɒri/ *noun*

market /'mɑːkɪt/ *noun*

pretty /'prɪti/ *adjective*

sand /sænd/ *noun*

sink /sɪŋk/ *noun*

storm /stɔːm/ *noun*

suitcase /'suːtkeɪs/ *noun*

supper /'sʌpə/ *noun*

surfboard /'sɜːfbɔːd/ *noun*

unusual /ʌn'juːʒuəl/ *adjective*

useful /'juːsfəl/ *adjective*

warm /wɔːm/ *adjective*

UNIT 5

art /ɑːt/ *noun*

biology /baɪ'ɒlədʒi/ *noun*

chemistry /'kemɪstri/ *noun*

classroom /'klɑːsruːm/ *noun*

dictionary /'dɪkʃənəri/ *noun*

diploma /dɪ'pləʊmə/ *noun*

exam /ɪg'zæm/ *noun*

fail /feɪl/ *verb*

music /'mjuːzɪk/ *noun*

paper /'peɪpə/ *noun*

pass /pɑːs/ *verb*

physics /'fɪzɪks/ *noun*

sport /spɔːt/ *noun*

take /teɪk/ *verb*

uniform /'juːnɪfɔːm/ *noun*

EP Vocabulary list

UNIT 6

bottle /ˈbɒtl/ *noun*
bowl /bəʊl/ *noun*
cup /kʌp/ *noun*
envelope /ˈenvələʊp/ *noun*
glass /glɑːs/ *noun*
gold /gəʊld/ *noun*
jumper /ˈdʒʌmpə/ *noun*
leather /ˈleðə/ *noun*
little /ˈlɪtl/ *adjective*
lovely /ˈlʌvli/ *adjective*
necklace /ˈnekləs/ *noun*
old /əʊld/ *adjective*
paper /ˈpeɪpə/ *noun*
plastic /ˈplæstɪk/ *noun*
pretty /ˈprɪti/ *adjective*
ring /rɪŋ/ *noun*
shoes /ʃuːz/ *noun*
silver /ˈsɪlvə/ *noun*
small /smɔːl/ *adjective*
soft /sɒft/ *adjective*
wood /wʊd/ *noun*
wool /wʊl/ *noun*

UNIT 7

boat /bəʊt/ *noun*
climbing /ˈklaɪmɪŋ/ *noun*
helicopter /ˈhelɪkɒptə/ *noun*
hiking /ˈhaɪkɪŋ/ *noun*
motorbike /ˈməʊtəbaɪk/ *noun*
mountain biking /ˈmaʊntɪn baɪkɪŋ/ *noun*
scooter /ˈskuːtə/ *noun*
ship /ʃɪp/ *noun*
tram /træm/ *noun*
underground /ˈʌndəgraʊnd/ *noun*
zip wiring /ˈzɪp waɪərɪŋ/ *noun*

UNIT 8

book /bʊk/ *noun/verb*
chair /tʃeə/ *noun*
cupboard /ˈkʌbəd/ *noun*
fridge /frɪdʒ/ *noun*
kind /kaɪnd/ *adjective/noun*
lamp /læmp/ *noun*
picture /ˈpɪktʃə/ *noun*
ring /rɪŋ/ *noun/verb*
sink /sɪŋk/ *noun*
sofa /ˈsəʊfə/ *noun*
washing machine /ˈwɒʃɪŋ məʃiːn/ *noun*
watch /wɒtʃ/ *noun/verb*

UNIT 9

badminton /'bædmɪntən/ *noun*
board game /'bɔːd geɪm/ *noun*
card game /'kɑːd geɪm/ *noun*
chess /tʃes/ *noun*
chess set /'tʃes set/ *noun*
class /klɑːs/ *noun*
climbing /'klaɪmɪŋ/ *noun*
cricket /'krɪkɪt/ *noun*
dance /dɑːns/ *noun*
diving /'daɪvɪŋ/ *noun*
fishing /'fɪʃɪŋ/ *noun*
fitness /'fɪtnəs/ *noun*
gold medal /gəʊld 'medəl/ *noun*
golf /gɒlf/ *noun*
karate /kə'rɑːti/ *noun*
puzzle /'pʌzl/ *noun*
skateboarding /'skeɪtbɔːdɪŋ/ *noun*
skiing /'skiːɪŋ/ *noun*
video games /'vɪdiəʊ geɪmz/ *noun*

UNIT 10

blog /blɒg/ *noun*
close /kləʊs/ *adjective*
contact /'kɒntækt/ *noun*
download /daʊn'ləʊd/ *verb*
friend /frend/ *noun*
guest /gest/ *noun*
link /lɪŋk/ *noun*
member /'membə/ *noun*
menu /'menjuː/ *noun*
message board /'mesɪdʒ bɔːd/ *noun*
neighbour /'neɪbə/ *noun*
old /əʊld/ *adjective*
post /pəʊst/ *verb*
record /rɪ'kɔːd/ *verb*
save /seɪv/ *verb*
search /sɜːtʃ/ *verb*
site /saɪt/ *noun*
web /web/ *noun*
upload /ʌp'ləʊd/ *verb*

Vocabulary list

UNIT 11

available /ə'veɪləbl/ *adjective*
bridge /brɪdʒ/ *noun*
cathedral /kə'θiːdrəl/ *noun*
details /'diːteɪlz/ *noun*
hospital /'hɒspɪtəl/ *noun*
information /ɪnfə'meɪʃən/ *noun*
library /'laɪbrəri/ *noun*
luggage /'lʌgɪdʒ/ *noun*
mosque /mɒsk/ *noun*
museum /mjuː'ziːəm/ *noun*
online /ɒn'laɪn/ *adverb*
palace /'pælɪs/ *noun*
park /pɑːk/ *noun*
police station /pə'liːs steɪʃən/ *noun*
post office /'pəʊs tɒfɪs/ *noun*
restaurant /'restrɒnt/ *noun*
shop /ʃɒp/ *noun*
shop assistant /'ʃɒp əsɪstənt/ *noun*
sports centre /'spɔːts sentə/ *noun*
stadium /'steɪdiəm/ *noun*
staff /stɑːf/ *noun*
statue /'stætʃuː/ *noun*
temple /'templ/ *noun*
theatre /'θɪətə/ *noun*
train station /'treɪn steɪʃən/ *noun*

UNIT 12

blues /bluːz/ *noun*
classical /'klæsɪkəl/ *adjective*
drum /drʌm/ *noun*
folk /fəʊk/ *noun*
guitar /gɪ'tɑː/ *noun*
jazz /dʒæz/ *noun*
keyboards /'kiːbɔːdz/ *noun*
pop /pɒp/ *noun*
rap /ræp/ *noun*
rock /rɒk/ *noun*
soul /səʊl/ *noun*
trumpet /'trʌmpɪt/ *noun*
violin /vaɪə'lɪn/ *noun*

UNIT 13

artist /ˈɑːtɪst/ *noun*

be /biː/ *verb*

break /breɪk/ *verb*

chef /ʃef/ *noun*

dentist /ˈdentɪst/ *noun*

dream /driːm/ *verb*

eat /iːt/ *verb*

fall /fɔːl/ *verb*

forget /fəˈget/ *verb*

grow /grəʊ/ *verb*

lend /lend/ *verb*

mechanic /məˈkænɪk/ *noun*

meet /miːt/ *verb*

model /ˈmɒdəl/ *noun*

nurse /nɜːs/ *noun*

photographer /fəˈtɒgrəfə/ *noun*

pilot /ˈpaɪlət/ *noun*

receptionist /rɪˈsepʃənɪst/ *noun*

ride /raɪd/ *verb*

sell /sel/ *verb*

tour guide /ˈtʊə gaɪd/ *noun*

wear /weər/ *verb*

UNIT 14

bookshop /ˈbʊkʃɒp/ *noun*

café /ˈkæfeɪ/ *noun*

chemist /ˈkemɪst/ *noun*

clothes shop /ˈkləʊðz ʃɒp/ *noun*

department store /dɪˈpɑːtmənt stɔː/ *noun*

market /ˈmɑːkɪt/ *noun*

shoe shop /ˈʃuː ʃɒp/ *noun*

sweet shop /ˈswiːt ʃɒp/ *noun*

supermarket /ˈsuːpəmɑːkɪt/ *noun*

grams /græmz/ *noun*

kilograms /ˈkɪləgræmz/ *noun*

litres /ˈliːtəz/ *noun*

centimetres /ˈsentɪmiːtəz/ *noun*

metres /ˈmiːtəz/ *noun*

kilometres /kɪˈlɒmɪtəz/ *noun*

pounds /paʊndz/ *noun*

pence /pents/ *noun*

euros /ˈjʊərəʊz/ *noun*

cents /sents/ *noun*

variety /vəˈraɪəti/ *noun*

pair /peə/ *noun*

bit /bɪt/ *noun*

slice /slaɪs/ *noun*

set /set/ *noun*

UNIT 15

acting /'æktɪŋ/ *noun*
book /bʊk/ *verb*
chat /tʃæt/ *verb*
clean /kliːn/ *verb*
collecting /kə'lektɪŋ/ *noun*
computer game /kəm'pjuːtə geɪm/ *noun*
cooking /'kʊkɪŋ/ *noun*
dancing /'dɑːntsɪŋ/ *noun*
do /duː/ *verb*
friend /frend/ *noun*
go out /'gəʊ aʊt/ *verb*
instrument /'ɪnstrəmənt/ *noun*
make /'meɪk/ *verb*
music /'mjuːzɪk/ *noun*
online /ɒn'laɪn/ *adverb*
order /'ɔːdə/ *verb*
pay /peɪ/ *verb*
photography /fə'tɒgrəfi/ *noun*
play /pleɪ/ *verb*
reading /'riːdɪŋ/ *noun*
repair /rɪ'peə/ *verb*
shopping /'ʃɒpɪŋ/ *noun*
singing /'sɪŋɪŋ/ *noun*
sport /spɔːt/ *noun*
things /θɪŋz/ *noun*
TV /tiː'viː/ *noun*

UNIT 16

article /'ɑːtɪkl/ *noun*
board /bɔːd/ *noun*
chat /tʃæt/ *verb*
dictionary /'dɪkʃənəri/ *noun*
exercise /'eksəsaɪz/ *noun*
guess /ges/ *verb*
interesting /'ɪntrəstɪŋ/ *adjective*
library /'laɪbrəri/ *noun*
list /lɪst/ *noun*
magazine /mægə'ziːn/ *noun*
message /'mesɪdʒ/ *noun*
mistake /mɪ'steɪk/ *noun*
spell /spel/ *verb*
textbook /'tekstbʊk/ *noun*

UNIT 17

back /bæk/ *noun*
blood /blʌd/ *noun*
body /'bɒdi/ *noun*
brain /breɪn/ *noun*
ear /ɪə/ *noun*
family /'fæməli/ *noun*
finger /'fɪŋgə/ *noun*
friends /frendz/ *noun*
health /helθ/ *noun*
heart /hɑːt/ *noun*
neck /nek/ *noun*
schoolwork /'skuːlwɜːk/ *noun*
sport /spɔːt/ *noun*
stomach /'stʌmək/ *noun*
toe /təʊ/ *noun*

UNIT 18

backpack /ˈbækpæk/ *noun*
compass /ˈkʌmpəs/ *noun*
first aid kit /fɜːst ˈeɪd kɪt/ *noun*
get back /get bæk/ *verb*
get up /get ʌp/ *verb*
give back /gɪv bæk/ *verb*
lie down /laɪ daʊn/ *verb*
map /mæp/ *noun*
pick up /pɪk ʌp/ *verb*
put on /pʊt ɒn/ *verb*
sleeping bag /ˈsliːpɪŋ bæg/ *noun*
snacks /snæks/ *noun*
take off /teɪk ɒf/ *verb*
tent /tent/ *noun*
torch /tɔːtʃ/ *noun*
trainers /treɪnəz/ *noun*
try on /traɪ ən/ *verb*
wake up /weɪk ʌp/ *verb*
walking boots /ˈwɔːkɪŋ buːts/ *noun*
wash up /wɒʃ ʌp/ *verb*

UNIT 19

add /æd/ *verb*
bake /beɪk/ *verb*
beans /biːnz/ *noun*
boil /bɔɪl/ *verb*
carrots /ˈkærəts/ *noun*
cook /kʊk/ *verb*
cover /ˈkʌvə/ *verb*
dishes /dɪʃɪz/ *noun*
do /duː/ *verb*
dry /draɪ/ *verb*
empty /ˈempti/ *adjective*
fill /fɪl/ *verb*
garlic /ˈgɑːlɪk/ *noun*
homework /ˈhəʊmwɜːk/ *noun*
make /meɪk/ *verb*
melon /ˈmelən/ *noun*
mess /mes/ *noun*
mistake /mɪˈsteɪk/ *noun*
mix /mɪks/ *verb*
oven /ˈʌvən/ *noun*
pear /peə/ *noun*
pepper /ˈpepə/ *noun*
potato /pəˈteɪtəʊ/ *noun*
prepare /prɪˈpeə/ *verb*
salt /sɒlt/ *noun*
spoon /spuːn/ *noun*
steak /steɪk/ *noun*

EP Vocabulary list

UNIT 20

castle /ˈkɑːsl/ *noun*

change /tʃeɪndʒ/ *noun/verb*

detective /dɪˈtektɪv/ *noun*

police officer /pəˈliːs ɒfɪsə/ *noun*

radio presenter /ˈreɪdiəʊ prɪzentə/ *noun*

receptionist /rɪˈsepʃənɪst/ *noun*

supermarket /ˈsuːpəmɑːkɪt/ *noun*

taxi driver /ˈtæksi draɪvər/ *noun*

transport /ˈtrænspɔːt/ *noun*

waitress /ˈweɪtrəs/ *noun*

Grammar reference

UNIT 1

PRESENT SIMPLE AND PRESENT CONTINUOUS

Present simple

We use the **present simple** to talk about things that are always true or that happen regularly. We often use it with words like *often*, *usually*, *every day*, *twice a week*, etc.

I usually ***work*** *hard.*
She ***learns*** *English at school.*
Does *he* ***work*** *here? No, he* ***doesn't****.*
Do *they often* ***go*** *to the cinema? Yes, they* ***do****.*

Spelling: third person *-s*

most verbs, add *-s*	*learn**s**, work**s**, live**s**, walk**s***
verbs that end *in -o, -s, -sh, -ch, -x* and *-zz*, add *-es*	*go**es**, miss**es**, watch**es**, box**es**, buzz**es***
verbs that end in consonant + *-y*, remove the *-y* and add *-ies*	*stud**ies**, carr**ies***
irregular verbs	*have –* ***has***

Present continuous

We use the **present continuous** to talk about things that are happening now or at the moment. We often use it with words like *now*, *at the moment*, *today*, *this week*, etc.

I'm teaching *my brother to swim* ***at the moment****.*
*They****'re playing*** *tennis now.*
You ***aren't practising*** *the piano much this week.*
Is the baby ***sleeping****? Yes, he* ***is****.*

Spelling: *-ing* form

most verbs add *-ing*	*play**ing**, go**ing**, learn**ing***
verbs ending in *-e*, remove *-e* and add *-ing*	*live →* ***living****,* *make →* ***making***
verbs ending in *-ie*, change the *-ie* to *-y* and add *-ing*	*lie →* ***lying***
one syllable verbs ending in a vowel + a consonant (except w, x or y), double the consonant and add *-ing*	*sit → si**tting**,* *swim → swi**mming***
two syllable verbs ending in a stressed vowel + a consonant, double the consonant and add *-ing*	*begin → begi**nning*** *(**but** open → opening)*
In British English, we double the final 'l' in travel	*travel → trave**lling*** *(American English: travel → traveling)*

Practice

1 Complete the conversation with the present simple or present continuous form of the verb in brackets.

Sara: What **(0)** ...are... you ...doing... (do)?
Martina: I **(1)** .... (paint) a picture of the trees.
Sara: But you **(2)** .... (not like) Art!
Martina: Yes, I know, but my friends **(3)** .... (play) football at the moment and I **(4)** .... (hate) that.
Sara: What sports **(5)** .... you .... (enjoy) doing?
Martina: I **(6)** .... (go) swimming twice a week. What about you?
Sara: My best friend **(7)** .... (play) hockey but I **(8)** .... (prefer) basketball.
Martina: I **(9)** .... (not do) anything now. Let's go for a walk.
Sara: Good idea!

2 Write complete sentences in the present simple or present continuous.

0 I / play tennis / at the moment.
...I'm playing tennis at the moment....
1 My dad / usually go to work by car.
....
2 We / learn how to play the guitar / today.
....
3 I / always watch TV / after dinner.
....
4 My friends / not swim in the sea / now.
....
5 My cousin / not have breakfast / every day.
....

UNIT 2

VERBS WE DON'T USUALLY USE IN THE CONTINUOUS

There are some verbs which we don't normally use in the present continuous:

- Verbs of thinking: *believe, understand, know, think*.
  Scientists ***believe*** *the Earth is 4.6 billion years old.*
  (**not** ~~*Scientists are believing*~~ …)
- Verbs of feeling: *like, hate, love, want, need, prefer*.
  I ***like*** *those monkeys over there.* (**not** ~~*I'm liking*~~ …)
- Verbs of owning: *own, belong*.
  That coat ***belongs*** *to me.* (**not** ~~*That coat's belonging*~~ …)
- Verbs to describe sensations: *see, hear, smell, taste*.
  We often use *can* with these verbs.
  I ***can hear*** *the sea from my bedroom.* (**not** ~~*I'm hearing*~~)
- When *think* means 'have an opinion' about something, we do not use the continuous.
  Scientists ***think*** *there are about 1000 wild pandas left.*
  (**not** ~~*Scientists are thinking*~~ …)
- However, when *think* means 'consider', we use the continuous.
  I'm thinking *of working in a zoo when I'm older.*
- We can use the present simple or the present continuous to say how someone looks or feels now.
  How ***do*** *you* ***feel*** *today? I* ***feel*** *better.*
  or *How* ***are*** *you* ***feeling*** *today?* ***I'm feeling*** *better.*

Practice

1 Complete the table with these verbs.

~~need~~ ~~run~~ believe understand
sing own buy hate climb
like work want know feel

Verbs we can use in the continuous	Verbs we don't normally use in the continuous
run, …	*need, …*

2 Choose the correct words to complete the sentences.

0 Jack's behind that tree. I **can see** (circled) / **'m seeing** him.
1 I **know / 'm knowing** the names of all the rivers in my country.
2 My brother **learns / 's learning** about the weather at the moment.
3 You **need / 're needing** to do your homework before Tuesday.
4 You're very quiet. What **do you think / are you thinking** about?
5 My friends **don't play / aren't playing** football today. It's cold.
6 Can you say that again? We **don't understand / aren't understanding**.
7 **Can you hear / Are you hearing** that strange noise?

3 Write complete sentences. Use the present simple or the present continuous.

0 Shh! I / think.
Shhh! I'm thinking.
1 I / not understand / this exercise.
………………………………
2 My friends / think football is boring.
………………………………
3 What / you / do right now?
………………………………
4 We / not want to watch the film.
………………………………
5 That dog / belong to my cousin.
………………………………
6 My grandma / feel / better today.
………………………………
7 I / not like this book very much.
………………………………

UNIT 3

PAST SIMPLE

Be

Positive	I / He / She / It **was** at home. You / We / They **were** at school.
Negative	I / He / She / It **wasn't** at school. You / We / They **weren't** at home.
Questions	**Was** I / he / she / it at home? **Were** you / we / they at school?
Short answers	Yes, I / he / she / it **was**. No, I / he / she / it **wasn't**. Yes, you / we / they **were**. No, you / we / they **weren't**.

Regular and irregular verbs

Positive	I / You / He / She / It / We / They **climbed** I / You / He / She / It / We / They **knew**
Negative	I / You / He / She / It / We / They **didn't want** I / You / He / She / It / We / They **didn't write**
Questions	**Did** I / you / he / she / it / we / they **travel** **Did** I / you / he / she / it / we / they **fly**
Short answers	Yes, I / you / he / she / it / we / they **did**. No, I / you / he / she / it /we / they **didn't**.

- We use the past simple to talk about things that happened or didn't happen in the past.
  Amelia Earhart ***decided*** *to fly around the world.*
  She ***didn't take*** *any passengers.*

Spelling: regular verbs

most verbs, add *-ed*	*play → play**ed*** *climb → climb**ed***
verbs that end *in -e*, add *-d*	*decide → decide**d*** *arrive → arrive**d***
verbs that end in consonant + *-y*, change *-y* to -i and add *-ed*	*carry → carr**ied***
one-syllable verbs ending in a vowel + a consonant (except *w*, *x* or *y*), double the consonant and add *-ed*	*stop → sto**pped***
two-syllable verbs ending in a stressed vowel + consonant, double the consonant and add *-ed*	*prefer → prefe**rred***
In British English, we double the final *l*	*travel → trave**lled*** (American English: *travel → trave**led***)

Practice

1 Complete this paragraph with the past simple form of the verb in brackets.

Last summer, I **(0)** ....visited.... (visit) Moscow with my family. We **(1)** .... (fly) from London. On the first day, we **(2)** .... (go) to the tourist information office and we **(3)** .... (ask) for information about the city. My sister **(4)** .... (want) to go to the zoo. My dad **(5)** .... (not want) to go there, so he **(6)** .... (go) shopping. The next day, we **(7)** .... (walk) to Red Square and we **(8)** .... (see) the Kremlin. We **(9)** .... (not go) inside the museum because it **(10)** .... (be) closed. We **(11)** .... (have) a fantastic holiday there.

SUBJECT QUESTIONS

We normally use *do* or *did* in questions.
Where ***do*** *you live?*
What ***did*** *you eat yesterday?*
However, we don't use *do* or *did* if the question word (*who*, *what*, etc.) is the subject. Look at these questions:

Subject: ***Who*** *helped you?* ***My mum*** *helped me.*

Object: ***Who*** *did you help? I helped* ***my sister****.*

Practice

2 Choose the correct words to complete the questions.

0 Who **did fly** / **flew** across the Atlantic in 1928?
1 What **did the boy see** / **saw the boy** at the cinema?
2 What **did happen** / **happened** to you? You're late!
3 Who **did eat** / **ate** the cake?
4 What **did he drink** / **drank he** with his lunch?
5 Who **did do** / **did** their homework last night?

UNIT 4

PAST CONTINUOUS AND PAST SIMPLE

Past continuous

Positive	I / He / She / It **was eating** a sandwich. You / We / They **were sitting** on the beach.
Negative	I / He / She / It **wasn't building** a sandcastle. You / We / They **weren't reading** a book.
Questions	**Was** I / he / she / it **shopping**? **Were** you / we / they **working**?
Short answers	Yes, I / he / she / it **was**. No, he / she / it **wasn't**. Yes, you / we / they **were**. No, you / we / they **weren't**.

→ **For the spelling of the *-ing* form, see Grammar reference Unit 1, p. 147.**

Past continuous and past simple

We use the **past continuous**:

- to describe activities happening at a particular moment in the past. Sometimes these activities happen at the same time. We're not interested when the activities started or finished.

  *Mum and dad **were cooking**, my brother **was playing** and I **was doing** my homework.*

We use the **past simple**:

- when one action follows another.

  *I **put** on my coat and I **left** the house. Then it **started** to rain.*

- when we refer to a shorter action or event that happened in the middle of a longer one or interrupted it.

  *I **was putting** on my coat when it **started** to rain.*

  → **See Grammar reference Unit 3, Past simple, p. 149.**

Practice

1 Use the past continuous to write complete sentences.

At 7.30 last night …

0 We / camp / in a field.

........We were camping in a field.........

1 It / rain.

....

2 Dad / build / a fire.

....

3 My brother and I / climb trees.

....

4 My sister / read.

....

5 My mum / listen to the radio.

....

2 Choose the correct words to complete the sentences.

0 I was studying in my bedroom when I (**heard**) / **was hearing** a strange noise.

1 While I was surfing, it **started** / **was starting** to rain.

2 My friends **played** / **were playing** football in the classroom when the teacher came in.

3 We drove to the beach and then we **had** / **were having** a swim.

4 At 6 o'clock Mum and Dad were cooking and I **did** / **was doing** my homework.

5 We **packed** / **were packing** our suitcases, when the phone rang.

3 Complete the email. Use the past simple or past continuous form of the verb in brackets.

> Hi Mark!
> We **(0)** ....arrived.... (arrive) here in New York yesterday. When we **(1)** .... (get up) this morning, the sun **(2)** .... (shine). It was a beautiful day, so we **(3)** .... (decide) to walk to Central Park. We **(4)** .... (sit) on the grass when I **(5)** .... (see) my teacher! She **(6)** .... (not be) pleased to see me.
> See you soon!
> Tim

UNIT 5

COMPARATIVE AND SUPERLATIVE ADVERBS

Adjective	Adverb	Comparative	Superlative
		regular	
slow	slowly	more slowly	the most slowly
easy	easily	more easily	the most easily
simple	simply	more simply	the most simply
beautiful	beautifully	more beautifully	the most beautifully
		irregular	
good	well	better	the best
fast	fast	faster	the fastest
hard	hard	harder	the hardest
late	late	later	the latest

We use **adjectives** to describe a noun and **adverbs** to describe a verb.

- We form most adverbs by adding *-ly* to the adjective.
  *quick → quick**ly**, careful → careful**ly**, easy → eas**ily***
- Some adverbs do not end in *-ly*.
  good → well, fast → fast, hard → hard, late → late

We use **comparative adverbs** to compare two things.
*My brother talks **more quickly** than me.*

- We use *more* with adjectives that finish in *-ly*.
  *Jack did the exam **more carefully** than Nick.*
- The opposite of *more* is *less*.
  *Nick did the exam **less carefully** than Jack.*
- We add *-er* to *fast*, *hard* and *late*.
  *Peter swims **faster** than Mike. Jim arrived **later** than me.*
- The comparative form of the adverb *well* is *better*.
  *My sister speaks French **better** than my mum.*
- We can also use *often* to compare things.
  *I play tennis **more often** than basketball.*
- We can also use *(not) as* + adverb + *as* to compare things.
  *Oliver talks **as loudly as** Phil.* (= *They both talk loudly.*)
  *Jane doesn't write **as quickly as** Paula.* (= *Paula writes more quickly than Jane.*)

We use **superlative adverbs** to compare one thing with three or more things.
*My dad walks **the most slowly** in our family.*

- We use *most* with adjectives that finish in *-ly*.
  *The maths teacher speaks **the most quickly**.*
- The opposite of *most* is *least*.
  *Kevin did his exam **the least carefully**.*
- We add *-est* to *fast*, *hard* and *late*.
  *Jason ran **the fastest** so he won the race.*
- The superlative form of the adverb *well* is *the best*.
  *My grandma cooks **the best** in my house.*
- We can also use *often* to compare things.
  *When I was young, I played football **the most often**.*

Practice

1 Write the adverb, comparative and superlative of the adjectives.

1 cheap, cheaply, ... , ...
2 heavy, ... , ... , ...
3 fast, ... , ... , ...
4 good, ... , ... , ...
5 serious, ... , ... , ...
6 wonderful, ... , ... , ...

2 Complete the sentences with the comparative or superlative form of the adverb in brackets.

0 Natalie ran ....*the fastest*.... (fast), so she won the race.
1 Laura won the competition because she danced .... (beautiful).
2 I watch films .... (often) than sports programmes.
3 My sister plays the guitar .... (well) than me.
4 Matt's mum helped him, so he finished the homework .... (easily) than us.
5 Luke's teacher was happy with him because he did the exercise .... (quickly).

3 Complete the sentences with *as* + adverb + *as*.

0 We all finished the exam quickly. I finished the exam ...*as quickly as*... my friends.
1 I arrived home late but my brother arrived home later. I didn't arrive home .... my brother.
2 My best friend speaks more quietly than me. I don't speak .... my best friend.
3 My parents eat very slowly. My dad eats .... my mum.
4 William watches TV more often than his sister. William's sister doesn't watch TV .... William.
5 My cousin is the best guitar player in my school. Nobody plays it .... him.

UNIT 6

POSSESSION

's (apostrophe + *s*)

- We use 's (apostrophe + *s*) for people and animals.
  That's my brother's hat. (**not** ~~*the hat of my brother*~~)
  Where's the cat's bowl? (**not** ~~*the bowl of the cat*~~)
- With singular nouns, we use *'s*.
  my mum's necklace, my teacher's ring
- With plural nouns, we put the apostrophe (') at the end of the noun.
  my friends' shoes (**not** ~~*the shoes of my friend*~~)
  my cousins' jackets (**not** ~~*the jackets of my cousins*~~)
- If the plural noun does not end in *-s* (e.g. *children, men, women, people,* etc.), we use *'s*.
  The children's bedroom is over there.

Determiners and pronouns

Determiners	Pronouns
my	mine
your	yours
his	his
her	hers
our	ours
their	theirs

- We use pronouns instead of determiner + noun.
  *Is that my pencil on your desk? No, **yours** is over there.* (= *your pencil*)
  *Is this your jacket? No, it's **hers**.* (= *her jacket*)
  *Who do these books belong to? They're **ours**.* (= *our books*)
- We can use '*a friend of mine/yours/his,* etc.' instead of '*one of my/your/his, etc. friends*'.
  *This ball belongs to **a friend of mine**. He lent it to me.* (**not** ~~*a friend of me*~~)
  *Neil finished his homework. **A classmate of his** helped him.* (**not** ~~*a classmate of him*~~)

Practice

1 Rewrite the sentences with the apostrophe (').

0 The dogs bowl is empty.
........The dog's bowl is empty........

1 Terrys gold coins are on the table.
....

2 The childrens shoes are near the door.
....

3 Both boys lunches are in the kitchen.
....

4 I can't find my sisters necklace. She'll be angry.
....

5 My cousins names are Ana and Eva.
....

2 Choose the correct word to complete the sentences.

0 That isn't Ben's book. **He** / (**His**) / **Him** is on the teacher's desk.

1 Nora saw Sue at the cinema. She's a friend of **she** / **her** / **hers**.

2 We don't live here. **We** / **Our** / **Ours** house is near the park.

3 I've got two cats. **They** / **Their** / **Theirs** names are Leo and Tiger.

4 Who does this jumper belong to? Is it **you** / **your** / **yours**?

5 I was shopping when I saw a classmate of **me** / **my** / **mine**.

3 Complete the second sentence with the correct pronoun.

0 I saw one of my friends yesterday.
I saw a friend of ..mine.. yesterday.

1 Jane went on holiday with one of her friends.
Jane went on holiday with a friend of ....

2 We played football with one of our neighbours.
We played football with a neighbour of ....

3 My sister borrowed one of my necklaces.
My sister borrowed a necklace of ....

4 My parents had dinner with some of their friends.
My parents had dinner with some friends of ....

5 I found some money in one of your shoes.
I found some money in a shoe of ....

UNIT 7

PRESENT CONTINUOUS FOR FUTURE

→ Grammar reference **Unit 1 Present continuous, p. 147.**

- We often use the present continuous to talk about things that are happening now or at this moment (see Unit 1).

  *Tim's in the park. He's **climbing** a tree.*
- We can also use the present continuous to talk about our future plans and arrangements.

  *I'**m meeting** Julie later. We'**re playing** tennis.*
- When we use the present continuous for future, we usually use a future time expression (*later, on Monday morning, at 6 pm tomorrow,* etc.) to show we're talking about the future and not now.

  *We'**re learning** how to ski.* (= now, at this moment)

  *We'**re learning** how to ski next weekend.* (= future arrangement)

Practice

1 Complete these sentences with the present continuous form of the verb in brackets. Then read the sentences again. Are we talking about 'now' or the 'future'? Write N (now) or F (future).

0 My friends ...are hiking... (hike) in the mountains. ...N...

1 We .... (travel) to Rome on Friday. ....

2 .... you .... (listen) to me? ....

3 My dad .... (not come) with us on holiday next week. ....

4 Be quiet! I .... (do) my homework. ....

5 How .... you and your friends .... (get) to football practice later? ....

2 Sara is talking to Vicky. Look at Sara's diary and complete their conversation.

DIARY		
Thursday:	**am**	
	pm	help Max with homework
Friday:	**am**	
	pm	go to dentist
Saturday:	**am**	Dad's birthday, have pizza
	pm	at Paolo's Pizzas
Sunday:	**am**	play basketball
	pm	study
Monday:	**am**	Maths test!
	pm	

Vicky: Would you like to come to my house after school today?

Sara: I can't, **(0)** ...I'm helping Max with his homework... .

Vicky: How about Friday afternoon?

Sara: No, **(1)** ....

Vicky: Are you free on Saturday?

Sara: It's my dad's birthday and we **(2)** ....

Vicky: And on Sunday?

Sara: In the morning **(3)** ....

Vicky: What about the afternoon?

Sara: Oh no, I can't! **(4)** .... We've got a maths test on Monday!

3 What are you doing at these times this week? Complete these sentences so they are true for you.

0 (after school)
...I'm doing my homework after school...

1 (tomorrow morning)
....

2 (Friday afternoon)
....

3 (Saturday morning)
....

4 (on Sunday)
....

5 (next week)
....

UNIT 8

FUTURE WITH *WILL*

Positive	I / You / He / She / It / We / They**'ll** (**will**) be very different in the future.
Negative	I / You / He / She / It / We / They **won't** (**will not**) live in big houses.
Questions	**Will** I / you / he / she / it / we / they drive cars?
Short answers	Yes, I / you / he / she / it / we / they **will**. No, I / you / he / she / it / we / they **won't** (**will not**).

- We use *will* to talk about things which we think are possible in the future.
  *Everyone **will live** in big cities in the future.*
  *We **won't live** in small towns.*
- We often use expressions like *I think*, *I hope*, *I'm sure* or *certain* with *will.*
  *I **think I'll work** in a big bank.*
  *I'm **sure** my friends **won't live** in the same town.*

Practice

1 Complete the predictions with *will* or *won't*.

0 We / live / to be 120 years old
We'll live to be 120 years old.
1 I / have / a big house and a fast car
....
2 My friends / move / away
....
3 My cousin / become / a famous film star
....
4 There / be / cities on other planets
....
5 We / not buy / things in shops
....

2 Put the words in order to make questions. Then write the short answer.

0 cheaper / Will / space travel / get / ?
Will space travel get cheaper? Yes, it will.
1 people / walk / everywhere / Will / ?
.... No, ...
2 use / Will / we / house keys / ?
.... No, ...
3 you / live / in another country / Will / ?
.... Yes, ...
4 your friends / at university / study / Will / ?
.... Yes, ...
5 Will / buy / a faster car / your parents / ?
.... No, ...

3 Complete the questions with *will* and the verb in brackets and then write your own answers.

0 Where will people build (build) houses in the future?
I think they will build houses under the sea.
1 .... students .... (go) to school in the future?
I'm sure ....
2 Where .... we .... (buy) clothes and shoes in the future?
I think ....
3 How .... people .... (travel) from one place to another?
I'm certain ....
4 .... there .... (be) more wars?
I hope ....
5 .... scientists .... (discover) new things?
I'm sure ....

UNIT 9

MUST, MUSTN'T, HAVE TO, DON'T HAVE TO

must / mustn't

Positive	I / You / He / She / It / We / They **must** go.
Negative	I / You / He / She / It / We / They **mustn't** go.

- We use *must* and *mustn't* to talk about rules and obligation.
  *You **must** switch off your mobile phone in class.*
  *You **mustn't** eat or drink in the classroom.*
- We don't often use *must* in the question form. We prefer to use *Do* (*I, you,* etc.) *have to …?*
  ***Do** I **have to** wear a swimming hat?*

Practice

1 Write complete sentences with *must* or *mustn't*.

0 ✗ you / walk on the grass
You mustn't walk on the grass.

1 ✔ they / fill in the form
....

2 ✗ we / forget Mum's birthday
....

3 ✗ my cousin / wear large earrings to school
....

4 ✔ you / practise for an hour every day
....

5 ✔ you / be careful
....

have to / don't have to

Positive	I / You / We / They **have to** go. He / She / It / **has to** go.
Negative	I / You / We / They **don't** (**do not**) **have to** go. He / She / It **doesn't** (**does not**) **have to** go.
Questions	**Do** I / you / we / they **have to** go? **Does** he / she / it **have to** go?
Short answers	Yes, I / you / we / they **do**. Yes, he / she / it **does**. No, I / you / we / they **don't**. No, he / she / it **doesn't**.

- We use *have to* to say something is necessary and *don't have to* to say something isn't necessary.
  *You **have to** bring sandwiches.* (= *you need to bring …*)
  but *You **don't have to** bring a drink* (= *you don't need to bring …*)

Practice

2 Complete the sentences with the correct form of *have to* and the verb in brackets.

0 Do you have to wear (wear) a school uniform?

1 Today's Saturday. I .... (not go) to bed early.

2 My mum .... (work) in London this week.

3 What time .... your sister .... (come) home when she goes out?

4 My uncle has got problems with his back. He .... (go) swimming every day.

5 We .... (not watch) the film, we can play a game instead.

must and *have to*

- *Must* and *have to* are similar.
  *I've got a test tomorrow. I **must** study.*
  or *I **have to** study.*
- *Mustn't* and *don't have to* are different.
  *You **mustn't** be late for class.*
  (= you can't be late. It's the rule.)
  *You **don't have to** wear swimming goggles.*
  (= it isn't necessary but you can if you want.)
- In the past, we use *had to* for *must* and *have to.*
  *I didn't watch the film because I **had to** study.*
- The past of *don't have to* and *do you have to* is *didn't have to* and *did you have to.*
  ***Did** you **have to** stay at school late yesterday? No, I didn't.*
  *My mum **didn't have to** go to work this morning, so she drove me to school.*

Practice

3 Choose the correct words to complete the sentences.

0 You **don't have to** / **mustn't** help me but you can if you want.

1 When I was younger, I **had to** / **must** go to bed at 8 pm.

2 No ball games, please! You **don't have to** / **mustn't** play football here.

3 **Do you have to** / **Must you** leave now? It's very early.

4 I **don't have to** / **mustn't** wear a swimming cap at my pool but I usually wear one.

5 Shh! My sister's sleeping! We **don't have to** / **mustn't** wake her.

UNIT 10

VERB PATTERNS – GERUNDS AND INFINITIVES

- When we use two verbs together in a sentence, the second verb is usually **a gerund** (*sleeping, swimming,* etc.) or an infinitive (*to sleep, to swim*).
  *I **want to meet** my new neighbours.*
  *I **don't mind helping** close friends.*
- We use **an infinitive** after some verbs.
  *We **hope to see** you soon.*
  *He's **learning to play** the guitar.*
- We use **a gerund** after other verbs.
  *He **finished doing** his homework and watched TV.*
  *My dad **enjoys playing** chess.*
- We can use **a gerund** or **an infinitive** after these verbs: *start, begin, prefer, like, love*.
  *We went to the beach but then it **started raining**.*
  or … ***it started to rain***.
  *My friends **began playing** that game two hours ago.*
  or *My friends **began to play** …*
- We also use **a gerund** after prepositions (*at, in, for*, etc.).
  *Thank you **for inviting** me to your party.*
  *I'm thinking **of buying** a new bike.*

verb + gerund	finish, don't mind, enjoy, miss
verb + infinitive	decide, choose, learn, help, hope, plan, want, need
verb + gerund or verb + infinitive	start, begin, prefer, like, love

Practice

1 Complete the sentences with the infinitive or gerund form of the verb in brackets.

0 I need ....to buy..... (buy) some new trainers.
1 I missed .... (see) you at the party.
2 My brother decided .... (study) maths at university.
3 I don't mind .... (get up) early at the weekend.
4 My friends enjoy .... (write) their blogs.
5 We finished .... (download) the film and then we watched it.

2 Complete the sentences with the correct form of these verbs.

~~invite~~	play	upload
join	make	fail

0 Thank you for ....inviting..... us to your birthday meal.
1 I'm interested in .... new friends.
2 My brother is very good at .... the guitar.
3 Don't worry about .... the exam. It's easy!
4 My mum's getting better at .... photos onto her blog.
5 I'm thinking of .... a computer club.

3 Complete the sentences with a verb in the gerund or infinitive form so they are true for you.

0 My friends and I are interested in ..finding information about.......... ..football players.......... .
1 When I leave school, I hope ....
2 I don't mind .... but I don't like ....
3 I started .... when I was younger.
4 I prefer .... to ....
5 I'm thinking of .... next weekend.

UNIT 11

DETERMINERS

a / an / the

We use ***a*** or ***an*** when we introduce something for the first time and when we talk about things in general.

*I visited **a** museum in Paris.*

*I bought **an** ice cream and **a** can of lemonade.*

We use ***the***:

- when we are talking about something already mentioned.

  *I visited a museum in Paris. **The** museum was very old.*
- before superlatives.

  *London is **the biggest** city in England.*
- before *first, second*, etc.

  ***The first** man to walk on the moon was Neil Armstrong.*
- when there is only one of something.

  *I went to **the sea** to swim.*

Practice

1 Complete the conversation with *a/an* or *the*.

Matt: Where did you go on holiday?
Jane: We went to St Malo. It's **(1)** .... city in France.
Matt: Did you have a good time?
Jane: Yes, we went to **(2)** .... beach every day and we swam in **(3)** .... sea. In the evening we ate in **(4)** .... very good restaurant near our hotel.
Matt: What was the name of **(5)** .... restaurant?
Jane: I can't remember. I bought you **(6)** .... T-shirt. It was **(7)** .... nicest one in the shop.
Matt: Thank you, Jane. You're **(8)** .... first person to buy me a present from their holiday.

both / all

- We use *both* to talk about two things.

  ***Both** Rachel and Ruth enjoy going to the theatre.* (**not** ~~*The both Rachel and Ruth*~~ …)
- We use *all* to talk about a total number of people or things.

  *We visited **all** the museums in the city.*

another / other

- We use *another* with a singular noun to talk about 'one other' person or thing. We write it as one word.
- *This café is closed. There's **another** one over there.*
- We use *other* with plural nouns to talk about people or things which are different from the ones we are talking about.

  *We wanted to see the palace and the cathedral but my sister wanted to visit **other** places.* (**not** ~~*another places*~~)

Practice

2 Choose the correct word to complete the sentences.

1. This pencil is broken. Can I have **another** / **other** one?
2. **All** / **Both** my parents work in the city centre.
3. My friends want to write about their last holiday but I've got **another** / **other** idea.
4. My dad's got five brothers and sisters. They **all** / **both** live near us.
5. I'd like to study **all** / **both** maths and science when I go to university.

Uncountable nouns

- Uncountable nouns (e.g. *information*) have got one form and they don't usually have a plural form. We can't count these nouns.

  *Could you give me **some information** about the city?* (**not** ~~*Could you give me one information…?*~~)
- To talk about quantity, we use *many* with countable nouns and *much* with uncountable nouns.

  *How **many suitcases** did you bring?*
  *We didn't bring **many suitcases**.*
  *How **much water** have we got? We haven't got **much water**.*
- We can use words like *a bit of, a piece of, two slices of, three bottles of, a lot of*, etc. to talk about quantity with uncountable nouns.

  *Can you buy **three bottles of** water?*
  *I'll make a sandwich. We've got **a bit of** cheese and **two slices of** bread.*

Practice

3 Choose the correct word to complete the sentences.

1. How many **eggs** / **milk** / **rice** are there in the kitchen?
2. I haven't got much **books** / **furniture** / **chairs** in my bedroom.
3. I can't go out because I haven't got much **coins** / **euros** / **money**.
4. We were late because there was a lot of **cars** / **people** / **traffic**.
5. Can I have two **sandwiches** / **bread** / **cake**, please?
6. Our teacher gives us too much **homework** / **exercises** / **exams**.

UNIT 12

RELATIVE PRONOUNS *WHO, WHICH, THAT*

- We use *who*, *which* and *that* with a short sentence (or clause) to give more information about people or things.
  A guitarist is a person ***who*** *plays the guitar.*
  Rock is a type of music ***which*** *is very loud.*
- We use *who* with people.
  A violinist is a person ***who*** *plays the violin.*
- We use *which* with things.
  Folk is a type of music ***which*** *is quiet.*
- We can use *that* for people or things.
  A drummer is a person ***that*** *plays the drums.*
  Waves is a music festival ***that*** *happens in the summer.*

Practice

1 Complete the sentences with *who* or *which*.

1 Jazz is a type of music .... comes from the USA.
2 A guest is a person .... visits your house.
3 A pop singer is someone .... sings pop music.
4 A park is a place .... often has lakes, woods and gardens.
5 Football is a sport .... is popular all over the world.
6 A band is a group of people .... sing and play instruments together.

2 Use *who*, *that* or *which* to make one sentence.

0 A singer was singing. He was very good.
The singer ....who was singing........ was very good.
1 A festival is here in summer. It is good fun.
The festival ....
is good fun.
2 A friend went to a rock concert. He had a good time.
The friend ....
had a good time.
3 There's a shop near my house. It sells jazz CDs.
There's a shop near my house ....
....
4 We went to a cinema. It had 12 screens.
We went to a cinema ....
....
5 A neighbour likes soul music. She sings with a band.
The neighbour ....
sings with a band.

CONJUNCTIONS

- Conjunctions are words which join two parts of a sentence.
  I enjoy playing basketball ***but*** *I don't like watching it on TV.*
- We often use conjunctions so that we don't repeat words.
  I've got a brother. I've got a sister. =
  I've got a brother ***and*** *a sister.*
- *Or, if, that, when, where* and *while* are also conjunctions.
  I like listening to music ***while*** *I do my homework.*
  Would you like fish ***or*** *would you like chicken?*

Practice

3 Choose the correct word to complete the sentences.

1 A cinema is a place **when** / **where** you can see films.
2 We can go to the theatre **or** / **but** we can go to the cinema.
3 I don't mind listening to music **but** / **and** I don't like going to concerts.
4 My sister thinks **that** / **if** rap is great.
5 Sunday afternoon is **when** / **while** I usually do my homework.
6 **Or** / **If** we don't do our homework, our teacher gives us more.

UNIT 13

PRESENT PERFECT WITH *EVER* AND *NEVER*

Present perfect

Positive	I / You / We / They**'ve** (**have**) **talked**. He / She / It**'s** (**has**) **decided**.
Negative	I / You / We / They **haven't** (**have not**) **gone**. He / She / It **hasn't** (**has not**) **taken**.
Questions	**Have** I / you / we / they **painted**? **Has** he / she / it **worked**?
Short answers	Yes, I / you / we / they **have**. No, I / you / we / they **haven't**. Yes, he / she / it **has**. No, he / she / it **hasn't**.

- We can use the present perfect to talk about our experiences before now.
  ***I've met** a famous singer.*
- We use *have/has* + past participle.
  *My sister **hasn't slept** in a tent.*
- With regular verbs, we write the past participle in the same way as regular past simple verbs. (for spelling, see Grammar reference Unit 3).
  *My mum **has worked** for a famous magazine.*
- With irregular verbs, the past participle does not end in *-ed*. (See irregular verb list p.167.)
  *I **have spoken** to a film star.*
- We sometimes use *ever* with present perfect questions to say 'in your life'.
  ***Have** you **ever climbed** a mountain?*
- We sometimes use *never* with present perfect statements to say 'not ever in my life'.
  *My grandparents **have never flown** in a plane.*
- We don't use past time expressions like *yesterday, last weekend, two days ago*, etc. with the present perfect. We use the past simple.
  *I **played** tennis **yesterday**.* (**not** ~~*I've played tennis yesterday.*~~)

Practice

1 Write the past participle.

1 arrive ....
2 enjoy ....
3 repair ....
4 stop ....
5 travel ....
6 walk ....
7 break ....
8 buy ....
9 fall ....
10 grow ....
11 lend ....
12 wear ....

2 Complete the sentences with the present perfect with *never* and these verbs.

~~play~~ learn grow miss meet cook

0 I ....have never played..... the violin.
1 We .... Chinese food at home.
2 My parents have got a big garden but they .... vegetables there.
3 My friends .... a famous person.
4 My grandma .... to speak English.
5 I .... the start of my lesson.

3 Write complete questions in the present perfect with *ever*. Then write the short answer.

0 you / swim / in a cold lake?
Have you ever swum in a cold lake?
Yes, ...I have.....
1 your brother / write / a blog?
....
No, ...
2 your friends / ride / a horse?
....
Yes, ...
3 your teacher / forget / your name?
....
Yes, ...
4 you / sell / things you don't want?
....
No, ...
5 you and your friends / win / a competition?
....
No, ...

UNIT 14

PRESENT PERFECT WITH *JUST, YET* AND *ALREADY*

→ Grammar reference **Unit 13 Present perfect, p. 159.**

- We can use the present perfect with *just*, *yet* and *already*.

  *I've **just bought** a new pair of shoes. Do you like them?*

  *I'm full. I've **already eaten** five slices of pizza.*

  ***Have** you **seen** that film **yet**?*

  *No, I **haven't seen** it **yet** but I'm going to see it tomorrow.*

- We use the present perfect with *just* to say that something happened a very short time ago. *Just* goes between *have* and the past participle.

  *Would you like something to eat? No, thanks. I'**ve just eaten**.* (= I ate something a very short time ago.)

- We use the present perfect with *already* to say that something happened before now, often sooner than we expected. We often use *already* in the positive. It usually goes between *have* and the past participle.

  Mum: You should do your homework.

  *Son: I'**ve already done** it.*

  (= The son has done his homework sooner than his mum expected.)

- We use the present perfect with *yet* to ask or talk about time until now. We often expect that something might happen in the future. We often use *yet* at the end of questions or negative sentences.

  *Dave: **Have** you **been** to the new café **yet**?*

  *Sue: No, I **haven't been yet**.* (= Sue might go to the café in the future.)

Practice

1 Rewrite the sentences with the word in brackets.

0 The new sports shop hasn't opened. (yet)
The new sports shop hasn't opened yet.

1 I've seen my best friend outside the library. (just)
....

2 Let's see a different film. I've seen that one. (already)
....

3 I'm hungry. I haven't eaten. (yet)
....

4 Rob can't play football. He's broken his foot. (just)
....

5 Have your friends arrived? (yet)
....

2 Choose the correct word to complete the sentences.

1 Can you lend me a pencil? I've **just** / **yet** broken mine.

2 We're having a lovely time in Paris. We've **already** / **yet** seen the Eiffel Tower and the Louvre museum.

3 It's Granddad's birthday. Have you phoned him **yet** / **just**?

4 Wait a moment! We haven't finished **yet** / **already**.

5 Dad's **just** / **yet** phoned. He's going to be late.

6 I've **already** / **yet** tidied my room. I'm not going to do it again.

3 Read the situation and write a question or sentence in the present perfect with *just*, *yet* or *already*.

0 Your friend fell and hurt her leg two minutes ago. What does she say?
I can't move. I have just hurt my leg.......... . (hurt)

1 You are in New York. You visited the Empire State yesterday but you'd like to see the Statue of Liberty. What do you say?
I .... (not/see)

2 A friend comes to your house and you are going to have lunch. What do you ask?
.... you .... ? (have lunch)

3 A friend lends you a book but you read it last month. What do you say?
I .... (read)

4 Your mum tells you to do your homework but you did it before. What do you say?
I .... (do)

5 You're friends are choosing a film to watch. What do you ask them?
.... you .... (choose)

UNIT 15

PRESENT PERFECT WITH *SINCE* AND *FOR*

→ Grammar reference **Unit 13 Present perfect, p. 159.**

- We can use the present perfect to talk about an action or situation which started in the past and continues in the present. We use *since* and *for* to say how long something has been happening.
  *We'**ve lived** in this house **since** March.*
  *We'**ve lived** in this house **for** four months.*
- We use *since* with the time when the action or situation started.
  *I'**ve had** this computer **since** 2013, January, my birthday, etc.*
- We use *for* with an amount of time, such as the number of hours, months, years, etc.
  *My dad's worked in that bank **for** eight weeks, six months, two years, etc.*
- We usually use *how long* with the present perfect to ask questions.
  ***How long have** you **had** your dog?*
  *We'**ve had** it **since** last year / **for** 11 months.*

Practice

1 Write the common time expressions in the correct place in the table.

10 o'clock three minutes Tuesday
13 April four months ages ever May
2011 10 seconds my birthday five days
breakfast years two hours I was young
two weeks a year

since	for
10 o'clock, …	

2 Complete the sentences with the present perfect form of the verb in brackets and *for* or *since*.

0 My neighbours have lived (live) in their house for five years.
1 My aunt .... (have) her cat .... 2007.
2 My brother .... (not / eat) meat .... a long time.
3 I .... (like) playing tennis .... I was young.
4 We .... (not / see) our cousins .... months.
5 My mum and dad .... (be) married .... 1996.

3 Write complete sentences with the present perfect and *for* or *since* so they are true for you.

0 (I / not play computer games)
I haven't played computer games since yesterday.
1 (We / not have maths)
....
2 (my best friend / live in this house)
....
3 (my mum / not cook a meal)
....
4 (my friends / know each other)
....
5 (I / not eat anything)
....

4 Write complete questions with *How long …?* and the present perfect. Then write your own answers with the present perfect and *for* or *since*.

0 you / know / your best friend?
How long have you known your best friend?
I've known him for four years.
1 your parents / live / here?
....
2 your best friend / have / his or her school bag?
....
3 you / study / in this school?
....
4 your favourite shop / be / open?
....
5 your English teacher / work / in your school?
....

UNIT 16

PRESENT PERFECT AND PAST SIMPLE

→ Grammar reference **Unit 3 Past simple, p. 149.**

→ Grammar reference **Units 13, 14 and 15 Present perfect, p. 159–161.**

We use the **present perfect**:

- to talk about an action that finished in the past but the result is important now. We are not interested in when the action happened.

  My brother's happy because he ***has won*** *a competition.*

We can also use the **present perfect**:

- with *ever* and *never* to talk about our experiences until now.

  I've never learnt *French.* (= until now, but I may learn it in the future)
- with *just, already* and *yet* to talk about things we have or haven't done recently.

  *We****'ve just finished*** *eating.* *I* ***haven't read*** *that book* ***yet****.*
- to talk about an action or situation which started in the past and continues into the present. We use *for* and *since* to say how long it has been happening.

  How long have *you* ***lived*** *here?*

  I've lived *here* ***since*** *2005.*

We use the **past simple**:

- to talk about an action that happened in the past.

  My brother ***won*** *a competition.*
- when we are interested in when the action happened.

  My brother ***won*** *the competition* ***last week****.*

We can also use the **past simple**:

- to talk about experiences which happened over a time in the past.

  When my dad ***lived*** *in France for a month, he* ***didn't learn*** *French.* (= this time is finished. My dad doesn't live in France now.)

  Remember, when we ask questions about a time in the past, we use *When …?*

  When did *you* ***learn*** *to ride a bike?*

  I ***learned*** *to ride a bike* ***when*** *I was five years old.*

Practice

1 Complete the table with these time expressions.

~~yesterday~~ ~~just~~ in 2008 already yet since 5 May when I was younger three days ago ever never for 18 weeks last week recently

Present perfect	Past simple
just, …	*yesterday, …*

2 Complete the sentences with the present perfect or past simple form of the verb in brackets.

1 I .... (buy) this bag when I was on holiday.

2 I .... (not be) ill for a long time.

3 My best friend was late for school this morning because she .... (miss) the bus.

4 We .... (send) an email to our teacher three days ago but she .... (not answer) yet.

5 My mum and dad .... (know) each other since they were children. They .... (go) to school together.

6 You .... (make) a lot of mistakes! Please write this story again.

3 Write complete questions with *How long …?* and the present perfect. Then write your own answer with the present perfect.

0 How long / live here?

How long have you lived here?

I've lived here for six years.

1 How long / know your English teacher?

....

....

2 How long / like your favourite band?

....

....

4 Now write complete questions with *When …?* Then write your own answer with the past simple.

0 When / start learning English?

When did you start learning English?

I started learning English four years ago.

1 When / learn to swim?

....

....

2 When / use a computer for the first time?

....

....

UNIT 17

PRONOUNS *MYSELF, YOURSELF, HERSELF, HIMSELF, OURSELVES, YOURSELVES, THEMSELVES*

→ Grammar reference **Unit 6 Determiners and pronouns, p. 152.**

I	myself	it	itself
you	yourself	we	ourselves
he	himself	you	yourselves
she	herself	them	themselves

- We use *-self* when the subject and the object of the verb are the same person.
  ***I** hurt **myself** when I was playing football.* (**not** ~~*I hurt me*~~.)
  ***My** friends enjoyed **themselves** at my party*. (**not** ~~*My friends enjoyed them*~~)
- We can use *by + myself, yourself,* etc. to mean 'alone' or 'without any help'.
  *I usually walk to school **by myself**.* (= nobody walks with me)
  *They did their homework **by themselves**.* (= nobody helped them)

Practice

1 Complete these sentences with *myself, yourself, herself, himself, ourselves, yourselves, themselves*.

1 My brother hurt .... while he was climbing a tree.
2 I've just cut .... with this knife.
3 Is it safe for those children to go swimming by .... ?
4 Do you and your friends need help or can you clean the kitchen by .... ?
5 If you're hungry, make .... a sandwich!
6 We really enjoyed .... at the party.

FIRST CONDITIONAL

If **+ present simple,**	***will/won't*** **+ infinitive**
If you **study** a lot,	you **will pass** the exam.

will/won't **+ infinitive**	***if*** **+ present simple**
You **will pass** the exam	**if** you **study** a lot.

- We use the first conditional to talk about things that will or won't happen in a situation.
  ***If** you **talk** about the problem* (situation), *you'**ll feel** better* (result).
  ***If** he **isn't** careful* (situation), *he'**ll hurt** himself* (result).
- When the sentence begins with *If* we use a comma. When we use *if* in the middle of the sentence, we don't use a comma.
  *You'**ll feel** better **if** you **talk** about the problem.*

Practice

2 Complete these sentences with the correct form of the verb in brackets.

1 We .... (go) skiing if it .... (snow) this weekend.
2 If you .... (not be) careful, you .... (fall).
3 He .... (get) ill if he .... (not stop) eating fast food.
4 If my friends .... (not leave) now, they .... (not catch) the train.
5 We .... (not stay) at home if the weather .... (be) nice on Saturday.
6 If Dad .... (not come) soon, he .... (miss) dinner.

3 Read the questions and write answers that are true for you.

1 What will your parents say if you're late home today?
If I'm late home, ...
....

2 What will you wear tomorrow if it's cold?
....
....

3 How will you feel if you pass all your exams?
....
....

4 What will you buy if you go shopping on Saturday?
....
....

5 Will you cook dinner if you get home before your parents tonight?
....
....

6 Will you watch TV if you finish all your homework?
....
....

UNIT 18

MAY / MIGHT

Positive	I / You / He / She / It / We / They **may** / **might go** to the beach.
Negative	I / You / He / She / It / We / They **may not** / **might not take** a ball.

- We use *may* and *might* to talk about future possibilities.

  *It **may rain** tomorrow.*
  *We **might go** for a walk later.*
- When we talk about future possibilities, *may* and *might* have the same meaning.

  *I **may** / **might** buy some new trainers tomorrow. Mine are very old.*
  *Jack's feeling ill. He **may not** / **might not** go to school tomorrow.*
- We don't often use *may* or *might* to ask questions about future possibilities. We usually use *will*.

  *What **will** you **take** on the school trip?*
  *I **may take** my sun hat and I **might take** my sunglasses.*
- We use *will* to say something is certain but we use *may* and *might* to say something is possible.

  *I'**ll bring** my walking boots on the trip.* (= I'm certain I'll bring them)
  *I **may bring** some playing cards or I **may bring** another game.* (= It's possible I'll bring some cards)

→ Grammar reference **Unit 8 Future with *will*, p. 154.**

Practice

1 Complete the sentences with *may* or *might* and the verb in brackets.

1 In the summer, we .... (go) camping or we .... (visit) a city.
2 I'm tired. I .... (not go out) later.
3 My brother .... (study) maths at university or he .... (do) chemistry.
4 My friends .... (not swim) in the lake this afternoon. It's too cold.
5 We're a little hungry. We .... (have) a sandwich.
6 Shh! You .... (wake up) Grandma.

2 Choose the correct word to complete the sentences.

1 I'm sure I **'ll** / **may** go swimming. It's really hot.
2 We **'ll** / **may** have pizza or we **'ll** / **may** have a hamburger. We haven't decided yet.
3 My mum **'ll** / **might** be able to drive us to the concert but she isn't sure.
4 Don't worry. I'm certain they **won't** / **may not** be late. They left 45 minutes ago.
5 I **won't** / **might not** go on the school trip. I'm not sure.
6 Where **will** / **may** you go on holiday? We may go to South Africa.

3 Write complete sentences with *may* or *might* and one of the verbs in the box.

~~watch~~	not rain	buy
not understand		get back
not go		

0 I don't know what we're doing this evening. We ....might watch.... a film.
1 I haven't got any sun cream. I .... to the beach.
2 We have to finish a project at school. I .... late this afternoon.
3 Look! The clouds are moving. It .... later.
4 It's my cousin's birthday. Her parents .... her a new mobile phone.
5 You .... this teacher because she talks very fast.

UNIT 19

PRESENT SIMPLE PASSIVE

Present simple *be*	+ past participle
I'**m** (**am**) / '**m** (**am**) **not**	**given** homework every day.
You / We / They '**re** (**are**) / **aren't** (**are not**)	**taken** to school by car.
He / She / It '**s** (**is**) / **isn't** (**is not**)	**taught** by Mrs Kingston.

- We use the passive to talk about what happens to something or someone.
  Cereal ***is*** *often* ***covered*** *in sugar or chocolate.*
  Packets of cereal ***are sold*** *all over the world.*
- We often don't know, or we aren't interested in, who or what does the action.
  The grain ***is taken*** *to the factory.* (We aren't interested in who takes the grain.)
  The cereal ***is eaten*** *for breakfast.* (We aren't interested in who eats the cereal.)
- We can use *by* to say who does the action.
  We are taught maths ***by*** *Mr Green.*

→ Grammar reference **Unit 13 for more information on past participles, p. 159.**

Practice

1 Choose the correct words to complete the sentences.

1 Bread **is sold** / **are sold** in that shop.
2 We **is given** / **are given** a lot of homework on Fridays.
3 My bag **isn't made** / **aren't made** of leather.
4 The World Cup **is watched** / **are watched** all over the world.
5 I'**m not paid** / **isn't paid** to help at home.
6 My friends **isn't invited** / **aren't invited** to the party.

2 Complete the sentences with the present passive form of the verbs in brackets.

1 My best friend .... (call) Jon. It's short for Jonathan.
2 Thousands of films .... (download) every day.
3 Walking boots .... (not need) for the school trip.
4 I .... (give) money for my birthday by my parents.
5 In my school, uniforms .... (not wear).
6 Cakes .... (bake) in the oven.

3 Rewrite the sentences in the present passive.

0 Someone cleans our classroom every day.
Our classroom ......*is cleaned*...... every day.
1 People speak English all over the world.
English .... all over the world.
2 We don't use the computers in our classroom.
The computers in our classroom
....
3 They don't cook the food in our school.
The food .... in our school.
4 My friends send me a lot of messages.
A lot of messages .... my friends.
5 They don't grow bananas in England.
Bananas .... in England.

UNIT 20

PAST SIMPLE PASSIVE

Past simple *be*	+ past participle
I / He / She / It **was** / **wasn't** (**was not**)	**given** a special award.
You / We / They **were** / **weren't** (**were not**)	**taken** to see a castle.

- We use the past passive to talk about what happened to something or someone.
  This museum ***was built*** *150 years ago.*
  Animals ***were kept*** *in that building.*
  Was *St Paul's Cathedral* ***built*** *by Christopher Wren?*

→ Grammar reference **Unit 19, Present passive, p. 165.**

→ Grammar reference **Unit 13 for more information on past participles, p. 159.**

Practice

1 Write complete sentences in the past passive. Remember to use *by* if you say who did the action.

0 This castle / build / a prince
This castle was built by a prince.
1 This photo / take / my sister.
....
2 The cakes / eat / my friends.
....
3 We / not invite / to Megan's party last week.
....
4 We / show / around the library / the tour guide.
....
5 You / not give / a present / your brother.
....

2 Choose the correct words to complete the sentences.

1 Our school **is built** / **was built** in 2005.
2 I **am driven** / **was driven** to school because my dad's a teacher in my school.
3 My mum's mobile **is stolen** / **was stolen** yesterday.
4 London **is visited** / **was visited** by millions of people every year.
5 These sandwiches **are made** / **were made** last night.
6 That book **is written** / **was written** many years ago.

3 Read the questions and write answers that are true for you.

0 What's your best friend called?
My best friend is called Nick.
1 When were you born?
....
2 What were you given for your last birthday?
....
3 What fruit is grown in your country?
....
4 When was your house built?
....
5 How much homework are you given?
....

List of irregular verbs

Infinitive	Past simple	Past participle
be	was were	been
become	became	become
begin	began	begun
break	broke	broken
bring	brought	brought
build	built	built
burn	burnt/burned	burnt/burned
buy	bought	bought
catch	caught	caught
choose	chose	chosen
come	came	come
cost	cost	cost
cut	cut	cut
do	did	done
draw	drew	drawn
dream	dreamed/dreamt	dreamed/dreamt
drink	drank	drunk
drive	drove	driven
eat	ate	eaten
fall	fell	fallen
feel	felt	felt
find	found	found
fly	flew	flown
forget	forgot	forgotten
get	got	got
give	gave	given
go	went	gone/been
grow	grew	grown
have	had	had
hear	heard	heard
hit	hit	hit
hold	held	held
hurt	hurt	hurt
keep	kept	kept
know	knew	known
learn	learned/learnt	learned/learnt
leave	left	left

Infinitive	Past simple	Past participle
lend	lent	lent
lie	lay	lain
lose	lost	lost
make	made	made
mean	meant	meant
meet	met	met
pay	paid	paid
put	put	put
read	read	read
ride	rode	ridden
ring	rang	rung
run	ran	run
say	said	said
see	saw	seen
sell	sold	sold
send	sent	sent
show	showed	shown
shut	shut	shut
sing	sang	sung
sit	sat	sat
sleep	slept	slept
speak	spoke	spoken
spell	spelled/spelt	spelled/spelt
spend	spent	spent
stand	stood	stood
steal	stole	stolen
swim	swam	swum
take	took	taken
teach	taught	taught
tell	told	told
think	thought	thought
throw	threw	thrown
understand	understood	understood
wake	woke	woken
wear	wore	worn
win	won	won
write	wrote	written

Acknowledgements

The authors would like to thank Annette Capel and Alyson Maskell for their support and guidance throughout the project.

The authors and publishers are grateful to the following for reviewing the material during the writing process:

Argentina: Celeste Hayet and Cecilia Rinaldi; Brazil: Litany Ribeiro; Colombia: Ellen Darling; Spain: Emma Heyderman; Turkey: Ali Bilgin, Naci Turgut and Mujgan Yesiloglu.

Development of this publication has made use of the Cambridge English Corpus, a multi-billion word collection of spoken and written English. It includes the Cambridge Learner Corpus, a unique collection of candidate exam answers. Cambridge University Press has built up the Cambridge English Corpus to provide evidence about language use that helps to produce better language teaching materials.

This product is informed by English Profile, a Council of Europe-endorsed research programme that is providing detailed information about the language that learners of English know and use at each level of the Common European Framework of Reference (CEFR). For more information, please visit www.englishprofile.org

The authors and publishers acknowledge the following sources of copyright material and are grateful for the permissions granted. While every effort has been made, it has not always been possible to identify the sources of all the material used, or to trace all copyright holders. If any omissions are brought to our notice, we will be happy to include the appropriate acknowledgements on reprinting.

Telegraph Media Group for the text on p. 56 adapted from 'Olympics of the mind: furrowed brows and frenzied thinking' by William Langley, The Telegraph 19 August 2012. © Telegraph Media Group Limited 2012;

Alex Rawlings for the text on p. 90 adapted from BBC news website 'Alex Rawlings, Oxford University Student Speaks 11 Languages'. Reproduced with permission of Alex Rawlings;

David Higham Literary Agents for the text on pp. 116–117 from Kensuke's Kingdom by Michael Morpurgo. Published by Egmont, copyright © 2010. Reproduced with permission of David Higham Literary Agents.

For the sound recordings on p. 84, Track 2.07 (1): The enchanted bagpipe, artist - Film & Music Co. Copyright © Pump Audio/Getty Images, Track 2.07 (2): Ancient temple – flute only, artist -Dominik Hauser. Copyright © Pump Audio/Getty Images, Track 2.07 (3): Marching Taiko Drums, artist - Cuttlefish Music. Copyright © Sound Express/Getty Images, Track 2.07 (4): Spanish guitar – Puerta de Malaga, artist - Arrington Music. Copyright © Pump Audio/Getty Images; p. 85, Track 2.09 (2): Auld Lang Banjo, artist - Cary "CKP" Kanno. Copyright © SoundExpress/Getty Images, Track 2.09 (4): Zaigrai, Moya Volinka, artist - The Russian Folk Ensemble Balalaika. Copyright © Pump Audio/Getty Images, Track 2.09 (5): Peruvian Cajon, artist - Beetle and Bugs. Copyright © Pump Audio/Getty Images; p. 107, Track 2.26: Bollywood Party, artist - David Banks, Electronic World Music Fusion. Copyright © Pump Audio/Getty Images.

Photo acknowledgements

p.10 (TL): amana productions inc/Getty Images, (BL): Alberto Pomares/Getty Images, (TC): Jonathan Kirn/Getty Images, (R): Juice Images/Alamy, (CL) & p.100 (4): MBI/Alamy, p.14 (BR): Peter Essick/Getty Images, (B main): DPK-Photo/Alamy, (CR): Jason Politte/Alamy, (TL): Stocktrek Images, Inc./Alamy, (TR): Jim Sugar/Science Faction/Corbis; p.16 (TL): yykkaa/shutterstock, (C): Joe Farah/Shutterstock, (CR): Manor Photography/Alamy, (TR): Tory Kallman/shutterstock, (BR): Pictorium/Alamy; p.17 (TR): Mike Hill/Alamy, (C): Eduard Kyslynskyy/shutterstock, (B): Stephen Belcher/Minden Pictures/Corbis; p.18 (TR): pisaphotography/shutterstock, (CR) & p.63 (TC inset): grzegorz knec/Alamy, (TL): Neil Armstrong/AP/Press Association Images, (BR): Hamik/shutterstock, (BL): Dan Thornberg/shutterstock; p.19 (California): Alexander Zavadsky/shutterstock, (Florida): Globe Turner/shutterstock, (New York): Globe Turner/shutterstock, (Texas): Gil C/shutterstock; p.20 (TL): Fotosearch/Stringer/Getty Images, (TR): Topical Press Agency/Stringer/Getty Images, (CR): Popperfoto/Getty Images, (BR): Barcroft Media/TIGHAR/Getty Images; p.22 (a): Leonid Serebrennikov/Alamy, (b): Pavel L Photo and Video, (c): Seth Wenig/Reuters/Corbis, (d): Eviakhov Valeriy/Shutterstock; p.23 (R): Juice Images/Alamy; p.26 (a): Clearview/Alamy, (b): Gary Blake/Alamy, (c), p. 42 (BR) & p.45 (8): LOOK Die Bildagentur der Fotografen GmbH/Alamy, p.26 (d): MichaelGrant/Alamy, (B) Image Source/Alamy; p.27 (B): Rick Gomez/Getty Images; p.28 (a): LatitudeStock/Alamy, (b) & p.103 (B): John Warburton-Lee Photography/Alamy, (c): WitR/shutterstock, (d): Ivan Pavlov/shutterstock; p.29 (CL): NASA Archive/Alamy, (BR): Beata Aldridge/shutterstock; p.30 (0): Super Prin/shutterstock, (1): Svetlana Foote/shutterstock, (2): Peter Wollinga/shutterstock, (3): Patryk Kosmider/shutterstock, (4), (5), (6): Eric Isselee/shutterstock, (7): Shchipkova Elena/shutterstock, (8): ArchMan/shutterstock; p.34 & 77 (TL): Monkey Business Images/shutterstock; p.36 (B): Jamie Grill/Getty Images; p.38 (a) & p.60 (BR): TetraImages/Alamy, (b):R.legosyn/shutterstock, (c): Janet S. Robbins/Alamy, (d): Marco Secchi/Alamy, (B main): Helen Filatova/shutterstock, (CR): Stocksnapper/shutterstock, (BR): Eddie Keogh/Corbis; p.39 (R): 2happy/shutterstock; p.40 (TR): Ian Lishman/Juice Images, (BR): stockyimages/shutterstock, (BL): Christopher Furlong/Staff/Getty Images; p.41 (TL), (TC), TR): Janine Wiedel Photolibrary/Alamy, (B): Bartosz Hadyniak/Getty Images; p.42 (BC): Hero Images Inc./Alamy, (TR): Lumii Images/Alamy, (BL): Ammit/Alamy; p.43 Strahil Dimitrov/shutterstock; p.44 (TL): Robert Harding Picture Library/Alamy, (TC): Martin Strmiska/Alamy, (TR): Chad Ehlers/Alamy, (BR): Charles Sturge/Alamy; p.45 (1): Rob Wilson/shutterstock, (2): Artur Achtelik/Getty Images, (3): Kumar Sriskandan/Alamy, (4) & p.64, (d): Chris Rokitski/shutterstock, (5): Tracey Whitefoot/Alamy, (6): DBURKE/Alamy, (7): NAN728/shutterstockp.46 (1): KKulikov/shutterstock, (2): Ljupco Smokovski/shutterstock, (3): AlexussK/shutterstock, (4): Sergio Stakhnyk/shutterstock, (5): Ad Oculos/shutterstock, (6): Miro Kovacevic/shutterstock, (7): Kankaitom/shutterstock, (BL): VIEW Pictures Ltd/Alamy, (BR): AlexRoz/shutterstock; p.48 (TL): Sam DCruz/shutterstock, (TR): NASA Archives; p.50 (T): Christos Georghiou/shutterstock, (BL): Science Photo Library/Alamy, (BR): NASA/Science Photo Library, 50 (BC): B.A.E. Inc./Alamy; p.53: Pawel Libera Images/Alamy; p.54 (a): Jupiterimages/Getty Images, (b): Cultura Creative (RF)/Alamy, (c): Rob Marmion/Shutterstock, (d): Unlisted Images/Corbis, (e): Bogdan Angheloiu/Getty Images, (f): Lasse Kristensen/Alamy; p.56 (TR): Tatiana Belova/shutterstock, (TC): cosma/shutterstock, (C): Galcka/shutterstock, (B): Elnur/shutterstock; p.58 (L): PhotoAlto/Alamy, (R): racorn/shutterstock; p.60 (TL): Mienny Photography/Getty Images, (TR): Blend Images/Alamy, (BL): Radius Images/Alamy; p.61: Paul Chinn/San Francisco Chronicle/Corbis; p.62: Friedemann Vogel - FIFA/Getty Images; p.63 (BC inset): Staff/Getty Images, 63 (main): VI-Images/Getty Images, 63 (BR inset): Shooter Bob Square Lenses/shutterstock; p.64 (a): Loop Images Ltd/Alamy, (b): TungCheung/shutterstock, (c): JM Travel Photography/shutterstock, (e): All Canada Photos/Alamy, (f): Marques/shutterstock, (g): apiguide/shutterstock, (h): Iuliia Timofeeva/shutterstock; p.65: Craig Dingle/Getty Images; p.68 (L): Matt Cardy/Stringer/Getty Images, (C): Corey Weiner/Alamy, (R) & p. 76 (C): Adrian Sherratt/Alamy; p.69: PYMCA/Alamy; p.70 (A): nkbimages/Getty Images, (B): isitsharp/Getty Images, (C): moodboard/Alamy, (D): Photononstop/Alamy, (E): Phil Boorman/Getty Images; p.71: James Pauls/Getty Images; p.73 (TL): Sheila Terry/Science Photo Library, (TR early): DEA/S. VANNINI/Getty Images, (CL): Danita Delimont/Getty Images, 73 (CR early): View Stock/Getty Images; p.76 (L): rista/shutterstock, (R): Mark Makela/Alamy; p.77 (CL): michaeljung/shutterstock, (TR): Tyler Olson/Shutterstock, (CR): Glow Asia RF/Alamy, (B): Novastock/Getty Images; p.80 (TL): Alan Wrigley/Alamy, (TC): Stefano Paterna/Robert Harding, (TR): Gianni Muratore/Alamy, (sweets): Steve Vidler/Alamy, (juice): Marcelo_Krelling/shutterstock, (B): Odua Images/shutterstock; p.82 (1): Yeko Photo Studio/shutterstock, (2): design56/shutterstock, (3): Tomislav Pinter/shutterstock, (4): Chukov/shutterstock, (5): sutsaly/shutterstock; p.83: monkeybusinessimages/Getty Images; p.84 (a): Ronald Sumners/shutterstock, (b): Peter Widmann/Alamy,